Praise f

T0161096

"His narrative is haunting and e   .... v. .... uccans and natural
scenery."   —*Shelf Awareness*

"'Me in place and the place in me,' Seamus Heaney declares in his poem
'A Herbal.' That idea is at the core of this deeply satisfying memoir of
one man's exile from and return to his Appalachian homeland. Jeremy
Jones shows the complexity of a region and a people too often reduced
to the crudest of stereotypes, and by doing so gains even greater self-
awareness. *Bearwallow* is a book to be savored."

—Ron Rash, *Serena* and *In the Valley*

"*Bearwallow* is a thoughtful reflection on what it means to be a
particular kind of southerner—one who went away and returned to see
his homeplace anew through fresh eyes. Jeremy B. Jones revels in what
many have known for years—that there is not now and never has been a
singular Appalachian experience. Jones's writing is clear-eyed, curious,
and reverent. This memoir is a pure pleasure to read."

—Beth Macy, *Dopesick* and *Factory Man*

"*Bearwallow* is a marvel of a book—intricate and wise. Jones folds the
past in with the present—his ancestors' stories in with his own and
those of the new generations of immigrants—tales told in beautiful,
meditative prose that stack up like the mountain ridges, one on top of
another in a seamless continuum."   —Mesha Maren, *Sugar Run*

"In prose vivid and fresh, Jeremy Jones gives us an intimate and in-
depth study of contrasting worlds—Latin America, the Blue Ridge
Mountains, old families, new Hispanic arrivals, the pull of home, and
the need to escape. . . . It is a story of both teaching and learning, of
roots, and of unexpected discovery. *Bearwallow* is a delight to read."

—Robert Morgan, *Gap Creek*

BEARWALLOW

BEARWALLOW

*A Personal History
of a Mountain Homeland*

JEREMY B. JONES

BLAIR

BLAIR

905 W. Main Street
Suite 19 D-1
Durham, NC 27701

The Library of Congress has cataloged the hardcover edition as follows:
LCCN: 2014005473

Library of Congress Cataloging-in-Publication Data
Jones, Jeremy B., 1981–
Bearwallow : a personal history of a mountain homeland / by Jeremy B. Jones.
pages   cm
ISBN 978-0-89587-624-9 (alkaline paper)— ISBN 978-0-89587-625-6 (ebook)
1. Jones, Jeremy B., 1981- 2. Edneyville (N.C.)—Biography. 3. Edneyville (N.C.)—
Social life and customs. 4. Social change—North Carolina—Edneyville. 5. Mountain
life—North Carolina—Edneyville Region. 6. Mountain people—North Carolina—
Edneyville Region—Biography. 7. Bearwallow Mountain (N.C.)—Biography. 8. Blue
Ridge Mountains—Biography. I. Title.
F264.E34J66 2014
975.6'92—dc23
2014005473

DESIGN BY DEBRA LONG HAMPTON
COVER DESIGN BY BROOKE CSUKA

To
Ray & Grace and Ray & Betty,
grandparents who spun in me
the earliest of stories

Author's Note

This book is a memoir, not only about my life, but also about the life of a place. In this way, it relies on both research and memory, on both myth and history. Drawing from many sources, I have tried to step as close to the truth as one can when the past is involved. I've unearthed what I can reach, and I've pieced it together here. In this piecing together, I have changed the names of many of the living, especially children, to protect privacy; historical names, however, remain intact. In some cases, I have rearranged or compressed the chronology of events to provide a clearer narrative for the reader. These changes do not affect the overall progression of the story, only keep it from being bogged down by sequences of irrelevant scenes. Beyond these alterations, I've gotten my hands dirty and made something true that I hope is worth reading.

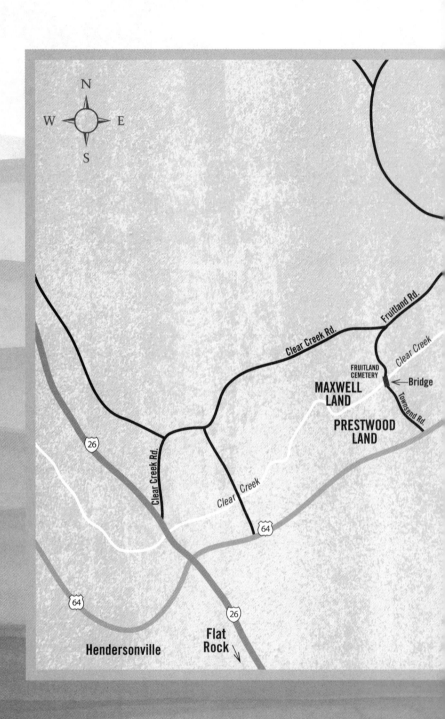

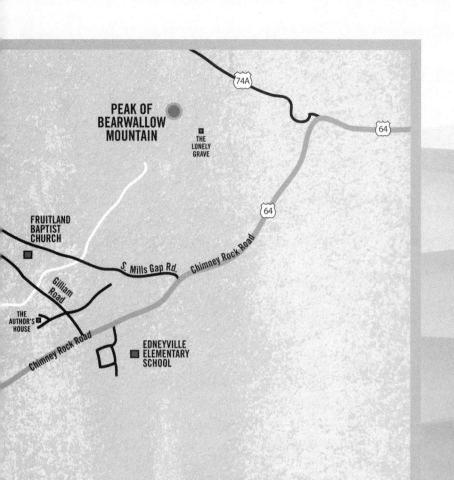

To come devotedly into the depths of a subject, your respect for it increasing in every step and your whole heart weakening apart with shame upon yourself in your dealing with it: To know at length better and better and at length into the bottom of your soul your unworthiness of it: Let me hope in any case that it is something to have begun to learn.

James Agee, *Let Us Now Praise Famous Men*

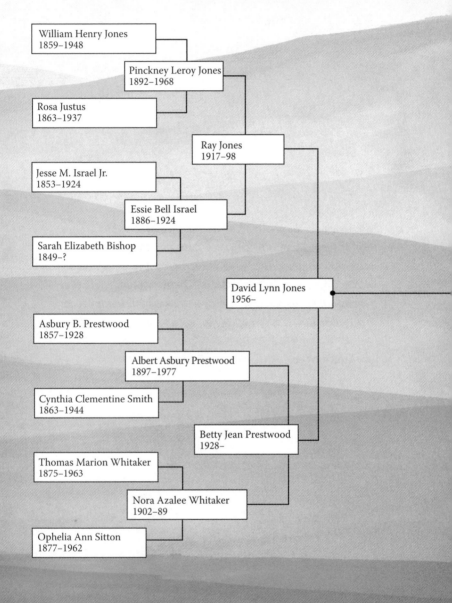

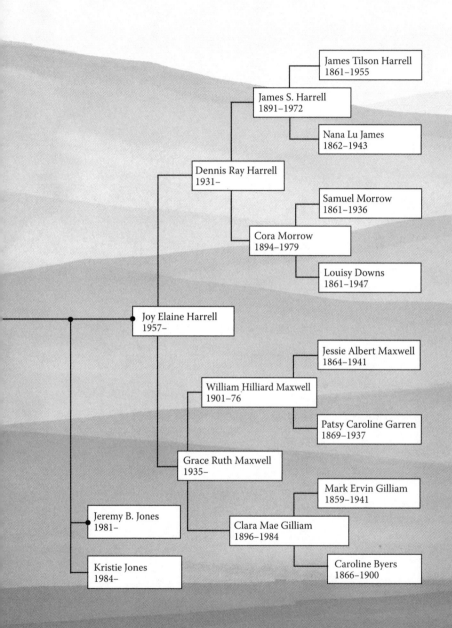

Prologue

Now the Lord said to Abram, "Go from your country and your kindred and your father's house to the land that I will show you." . . . Abram was seventy-five years old when he departed. . . . Then the Lord appeared to Abram, and said, "To your offspring I will give this land."

As far as I know, my Abraham forefather made no covenant with God. He wasn't promised a piece of land near the Euphrates, didn't march through the desert with family and slaves and animals in tow, trusting in unseen land. No, my Abraham was Dutch, not Hebrew, and something more of a leprechaun. Not short or red-headed or ever-clad in green, but the kind of man who buried pots of gold in the woods.

Like the Abraham of antiquity, Abraham Kuykendall trekked across lands—leaving New Amsterdam in the mid-eighteenth century, gliding south through Virginia and the Great Wagon Road, and eventually boring into western North Carolina. There, he married, began fathering children, and took up arms for the American Promised Land. After the war, he and Elizabeth and his tribe of eleven children built a sturdy life on the edge of Cherokee country. Abraham became some-thing of a frontier father figure. He was appointed commissioner, over-seeing the building of the courthouse and prison, and was then elected justice of the peace.

But this was all before his claustrophobia. Before he set off into the wild at age seventy-five with a young temptress to brew whiskey. Before he threw all his gold into the earth in the middle of an empty night.

As more pioneers pulled wagons in to lay claim to the open land around him, he itched for space. His world wasn't yet crowded, but Abraham felt squeezed by the sprouting houses and filling streets—by the shift from frontier to development. He knew the Hopewell Treaty of 1785 had opened up the Blue Ridge Mountains to settlement. Across his western horizon, those blurry mountains stretched out, empty and unknown and tempting. And Abe was restless.

Then Elizabeth died. So at nearly eighty years old, Abraham promptly married a beautiful young woman named Bathsheba, and together they packed everything up and lit out, deeper into the moun-tains, to an area labeled on the map only as "the Wilderness."

1

Debbie and I share a single-wide behind the school. No matter the drab off-white exterior, she has decorated the inside with bits of Mexico, its flag hanging over a small metal desk, posters of Mayan ruins and Simón Bolívar sticking to the walls, a donkey piñata and red and green streamers dangling above the bookcase. In the center of the room stretches an empty table, corralled by multicolored plastic chairs.

This is our classroom—our "mobile unit," as it is designated by the school. I try to envision it full of children, to picture some of them reclining on the beanbags with *Clifford the Big Red Dog* in hand, but no students have arrived yet. So I grab my lunch and drop down the wooden ramp outside. As I head toward the main building, the scent of manure from the cattle farther down the hill cuts through the early-morning fog.

Along the hall inside, the clamor of first-day cubby packing and desk arranging and book assigning rises and falls from the classrooms. I pass by them all to arrive at the middle of the building. There, I freeze, stopped in my tracks at the door of the teachers' lounge.

Fifteen years ago, this spot a few steps from the girls' bathroom marked a boundary never to be crossed; it was a portal through which teachers disappeared, daring us to drift from our quiet line hugging the cinder-block wall. I never drifted, always waiting in my place until my teacher reappeared smiling, like an actress who didn't realize she'd stepped back on stage. Then, in a flash, she'd reset her face, dispose of the soda, and drive our herd onward.

Twenty-four years old now, standing in this same dim hall, knowing all my former teachers still roam somewhere within this squat brick building, I hesitate, fearing a stern "Stop!" at my back or, worse, a narrowed brow awaiting me on the other side of the door. But, I turn the knob, half hoping to find waterfalls and roulette tables and electric harps inside.

Instead, one of the custodians rests on a faded brown loveseat with her arm draped around a vacuum cleaner as a copier hums in the corner near the sink. I nod hello, drop my Tupperware in the fridge, and reappear in the hall: no soda, no involuntary smile.

Still, I perform. My dress shirt and the ID dangling around my neck are meant to aid in this new role. I am now Mr. Jones, ESL teacher, even though I mostly still feel like a kid pining after PE.

Strangest, perhaps, about being back in this building is that hardly anything has changed, save me. Since high school, I have drifted, leaving these mountains for college and eventually landing in Central America. Yet now I stand back in this hallway as if I've stepped out of a time machine. The place smells the same, and inside the classrooms wait many of the same faces. But these women are no longer Mrs. King and Mrs. Salatino and Mrs. Lyda; they're Angie and Sharon and Nancy. It's bizarre and comfortable all in the same breath.

Before I get far back down the hall, I see Mrs. Lunsford—Debbie—approaching.

"Want to go for a ride?" she asks.

"Um, sure?"

Debbie was my third- and fourth-grade teacher, but now we're ESL colleagues. While we share the trailer—"the condo," she calls it—she will work alongside other teachers in the inclusion classrooms within the main building. I am supposed to pull out the "newcomers"—the students who have just arrived in the country—to work in small groups

out back in the condo. But this first week, she says, we won't have much
to do except carry out standardized testing, something neither of us is
eager to start. So we apparently will go for rides instead.

"Manuel isn't here," she says. "But he should be. I can't imagine
why he wouldn't be here on the first day, unless he missed the bus. Or
the bus missed him. He loves school and is one of my best readers. He
had perfect attendance last year. I called the number we have, but it's
disconnected or changed, and I can't believe his family would've left."

"Oh," I say, untangling my ID and the electronic building key that
are wound around my neck, trying to keep up.

"He doesn't live far. It's easiest to just go see." She turns to look
down the hall. "We should probably tell the office, but they won't miss
us. Plus, we're not supposed to drive students around anyway. No one
needs to know, right?"

"Okay, sure, no." I stop short of a *ma'am*.

And we're off, marching down the hall toward the back door,
which leads down the hill to the cattle and woods and the big-kids'
playground, something that has also changed—the monkey bars have
vanished, and everything now rests atop soft mulch. We skip the playground, circle past the dumpsters, and circumvent the office to climb
into Debbie's car waiting up the hill. I ready myself to break a rule on
my first day of school.

The dirt road just above the school's property tunnels through forest before finally hitting pavement. Soon, we run into Ridge Road and
turn right toward the mountain. As we snake along the mostly flat and
empty road, Debbie points out a couple of trailers and small houses
where other students live. I haven't met any students yet, but from conversations with Debbie, I'm beginning to attach anecdotes and details
and, now, houses to a few.

The road is speckled by double-wides and brick houses with
broken-down cars and trucks outside; satellite dishes haphazardly attached to roofs aim above the rounded mountains, which peek through
the thin veil of gray and reach above the forests, soft and rolling.

"It's just up here, I think," Debbie says as we slow. No other cars follow us, so we nearly stop in the road as she tries to read the mailbox. We see no name, no numbers. "I think this might be it—this looks familiar."

The trailer sits parallel to the road, but the open land surrounding it and leading toward the mountains gives the sense that the structure may have simply been dropped in this spot. There isn't a driveway to speak of, but simply a short stretch of worn-down grass. We park in the yard and climb out.

"His parents don't speak any English," Debbie says, which lets me know that once we knock on the door, it's up to me. She doesn't speak much Spanish—none of the teachers at the school does—and so I walk to the door piecing together this new life I've stepped into. A month ago, I walked down cobblestone streets to students' adobe houses in the colonial town of Gracias, Honduras, dodging horses and oxen. Now, I'm emerging from a new Ford SUV to walk through what must have once been a hayfield to help a young Mexican student get to a tiny brick school in Appalachia.

No one comes. I knock again. Nothing. As we turn back to the car, the door opens. I had warmed my tongue with Spanish, but upon the sight of the gray-haired white man standing in the doorframe, I still the "*Buenos días*" waiting in my mouth. In fact, I stop altogether, so Debbie speaks instead: "Sorry, we must have the wrong house."

He looks past us, then nods slowly before turning back inside and closing the door.

Once we're back on the road, Debbie drives us farther from the school, closer to Sugarloaf Mountain. I scan the horizon behind the fields and houses and apple orchards, looking at those mountains I've looked at most of my life, wondering if I might see something new in them now. Wondering if I can make a home here.

"This one," she says as we approach another trailer. We park in grass again.

After a knock, a square Latino boy appears in the door, wearing a Batman T-shirt and jeans. I ready my Spanish again, but Debbie speaks before I get going: "Hey, Manuel."

"Mrs. Lunsford?" he says, eyes wide, a prepubescent creak in his voice.

"Ready to go to school?"

He smiles.

"Run get your backpack."

Manuel is evidence of the change to this place since I was a student in Mrs. Lunsford's classroom. A couple of decades ago, most of the Latino students at Edneyville Elementary dropped in unannounced. We knew them in flashes—they'd spend much of the day learning English outside the classroom, returning only for PE and art. Then, one day, seemingly without warning, their desks would stand empty, their books and journals and colored erasers unclaimed. Some returned the next year, others never again.

Those students were the children of migrant workers, arriving in the mountains in the fall to pick apples, then vanishing to follow a harvest line of peaches and oranges south. But today, many of the Mexican students have been here for years and are no longer perpetually uprooted. They have homes instead of camps. Their parents work mostly stable construction or landscaping jobs. Manuel thus walks into his fifth-grade classroom to smiles and *heys* from children he has known for years. A labeled desk awaits him.

The other students, though—the ones without labeled desks—will be mine. The migrants, the newly arrived, those carrying nothing but the voice of their homeland. Even before I meet them, I wonder how I might relate. I'm a young man back in the mountains my people have haunted for over two hundred years. My family tree digs deep into the soil—I've taken up in a house on a road named after my forefolk—and yet I'm somehow trying to reroot myself after moving away. I have decided to imagine myself something of an ambassador to my students, someone who knows this place but speaks their language. Someone with a foot in two worlds.

I spend the rest of the day walking from class to class with Debbie, meeting a few of my students, along with many of hers. Each time she turns to me to say, "And this is Mr. Jones," I nearly turn around myself, in search of my father.

As we wander into a kindergarten classroom, Debbie asks the teacher if we might speak with two students, Angel and Marco. The teacher, though, points out a couple of girls not on our list—students on no one's list until this morning.

"I don't think they speak any English," she says.

Four children shuffle over. Debbie squats to say hello. Angel and Marco respond in kind. The girls, though, stare with big eyes. I greet them in Spanish, squatting, too, asking questions to try to warm them up.

"*Bien,*" they whisper.

I coax out names: Maricruz, Ana. Even though we will soon test each of these students to gauge their English abilities, dividing them accordingly between Debbie and me, it seems immediately clear Maricruz and Ana will come with me. They wear the look of the lost, of the displaced. I explain that later in the week they will go to class with me to practice English. They barely nod, tugging on pockets, studying my shoes.

A round, red-headed boy walks by. "She don't talk." He points at Ana.

"Jimmy, back to the carpet," the teacher calls to him. He shrugs at me and runs off.

"You're going to have a lot of fun today," I try to convince them in Spanish, shaking each of their hands like we've just secured a business deal. Maricruz grins at the exuberance with which I shake, lifting her arm high into the air. Angel and Ana, though, exchange baffled looks.

"*Nos vemos,*" I say, smiling—"See you later."

They fade silently back into the groups playing with blocks on the carpet. As we leave, Ana looks back at us while Jimmy jabbers at her.

⋙

On the short drive home, I watch Bearwallow Mountain rise as I turn on to Gilliam Road. It, too, seems unchanged: the bald peak, the soft dip on top. I drive right at it before turning into our driveway, passing the field boxing in the two horses. Sarah won't be home for at least another hour, so I decide to tune up my bike to set out after that mountain.

The bottom land behind our house stretches downstream along Clear Creek to open eventually upon my family's plot. As a boy on that land, I kept my eyes on Bearwallow, its peak often smothered in snow while my yard hoarded only dead leaves and grass. I spent many an empty winter morning watching the mountain float in the distance. I conjured a giant black bear, silent but strong, patrolling the peak. Even though I never climbed the mountain as a boy, I could see the bear as I stood down in the valley. He circled the peak, a mysterious mix of gentleness and power, always keeping his distance behind trees and high grass.

Because Bearwallow's peak is an immense meadow, it was easy for me to spot it even without snow, standing like an enormous green molehill among the surrounding forested mountains. I watched it as we drove into town or to the general store or to school. I could find it wherever we were. It was my North Star.

It was years before I ever crossed the mountain. I left for college, where I started road biking, setting out from my dorm for long loops through the dead mill towns that accent the Piedmont of North Carolina—brick shells disintegrating beside the foundations of strip malls. I worked my way into that land, into its past, on the saddle of my futuristic titanium bike rigged with a tiny computer. It was my time machine. And soon it pulled me to Bearwallow.

When I returned to the Blue Ridge Mountains for holidays, I threw my bike on top of my car. Once home, I'd pull it down and make my way up and down the winding roads of Edneyville, seeing the land of my boyhood anew, in slow motion.

One summer, I set out from Fruitland Baptist Church and took off after Bearwallow once and for all. Out Old Clear Creek Road, I passed apple orchards and families I'd known my whole life. For some miles, the road rolled easily alongside pastures of indifferent cows and gentle, thin streams. Before long, though, I turned left on Bearwallow Mountain Road, aiming directly at the mountain, and the grade changed.

The climb was more than I expected. Accustomed as I was to riding in the relatively flat middle of the state, Bearwallow was immediately demanding. I feared I hadn't built enough momentum to make the climb. Then, after a few grueling minutes, I realized it wasn't a question of momentum as much as endurance. Endurance I didn't have.

I lumbered up the weaving road. I could have walked faster (and easier) than I rode, but I kept rolling, standing on the pedals as if riding a stubborn old horse, blood vessels knocking at my skin and sweat blurring my vision. I was alone, closed in by woods and one empty road that seemed it would never end.

Then the trees in front of me shuddered, an angry patter of leaves built, and I nearly stopped altogether for curiosity. From the stretch of pines alongside the road, a dog charged as if out of thin air. I leaned into the pedals and tried to fashion any speed I could as it barreled toward me, snarling and barking. I rocked the bike by pedaling harder and faster and took on my mean voice, hollering "Git!" over and over as my puny pace slowly picked up. I tried to keep my eyes straight ahead and think only about speed, about distance. And soon I was scaling the mountain, the dog's barks falling away into the valley.

Eventually, the land softened slightly. With each revolution, I thought only about the ten feet in front, not the seemingly endless slanted land above me. No Trespassing signs hung nailed to trees leading into deep forest. I considered turning around—the steep grade much more inviting behind rather than in front—but I kept on, trying only to keep myself upright and moving.

When I finally reached the top, I stopped, unclicked from my pedals, and decided to beg forgiveness of my legs before dropping down the backside of the mountain. Bearwallow's meadow allowed a panorama that swept broadly across Edneyville: un-geometrical patches of farmland, armies of apple trees, tangled-up roads cutting through it all.

Yet I was most immediately struck not by the wide view but rather by the silence there on the mountain.

No car had passed me as I climbed, and while there were a few houses along the way, the only sounds I heard during the ride, aside from the angry dog, were my heavy breathing, the streams hidden in the woods, and the rustling of wind and animals. Atop this mountain that had stood in the distance of my childhood, I found an eternal quiet. And I wanted to stay.

Even though many other mountains in Edneyville offered better views and more exhilarating descents, Bearwallow became my most ridden route during trips home. The mountain seeped into my head as I drove the wide interstate home toward the Blue Ridge; I already imagined my climb to the top, the taxing ride into stillness. While the rush down the backside made the painstaking climb worth it, my favorite part was cresting the peak. As my bike neared the pinnacle, I always anticipated the moment when I would sit balanced exactly on top, when gravity was not pulling me the way I'd come or drawing me ahead.

During most other mountain rides, I cherished the shifting, the sudden rush of falling, as I crested the peak. I didn't stop to take in sights; instead, I fed on the great swing in momentum and flew down those mountains at forty miles per hour. On Bearwallow, though, I stopped the speed I'd worked so desperately to create during the last six miles of road and two thousand feet of elevation gain. I waited for the balanced moment and hopped off so I could stand for a spell on the peak. The trees breathed with the wind and water trickled down the mountain, but everything felt still, like I'd found some secret: a whole place forgotten.

~

I haven't been back up the mountain since we returned, but I feel pulled to it. I tighten what's loose and grease what's dry and dispose of the Mr. Jones uniform to slap on spandex. A smarter man would choose an easier inaugural ride—I haven't ridden seriously for years—but I'm passing the church and dropping down Old Clear Creek and steadily climbing in the direction of Bearwallow anyway.

As the mountain grows larger and the road aims upward, I realize I've made a mistake. I'm already out of breath, beginning to cramp, and the steepest has yet to come. But I keep on because I want to sit still on the peak, to feel returned.

Nothing seems to have changed along the route except that a few more No Trespassing signs cling to the trees and a couple new houses hide in the heavy woods. As I inch onward, the same dog recognizes my smell or the sound of my bike and bursts through the trees to chase my ankles. I unclick my cleat to threaten a kick, but it is an act. I holler "Git!" but only because it's my part in our drama.

I have to climb off the bike twice to catch my breath and keep from tipping over. Each time, I walk beside it like I'm herding a lazy cow before I finally talk myself into another go, forcing my legs to slowly power the bike upward.

When I finally near the top, the trees fade away and the skyline opens up, as if I've taken off from the earth and am now floating. Immediately, the silence envelops me. But before I dismount and finish my last bit of water, I notice the machinery and the signs and the miles of winding, darkly stained wood fence stretching across the entire meadow. Dirt roads still in progress carve up the landscape. Just off the main road, a fountain splashes over the silence and a ten-foot rock sign towers above me, reading, GRAND HIGHLANDS.

Across the land, smaller signs denote the dozens upon dozens of lots for sale. There are no houses, only signs, empty bulldozers, front-end loaders, and smoldering felled trees. Wisps of smoke drift off the mountain as I, after a life away, stand out of breath on top of the bald mountain and look around for any sign of the bear.

2

In high school, a friend developed a theory he called "the Pull." This, he claimed, was the phenomenon that kept people in or always coming back to our small mountain town. As if by a massive magnet hidden beneath the soil, people were affixed to these mountains. While some of us wanted nothing more than to get out, others were caught, as the theory went, and would never leave. Many never tried. They were pulled in to never escape. They married right after high school, many of them pregnant within a year. But even those who felt sure they weren't ensnared—who tried to leave, to explore or plant roots elsewhere—were pulled back eventually. They drifted out of college or ran out of money or broke down, and then moved back. For good. Nothing was to be done about the Pull, if you were within its grasp.

I wasn't. I left the mountains following high school, and after college, I disappeared entirely. I stretched myself farther from the Blue Ridge, finally landing in what I imagined to be a world away, burrowing into a rural piece of western Honduras originally named Gracias a Dios—"Thanks to God."

A hundred years before my forefather Abraham set out into the

13

Wilderness, Spanish conquistadors set out into the ever-rising high-lands of western Honduras, which on gray afternoons of the wet season reached into the clouds, leaving only a wall of green from the ground to the hidden sun, a frightening and alluring eternal presence. The mountains tempted, spoke of magic, and so the Spanish climbed and cut their way, winding from peak to valley, eventually arriving at an oddly consistent, flat piece of earth surrounded by looming land. And there they stopped.

They didn't think of the immense, cloudy heap into which the plateau crashed—a mountain the Lenca people called Celaque, or "Box of Water." They didn't worry about the tangled forests and mossy trees awaiting them, growing together like the treacherous climax of a fable. They only raised their hands to the sky at the sight of even land and said "*Gracias a Dios*" for space enough to live.

And there, some three hundred years later, I settled, too. Sarah and I rented a small apartment at the entrance of town, near the *gasolinera* and the only road out of Gracias. We began teaching in the small elementary school. To the town, Sarah became something sounding like *Sadah* and I became "Mister," sounding like *Meester*. We began to make a home in a place somehow poor and infertile in a region of volcanoes, a place somehow ever-coated in dust despite the deep green of Celaque rising at its back.

It was in Gracias, leading fourth-graders through the cobblestone streets and across the snaking rivers, that I somehow found myself working back to Bearwallow. I began to see traces of home everywhere. At first, it was only in the land. The sweeping mountains of western Honduras, while a bit more jagged and lush than the Blue Ridge, felt immediately reminiscent of home, cousins to the mountains I'd left. Their aged, soft presence backed every step of my daily life.

Random moments tripped my brain and pointed it toward my mountains. Uncovering local folk songs with my students had me digging out similarities to Appalachian tunes; hearing ghost stories of men on the mountain made me think of my forefathers; leading my students to search after a fabled enormous snake living inside the mountain moved me to recall my mythical bear patrolling that eternal peak.

I even began to pick out qualities in the people that turned my head toward home. It was as if I'd found some sort of wide-reaching mountain-ness. The consistently private-but-kind nature of the locals felt akin to the manner of the people of western North Carolina, as if the history of mountain survival shaped generations and daily interactions. As if the harshness and isolation of wrinkled, towering land led people to distrust the outside and forced them to rely on community. These people, it seemed, were my people.

Some mornings in the first-grade classroom at the elementary school, I passed around white sheets of paper along with our basket of broken and half-naked crayons so the students could draw while I collected myself in the front of the room. Nearly all of them reached first for the green (thereby starting a few feuds). They aligned their pages on their desks and then, with crooked, sharp lines, pulled the crayons up and down and up and down along the top of the whiteness.

No one, nothing was added to the page until the lines of the mountains stood firmly in the backdrop. It was impulse. We hadn't spoken about representing the physical parts of the world around us—I was just trying to keep them busy while I pieced together lesson plans—but the mountains were always first, as if the children were born knowing of the land's longevity and history. The mountains spread as a green outline across the entire piece of paper—always mountains before houses, before mothers and fathers, before the students' round-headed, long-armed representations of themselves. It was a strange image to witness: a room of small Honduran children hunched over their papers and wobbly wooden desks, scratching thick, green lines into an empty world.

As I walked the impoverished edges of town and sat by the market in the center of Gracias and explored the wild mountain shadowing us, I found residues of home. The men driving oxen down the mountain, the women cooking over wood stoves in the hollows of Celaque—that world felt like a history lesson of Appalachia, like I'd been dropped into an alternate-universe version of the world of my grandparents. Even the soft, tapered accent of western Honduran Spanish rang with resonance of home. Was I making it up?

Here I was in another world, somewhere that seemed to spring from the mind of Gabriel García Márquez—a puma wandered into town from Celaque; butterflies swooned over the flowers on the playground as children burst wildly through; a toucan rested on a tree outside my classroom as we took a vocabulary quiz—and I could think only of my bear and my mountain.

~

A few years before landing in Honduras, Sarah and I had set out from my university for lunch one day. We stopped in the parking lot of a grocery store to get money from an ATM, and as we did, I noticed the hood of my Rodeo coughing smoke. I pulled forward. The car jerked and stopped, the smoke a final sigh.

I remember climbing out into the half-full parking lot and cringing at the irony of being broken down in my college town. Both of my grandfathers, with their bare high-school educations, could likely have fixed the car, or at least diagnosed the problem. All I really knew to do was open the hood and look around. But I could talk about Faulkner and iambic pentameter.

A man eventually stopped to help us. He hopped from his muddy truck with his two young children in tow. He bid us hello and immediately bent down, reaching to touch the green goo pooling beneath the car.

"Your radiator's busted," he announced, standing back up and wiping the green on his jeans. He sent his son to fill a jug with water next door at a bank as Sarah and I stood by the steaming car in the middle of a parking lot in the middle of North Carolina.

"Where y'all from?" he asked.

"Henderson County," I said, "farther west."

"Oh, so y'all's mountain folk."

We nodded slowly. Unsurely.

"Mountain folk's good people," he said.

Despite hailing from the Blue Ridge, I hadn't ever considered that any qualities could make me "mountain folk"—that geology had affected my personal characteristics or shaped me in any way. It seemed such a curious notion; if the land had marked me somehow, I didn't know how. I started wondering if others somehow knew me to be mountain folk from my walk or gestures or tongue. Was I "good people" because of plate tectonics?

In Honduras, the voice of our Good Samaritan mechanic crept back into my head over and over: *So y'all's mountain folk.* In that foreign world, I easily spotted how the mountains rubbed the people. They'd been shaped by life in the highlands. I heard it in their voices; I saw it in their eyes. But I couldn't do the same with myself. How was I marked? How was I mountain people—how was I my people?

So after digging in and planting roots on the edge of Gracias a Dios, Sarah and I decided to pack it in and return to the Blue Ridge. I took this job at Edneyville Elementary School; Sarah and I married and moved into a small house off Gilliam Road, dead in the view of Bearwallow Mountain.

The large upstairs window exactly frames the mountain's silhouette. The sun dips behind the bare peak in the evenings, strewing deepening yellows through the house.

Sarah can't entirely acclimate to the night's full darkness and the bare silence out here. Even though she was born exactly thirty days after I was, in the same hospital, she grew up in Hendersonville—what we in Fruitland and Edneyville call "town." Our whole lives, we lived fifteen miles apart in the same county, but the worlds around us were distinct. I spent my childhood running through woods and fields below this little house. I couldn't see any houses from mine, but I knew how to get to my cousins' by blazing my way through the woods. She lived on Fourth Avenue in a large, hundred-year-old house only a few blocks from Main Street, with people on all sides. She played with a diverse mix of friends and neighbors in yards and parks. I played Vietnam with my cousins and plastic guns in the creek and the hayloft of the barn.

She comes from a line of doctors and lawyers. I come from a family a few generations removed from farming. Both my grandfathers turned it into a hobby rather than a livelihood, finding new jobs delivering the mail and working in a textile plant. Her grandfathers owned their practices, one law, the other medical.

Growing up in town, she slept to streetlights and passing cars and voices. Our apartment in Honduras stood off the main entrance to Gracias, so sporadic light seeped through the windows and we heard pickup trucks rattling along the cobblestones. Now, we're living in the middle of my native nowhere.

The house stands a ways off Gilliam Road. We're renting the property from Fred Pittillo, who bought it for the bottom land reaching out below the house. The land had been a horse farm, but now only a couple horses loaf around the front pasture. A handful of cows graze on the sloped land behind the house, and the old barn next to the house stands empty. Fred uses the acres and acres of flat land running behind the house and along the creek for his sod business. Since dairy cows no longer pay bills, nearly all of the even pastureland along the creeks of Fruitland and Edneyville is rented to Fred for sod, much of which is used on the high-dollar golf courses springing up on the mountain peaks. Since he wants only the lowland, Fred is selling the house on the hill and its barns for a large sum of money. But he hasn't had much interest, so he lets us pay a little to stay and maintain the grounds.

We have a couch and a bed and two dogs that are too big for their own good. Too big for the house, at least. Most afternoons, I come home from school and set out with them toward Clear Creek. They bound through the sod field and past the cattle chewing indifferently on the hill, leading me in the direction of my family's land.

⌒

After a month of school, I have a steady stream of students in my condo. In the mornings, I bring a short line of kindergartners—Maricruz, Angel, and Ana—bouncing into the trailer to sing silly songs. By the afternoons, fifth-graders sit around the table with books opened. The range keeps me on my toes—and feet—all day long.

Last week, Maricruz asked me if I live in the trailer. It seemed a fair question; most of my students live in mobile-home parks. But I often wonder what they think about a young white man bringing them to his house every morning to sing songs in a strange language. I am *Señor* Rogers.

Four other trailers rest out back around mine. They were all moved in a few years ago to ease the crowding from the influx of students. I'm trailer number 1, in front of the trailers for art and reading and music and dance. We trailer dwellers have our own intercom system, as suits our own little banished nation. Occasionally, the office forgets to inform us of important events, like the fire drill this morning that I apparently taught straight through. We joke of seceding.

While I don't mind the condo, I am happy to leave it every hour or so to fetch my next group of students. It allows me a brief walk outside before, like a mother duck, I pass from classroom to classroom, waiting in the doorways for my students to spot me and fill in the line growing at my back.

As I expected, my students are here for apples, mostly. Their fathers and mothers work in the orchards and packing houses that dominate the landscape of Edneyville and Fruitland, and they live in the trailer parks pocketed in the mountain valleys. Some of them pick beans or tomatoes, but the majority have crossed the border and trudged north into the mountains of North Carolina for apples. I wonder about their arrival. They rarely talk of the journey, but I catch pieces here and there. The desert, they seem to believe, lies just outside our mountains. Leaving the Blue Ridge means arriving into endless desert, and finding one's way through this desert means Mexico. Mexico, desert, Blue Ridge. A sandy Cumberland Gap.

Antonio, a third-grader who came to the States four months ago, at the end of the last school year, shows up in the middle of my day. I was told that he and his dad crossed the border and worked their way here to live with the dad's brother. Debbie says Antonio cried when he sat in front of the computer in our condo for the first time. He also had a broken arm that no one knew about, suffered during the journey. After a week of pain streaming across Antonio's face, Debbie insisted the father take him to the hospital, no matter his fears of deportation. The next week, Antonio wore a hard cast, which the other kids signed in bright, bubbly letters.

He's considerably happier this year because his sister and mother have arrived from Mexico after a tense kidnapping and ransom dispute between *coyotes* at the border. They've all moved into a trailer on the side of Bearwallow Mountain.

Today, my other third-grade student, Carlos, is absent, so Antonio and I sit alone at the table in my classroom, staring into his open social studies book. His class is studying the Civil War, and so we wade into the chapter, with its illustrations of battles and maps showing borders and loyalties. I try to further simplify the text to help Antonio work through the words and stories. He follows along indifferently as I outline the sides and motivations of the bloody and lionized war.

As Antonio stares out the window overlooking farmland, I quickly decide my real goal must be to help him decipher the past tense, not to unpack all the details of the War Between the States. After a few slow pages, we close the book. Tomorrow, we'll move on to a picture book about a taxi driver in New York City with a talking dog riding shotgun.

After I walk Antonio back to his class and amble toward the teachers' lounge to grab my lunch, the image of a square, crew-cut boy who used to roam these halls fills my head. Willie Griffin. I haven't seen Willie in years, since high school, but his third-grade self stomps around my gray matter as I heat up spaghetti in the old microwave by the copier.

⌇

Willie Griffin started calling me "Cripple Finger" in the second grade. I didn't mind too much because I liked him. It seemed a friendly nickname—I figured he and I were friends. Plus, I was kind of scared of the sturdy, square kid with the buzz cut. He was big and rough, his temper sharp as nails.

Willie found this nickname for me in second grade, but my cripple finger had come about the year before, on an unusually warm December day, the kind of day that is wrong enough to be right because it falls out of nowhere, threatening to erase all memory of winter. The sun shone evenly across dead leaves like a faded photograph, and because the weather was so unseasonable for the mountains of North Carolina, I was in the yard, out by the well, helping Daddy split wood. I remember thinking that it was New Year's Eve's eve—I had learned what the word *eve* meant the day before, but I still wasn't sure how to connect *eve*'s meaning with Eve of Adam and Eve. Had she preceded something? Me? The Fall?

Our wood splitter was a thing of steel. Had the back not looked like a complicated weapon—engine like an outboard motor, tubes running to the oblong, red, missile-like casing that housed the hydraulic arm—it could have appeared as a long, monstrous tricycle. Two large wheels were in the back, while the front stood on a stout black leg that could be raised and lowered. With the leg retracted, the machine could be hitched to the back of a truck and rolled wherever needed. But once the metal leg was set down, the wood splitter was solid and sturdy and ready for work. When the long lever, which looked like a car's stick shift, was pushed forward, the hydraulic arm extended from its red housing, a square push block on its end advancing steadily toward an ax-like blade waiting at the edge of the machine.

As a boy of seven, my job was to push that lever, sending the hydraulic press toward a round log Daddy would lay at the end. The log waited, resting against the blade, until the pressure of the ever-advancing arm and the sharpness of the blade squeezed it and it creaked and cracked and finally split down the middle, falling in halves on either side of the machine. I would then pull the lever, and the arm would slowly return to me and its red casing. Usually, Daddy would then put one of the split logs on the machine again so that I could send the press back toward the blade to cut the halves into quarters—blocks of wood the shape of watermelon wedges. If the wedges were small enough, I'd help carry them to the growing pile of firewood while the arm returned, but they were usually too big, so I stood by the wood splitter watching the hydraulic press disappear into its place while Daddy stacked the freshly cut wood.

I'd been working the lever for months. Every time Daddy hooked the wood splitter to his Bronco and pulled it into the woods, following the old logging trails, I wanted to be there, hand on lever. He'd cut, split, and pile the wood, eventually heaping trailer loads of it onto the back porch for the coming winter.

I became nonchalant with the pushing and pulling, and that warm winter day, I wasn't thinking. Or maybe I was, but about something other than the task at hand. About Eve, maybe. As Daddy carried split timber to our pile and I pulled the lever to return the arm to its place, I laid my left hand casually on the red casing that housed the arm and push block. As the greasy hydraulics pulled the push block surely back to its home, my pointer finger and thumb were squeezed tight in the closing gap.

The vibrations of my scream rushed through the woods so that Granddaddy heard them clearly where he was piddling in the tractor shed. When he saw the dust billowing from the road to our house, he reckoned something was wrong and jumped in his truck to follow Daddy's Bronco down Highway 64. I don't remember that scream, nor do I remember the pain, only the towel wrapped around my hand as Daddy ran red lights in town on the way to the hospital. I remember the sudden strangeness of realizing that something as firm as a finger could be smashed.

By the time Willie found his nickname for me, my finger had passed through a surgery and a few casts and was shorter and more crooked than the others—a little longer than my pinky. It no longer needed bandages or pins, but since its nail grew off to the side of its short tip, its seeming crookedness invited Willie's nickname.

Willie was one of those boys who was jerky in his movements, who had a quick temper that sent all the blood in his choppy body to his face. A boy about whom people tended to say, "He just doesn't know his own strength." A boy who would take wrestling too far or throw a punch during kickball. And so I forced a laugh at the nickname "Cripple Finger" and didn't worry when my mama didn't like that a classmate called me such. Plus, Willie Griffin was a good friend to have—he was learning karate.

He called me Cripple Finger in second and third grade. In third, in Mrs. Lunsford's class, I learned to hide my finger pretty well by making a natural-looking, loose fist when my hand was unoccupied. I don't remember thinking of it much then; I was young and had been told that the finger might grow along with the others. The doctors weren't entirely sure about how badly the growth plates were damaged. I knew I could play four-square and swing on the monkey bars. Even with a twisted finger, the world made sense. Things were right; kickball happened on Fridays and cursive still seemed unnecessary.

But for Willie, one day in third grade shook the earth from its axis. We finished social studies and began to pack up our materials and dig through our cluttered desks to find lost books for library time. All of us but Willie. He didn't bother raising his hand; he just hollered out his question across the classroom: "And then we won the war?"

I only halfway heard him. As far as I was concerned, social studies was over and I planned to be ready for the library as fast as possible. No one stopped sifting through the desks. We had more important things to worry about, like who would be line leader.

Mrs. Lunsford tilted her head to the side. "No, no, the North won that battle, Willie, and then the South—General Lee—surrendered. Does anyone remember what *surrender* means from our word list?"

Tiffanie sat straight up in her chair and shot her hand into the air, but Willie kept on: "But . . . when did we finally win? When did we beat 'em once and fer all?"

"The North won the war, Willie," she said.

Most of us had found our library books and were trying to look quiet and well-mannered so we could be called to line up. Willie, though, only stared at Mrs. Lunsford. The whites of his eyes turned pink, and the pink of his face turned white.

Some days, we were permitted to walk in the hall alone without a teacher guiding our line. And this, apparently, was one of those days because Mrs. Lunsford said "Off we go" to Tiffanie. We filed out, but Willie still sat at his desk, motionless. As I left the room, I turned to see him—hands flat on his desk, a question on his face he couldn't get out. Mrs. Lunsford approached him, but he didn't look up.

I'd already picked out a book about a team of scuba divers traveling through the South Pacific when Willie came into the library, his eyes red, his cheeks wet, and his head lowered. He looked smaller than normal, smaller than Willie Griffin ought to. Mrs. Lunsford had her arm around his square shoulders, and she bent to whisper something in his ear. He sulked toward the books as though his shoes were full of water. Mrs. Lunsford walked over to the librarian. The two women smiled, their arms casually crossed, as Mrs. Lunsford said something. They were adult smiles, hinting at some shared knowledge or wisdom unavailable to children.

I wanted to ask Willie what was wrong, but I was scared and only watched him drag himself by. Although I'd never seen big Willie Griffin cry, that was the only explanation for his flushed, wet face. I'd seen his face red plenty of times, but out of exertion or anger or laughter. Never tears.

He stopped walking in front of a nonfiction bookcase. He was completely still for a long while, and then, suddenly, he started stomping his feet like he was marching in place. He put his hands over his eyes, stamped his boots as hard as he could, and sat right down in the middle of the library floor. The previous year, in second grade, Willie had stood in that very spot with his Alabama T-shirt on. The band members were pictured on the front—long, wavy hair and tight jeans. He had gone to a concert the day before, for which his parents allowed him to miss school. When he returned to class after the concert, he stood proudly in front of us in the library and sang Alabama's hit "Song of the South."

Willie cried all day, off and on. Sometimes, he sobbed. Other times, he pitched a tantrum. He cried like it was too dark to see. He cried like his foundation had vanished. He cried on Monday and Tuesday. On Tuesday, we didn't even talk about the war, but he probably hadn't slept and probably hadn't eaten and probably hadn't said a word but for the one constantly in his head: *why?*

I was confused. Confused not only because the biggest and roughest kid in class was crying, but because I knew the South lost the war. I figured everyone did. Willie, though, lived up on Bearwallow Mountain and didn't come down but for school and groceries. Up there, they flew a Rebel flag like it brought up the sun every morning and laid it to rest at night.

~

Willie and I learned quite a bit about "the War" in the third grade. The abstract went like this: The South had slaves. The North didn't. They beat us up because we didn't have guns or shoes, and made us free our slaves. They had factories, and we had farms. They had machines, and we had cotton. We all nodded our third-grade heads solemnly; we knew slavery and racism were bad.

But when Willie broke down and lost his bearings, he wasn't crying over slavery. His tears had nothing to do with the knowledge of freed blacks or a childish fear that racism could unleash the fury of the North. No slaves lived on Bearwallow when we were in third grade, and there probably never were any.

He and I knew only three black kids.

One was Dea Pepper. She and I played soccer together. Her dad—a happy, motivating man—was our coach. Dea and I were both fast, the fastest on the team, and I have a clear memory of our chasing a soccer ball at Jackson Park one Saturday. Our bright yellow uniforms, my wristbands. Dea beside me taking long strides with her skinny legs. I took shorter ones, but we were neck and neck. The other team (as well as our own) was far behind. We raced after the ball like nothing else mattered; there was no world, not even a net or game or score, only the ball, rolling away. I don't remember who reached it first, but I see Dea's arms pumping and my long, bright socks.

Alona, a fireball who stapled her tongue in first grade, had a funny smile but a temper that was quicker than Willie's. She must have respected and feared her grandmother because calling Alona's grandmother was a threat that teachers held over her head with great success (and consistency).

And Olaitan. Olaitan was the only other boy in third grade as big as Willie. He was square and stout. And Nigerian. Willie, Olaitan, and I played basketball together in elementary school, and my daddy was our coach. Neither Willie nor Olaitan had a basketball bone in their bodies; they had big, take-up-most-of-the-lane bodies. Daddy always drove Olaitan to and from games in the Bronco.

Olaitan didn't come to Edneyville from his faraway land until second grade. He talked a little funny. He smiled a lot. And while he mostly dressed like us, there was one day when he wore traditional clothing from his region of Nigeria.

We all were to give reports on countries we'd been studying, and Olaitan chose his homeland. I chose the Netherlands because I imagined wooden shoes would be cool. I knew nothing of my Dutch Abraham and his buried treasure then.

For extra credit, we were allowed to dress like someone from our country. I had a hard time finding wooden shoes. I don't remember Olaitan's presentation, but I remember him afterward on the blacktop in bright garb; we were playing four-square, and he wanted in, but the teacher instructed him to change clothes first so as not to ruin his get-up. We were all yelling for him to come play, to hurry, and he rushed inside as quickly as he could to change.

Olaitan was exciting and novel. Everyone wanted to be his friend. We all wished we had Nigerian clothes. We all wanted to take a field trip to Africa. We even tried to imitate his accent. Willie, Olaitan, and I always put our hands in the center of the huddle before basketball games and yelled, "Go Yellow Jackets!"

Willie's third-grade breakdown was over pride. He may have lived on a mountain where men still said *nigger*, but *Yankee* was a far stronger word. He believed in a world in which the good guys won, a world in which the South held off "Northern aggression." He couldn't accept a world in which the Yankees had actually won, had put the South down. The ominous Yankee was the villain in both Willie's dreams and living world.

I appreciated his utter investment in Southern-ness. But I couldn't understand his collapse. He and I shared an accent and town and school, yet I couldn't fathom crying over history. History was dead, from a book, just like math equations and spelling rules. The knowledge that it brought could be processed or noted or tested, but it didn't have the power to reshape or crush worldviews. History and I were disconnected; it was static and I malleable.

Although I'd never been up north, so far as I knew, the North and South were simply two sides of a coin—two pieces of land separated by a visible line, something red and straight. Place didn't define but was rather defined by those upon it.

But the South was who Willie was, Alabama's "Song of the South" his soundtrack. Yet Willie's idea of the South wasn't explicitly linked to region or history; instead, it was something rural and wild. He wanted a Chevy truck and camouflage pants. He dreamt of deer hunting and Rebel flags. All he knew of being Southern was what he saw around him: thick forests and strong men.

Willie's South was Bearwallow Mountain. And Willie's South wanted to be left alone.

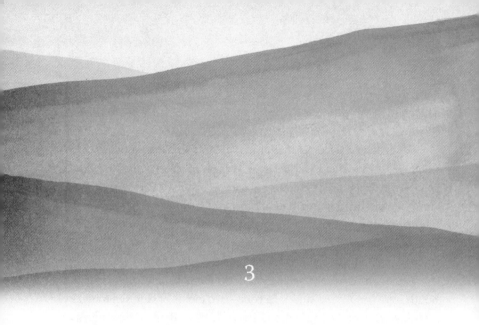

3

"Oh yeah, that place is going to take over the whole mountain," Jayne says as I drop quarters into the drink machine in the lounge. She and Terry, both second-grade teacher assistants, sit on the couch by the window eating, making a mismatched pair. Jayne, a woman who could butcher a hog, then serve it for dinner, leans comfortably back into the couch, scratching her cropped blond hair with a pencil. Terry, tall and tan and thin, perches on the edge of the couch, her blouse and skirt impeccably matched and her legs crossed.

"How big is it supposed to be?" I ask, fetching the Dr Pepper and my change.

"Right now, it's supposed to be two hundred acres," Jayne says, "but them lots are so small, they're liable to squeeze two thousand houses up there."

One of the perks of not having a classroom of kids is hiding out in the teachers' lounge during lunch. Classroom teachers have to sit in the raucous cafeteria and mind the children, but I dip in here for thirty minutes of quiet. Or gossip.

"It's a shame," Terry says.

"Whose land was it?" I ask, settling into the armchair.

Terry shrugs, but Jayne answers: "Belonged to a couple families, I think. The Barnwells have some land up there. So do the Griffins—you went to school with Willie, right?" I nod. Jayne's son and I are the same age; we both went to school with Willie. "But they haven't sold. They're right up there on the edge of it. You know Ann Cody's place is up there, don't you?"

Ann Cody is a teacher assistant in a kindergarten classroom. When I was a boy, she was the school's janitor; she kept a picture of Elvis on the door to the custodial closet. But since I left, she has earned a degree and now works in the classroom helping five-year-olds recognize and read words from the Dolch word list.

"No, I didn't know that."

"Well, you might ask her about it. But I don't know who all sold the land to the developer. Reckon they made a pretty penny."

"I heard about one guy," Terry chimes in, "who sold off his family land up there. I don't know his name. I hear he got nearly a million dollars. But he didn't want to leave the mountain, so he moved into this little hunting shack he had down the mountain. Can you imagine? A millionaire living in a shack?"

"Lord, that's all I need. I'm going to get me a shack so everybody thinks I'm rich," Jayne says.

"I done got me one," Terry laughs, standing.

They toss their trash and leave me in hiding for another ten minutes before I head back to the trailer.

⌒

Antonio and Carlos don't like "The Lion Song." The second-graders couldn't get enough of it this morning, doing the hand motions, trying out the noises and the new words. But Antonio and Carlos, the third-graders, prefer to sit. They wonder if we might play the bingo game again.

"Let's sing the song first," I say in English, readying the CD player.

I try to speak exclusively in English during our class time, repeating words often. Antonio sometimes tries to respond in English, relying heavily on what sounds like one word: "*Idunno.*" Carlos, though, speaks only in Spanish to me. He mostly seems relieved to speak at all. No other students in his classroom speak Spanish, so when Antonio and I appear at the door to take him back to the condo, he smiles and has to pin his arms to his sides to keep from all-out running for us. No matter my no-talking-in-the-hall rule, he lets loose like a rolling pot of water: "*¿Qué vamos a hacer hoy? ¿Ya fuiste a recreo, Antonio? Vimos una película hoy.*" "What are we doing today? Did you already have recess, Antonio? We watched a movie today."

In Honduras, I had no curriculum. I pieced together plans from talking with the Honduran teachers over coffee and scouring *National Geographic*'s website in the Internet café and taking field trips to the botanical gardens. On my first day at Edneyville, I opened up brand-new materials: posters, books, CDs, flashcards, teacher guides. While I try to remind myself of daily objectives and assessment methods, I often let the whole session devolve into a conversation about a trip to the flea market, a term I didn't realize translated so smoothly into Spanish until yesterday. *La pulga*, the flea.

Both Antonio and Carlos have been in the country for less than six months, so anything exciting about this new life in a rural stretch of apple country seems worth some of our time. Plus, Carlos spends much of his day in silence, surrounded by foreign sounds. I pepper the conversations with new English words; they write new ideas. Today, though, I first make them sing. We're going on a lion hunt.

This curriculum gives students flashes of the world—one day we're in the jungle, the next under the ocean. Many of the stories reveal cultural traditions spanning the globe, often through the lens of an immigrant—narratives of Chinese New Year celebrations in New York, of preparing Peruvian food in California. Of course, none of the stories explores *La Pulga* along Highway 25 near the town of Fletcher, or the squeaky fiddle music of the Blue Ridge Mountains. The curriculum helps them to see the larger world, to process being of two minds, in two places, but it doesn't situate them within these hazy mountains. This, I figure, is my job, my ambassador role. But I'm not sure how to do it. I'm trying to situate myself back here.

Last week, I bought a banjo, in part to find a way to grab hold of this place. A Saga, it's called. While I can't make it run smoothly yet, I thump along slowly in the afternoons after school, trying to find enough notes to build a melody. I've propped it on a guitar stand in a corner room on the second floor of our house.

The room's pair of windows give me glimpses of two sides of this land. One reveals the peaks—the top half of Fruitland Baptist's steeple, the soft lines of Bearwallow and Pilot and Sugarloaf mountains. The other window frames the valleys—the sloped pasture dropping into the sod fields that run alongside the creek to my family's land. My banjo and I sit in between.

Not long after we moved in, Dad helped me carry a desk into this room. I wanted somewhere to write. As he and I twisted and lifted the thing up the staircase, I slipped taking a step and dropped the desk's full weight on his finger. My daddy is a gentle man, like his father and grandfather (my great-grandmother Azalee always called Daddy "the compassionate one," which isn't to say he is not tough—and that's not to sound like every boy's defense of his father). He grew up with three brothers in the woods farther down the creek, and he broke his fair share of bones and carries scars from a wild childhood. But I hadn't seen my father hurt in a long time. He doubled over in our living room, a slice across his finger from the desk's wooden edge.

Eventually, he sat down holding his hand as water squeezed its way from his eyes. I stood in the middle of the room, not knowing what to do, thinking that he was about five years older than I am now when I crushed my finger in the wood splitter in our front yard.

He and I didn't talk much about my finger after it healed, but I know my childhood changed. He felt responsible, and in many ways, that meant I didn't have the same chores and boyish responsibilities. He split wood alone and rarely asked for help when he fiddled in the basement, fixing things and cutting boards. Of course, I didn't mind getting out of work at the time, but I knew the boys around me were required to apprentice with their fathers in such tasks. I cut the grass and helped paint, but he sheltered me from potentially threatening jobs. And now as a man in my first house, I wonder what I've gained and lost from the cripple finger.

Even though the growth plates at the base of the finger continued to function after the accident, the outermost joints stopped growing entirely. The finger grew, just never as long as it should have. It stayed crooked at the tip. The foundation grew, but the peak was stunted.

I mostly forgot about it. I played sports through middle and high school, having no problem with left-handed layups or two-handed backhands. I couldn't type the way we learned in keyboarding class because the finger was too short to reach the *T* key from the home row, but for most tasks, I didn't notice my finger.

I learned to keep it hidden—even from myself. Rarely did anyone notice its shortness because when I slightly balled my hand, the bottom half of the finger looked normal. Even today, people don't seem to realize my left pointer is short and crooked. I am practiced at concealing it—laying my thumb over its tip, holding a pen, resting it bent on my knee. Oddly, though, children seem to take note of it rather quickly. Perhaps this is because my students look at me for longer stretches of time than other people, or perhaps kids feel no shame about asking such questions: "Mr. Jones, what's wrong with your finger?" There's no hiding it from them.

When I turned sixteen, I talked my parents into buying me an acoustic guitar—a Gibson Epiphone—from a pawnshop in town. I had images of playing Neil Young and Oasis tunes in my bedroom and strumming resonating ballads on a stool in front of unknown faces in a dim coffee shop (even though there was none for miles). I wanted to take the guitar back to my room, pull the pick across the strings, and empty serious and poetic sound from the hundred-dollar used instrument.

When I took it out that first afternoon and sat on the edge of my bed with a chord book lying open on the carpet, I pressed my fingers as hard as I could into the strings, trying to find clear sounds. I plucked each string, pushing harder with my left hand to clarify the sounds. I then tried to form G and C chords. But after a few hours of contorting my left hand, I finally realized that the injured joints of my pointer finger weren't able to form a C or bend gracefully over any string without entirely muting it. I folded and crumpled my hand all afternoon, trying to find a way to force the finger to work like it ought to.

By evening, I sat on the floor, the guitar lying silent beside me, and cried. I'd never really cried over my finger. I'm sure I cried for the pain when I injured it, but after the surgeries and casts, I accepted it and tried to forget that warm December day. I learned to use and hide and never share my cripple finger.

But I'd been thinking about that guitar for months. I had plans of forming a band; I'd created a reality for me and the guitar. That evening, while I leaned against my bed and cried, I wasn't shaken by disappointment but by anger. I couldn't look at my finger; it disgusted me. I pushed the guitar away and left it in the corner.

It stayed in that corner the entire next day. But once my eyes dried, I stared at it and the book and visualized ways to make my hand work. I picked the guitar up again. I considered spinning it around—using my right hand to form the chords—but I didn't know how to string a guitar, and the thought of restringing it upside down was daunting. Plus, strumming with my left hand felt awkward and foreign to any kind of natural rhythm.

I tinkered and twisted and reformulated some of the chords like a puzzle with missing pieces. I found that I could form many of the chords without using my pointer finger, by ignoring it completely and leaving it below the neck of the guitar, pointing at nothing. After weeks of forming calluses, I could work my way through Gs and Cs and Ds, albeit slowly. I even started to find ways to use my hurt finger. It could reach the strings at the top of the guitar without needing to bend much. Its rigidity even proved useful when forming barre chords.

After a few years, I did find myself on a stool, then eventually on small stages opening for a friend's band, playing the simple and bad songs I'd written. Once I felt at home with the guitar, I started picking up other instruments: a twelve-string guitar, a bass, an Andean charango Sarah

brought me from Peru, some strange instrument made of wood and
snakeskin that my sister brought me from a college trip to Thailand.
And now I have a banjo standing in the corner.

⚋

It's a strange thing, the banjo. Some skin and strings. It looks as if
its maker couldn't decide between percussion and chordophone, and
just threw the two together. And then there's this string that doesn't
even reach the full length of the neck, stopping short at a peg sticking
out halfway up. The whole thing makes me think of an open hand—
four tuning pegs at the top and a thumb on the side.

My Saga has no back, no resonator to catch the sounds and roll
them around. When I decided to buy a banjo, I looked for this pre-
bluegrass breed because it felt distinctly Appalachian, clearly affixed to
the region's history. I bought old CDs of North Carolina banjo players
like Fred Cockerham, Clarence Ashley, and Bascom Lamar Lunsford.
The recordings were simple and crinkly, but they sounded right.

Much of the banjo music that I have was recorded in the 1960s by
people who had come to southern Appalachia to learn to play those
fiddle tunes. They wended through the mountains, staying with Appalachian families so they could capture the music on amateur recording
equipment. They wanted the music as an example, as a study guide for
when they returned north and sat down with their banjos and fiddles
and dulcimers. But now many of those people have formed a collective
and sell their recordings online. The profits go to the families of the
documented musicians. To me, the music feels wholly present; the fuzz
and waning audio quality sound like the living, breathing past.

I suppose I've been looking for this—a connection to the region—
since I returned to the Blue Ridge. The banjo sitting on my lap seems a
tangible bit of Appalachia. In Honduras, I felt at times like the hydraulic
arm from the wood splitter. I was slowly and steadily being pulled back
to my place.

And here I am, nearly re-placed in the body of my boyhood. I've
taken a job at my elementary school. I'm teaching beside my former

teachers, living just up the creek from family land. It's as though I'm searching for a taut line leading to southern Appalachian identity because I'm not sure what it is that makes me from here—what connects me to these mountains. *How am I mountain folk?*

The playing style I'm learning is called clawhammer. It has many variations, mostly depending on one's location in the mountains, but generally the fingers remain bent like a claw. They come down—always down—upon the strings, the nails thumping the notes. The thumb stays hooked and catches the banjo's fifth string during the strokes, creating a steady clip to the music's progression. Bluegrass banjo players pick, but clawhammer players rap.

Bluegrass is a fairly modern sound, a twentieth-century invention. It has roots and connections to Appalachia but is played all over the state and country. Earl Scruggs, most often referred to as the "inventor" of the three-finger bluegrass banjo-playing style, said he came upon the technique sitting on his porch, just an hour from where I live, near Kings Mountain. He said he couldn't keep his fingers from a-wiggling, and soon they began to pick out steady rhythms. "Scruggs style" is the rolling bluegrass sound most often associated with the banjo. The resonator attached to the back gives the instrument its reverberation.

But my banjo has nothing on its back to bottle up the notes. They shoot out the back, lonesome and true. This clawhammer style seems to be fading away. I hear it on my distorted discs. The musical style is simply called "Old-Time." And to me, that's all the more reason to grab on with both hands, to imagine it has something to tell me of what it is to be born inside these old mountains. So I sit by the window overlooking the steeple and Bearwallow and teach my hand to move naturally in steady rhythm.

～

I'm learning to play traditional folk songs, many of them Civil War–era banjo tunes such as "The Southern Soldier." And while some of them such as "Flight of the Doodles" document Southern victories in the war, others including "May God Save the Union" show a mountain loyalty to the United States. These banjo tunes send me into my land's complicated past.

North Carolina was the last state to secede from the Union. Debates and politicking abounded before North Carolina officially left. This was especially so in the mountains, where there were many Union supporters and few slaves. Most western North Carolinians were too poor for slaves. Large plantations were virtually nonexistent—the slanted land couldn't support them. Farmers and their families worked their own land. It didn't make monetary sense to buy a slave when ends barely met as was.

Although there were some slaves in the mountains, the mountain slave owner wasn't a farmer but a doctor or lawyer, a politician or merchant, often here to escape the Charleston heat. Of the small number of slaves in western North Carolina, most were servants or couriers, cart drivers or shop workers. They made up roughly 8 percent of the mountain population. Some counties had more; others had virtually none. Those numbers were dramatically different from the rest of the state; slaves comprised more than half of many eastern North Carolina county populations.

Thus, the mountain debate over secession required more than a simple up-or-down vote on slavery. Slavery didn't affect most mountaineers, so the politicians used other means of conversion. The reasoning most Confederate leaders and supporters employed had to do with what Willie grew up hearing—Yankee aggression upon the South, the central government controlling every man. However, these mountains held many pockets of strong national loyalty, of Union support.

Edneyville was home to the bloodiest prewar conflict in all of North Carolina. Before the polls opened for local elections, residents reported free-for-all combat between Unionists and secessionists. Throughout Edneyville, at the foot of Bearwallow, there were skirmishes, as well as looting and pillaging by Unionists. The captain of a local Confederate company complained to the governor that not one man in the area had volunteered to join his unit: "They are deadly hostile to our raiseing [sic] volunteers and the whole defence [sic] of the south as any portion of Pennsylvania." He even reported that some neighborhoods were hiring night guards because Union supporters were burning the houses of their Confederate neighbors. I doubt Willie knew that more than a century prior, his crying could have actually gotten him killed up on Bearwallow.

Ten miles from Edneyville, in Hendersonville, sentiments were strongly Confederate but equally violent. Secessionist forces intimidated a Unionist candidate, threatening to pull him from the stump and ride him out of town on a rail. They promised to hang or shoot anyone who voted Union. Several people who did were mobbed.

On May 20, 1861, North Carolina decided to break from the Union. In Hendersonville, a young secessionist exchanged shots with a Union supporter and then chopped down a pole flying the American flag. Many mountaineers favored secession once North Carolina left—one man said he felt "awful Southern"—but they adopted a watch-and-wait attitude, imagining the fighting wouldn't last long.

Western North Carolina was spared major battles, but the people still felt the war's effects. One of the banjo tunes I learn and play, "The Southern Soldier," documents young boys leaving home to fight:

> I'll place my knapsack on my back
> My rifle on my shoulder
> I'll march to the firing lane
> And kill that Yankee soldier

But other songs reveal the mixed loyalties of the region and its people. "Brother Green" speaks of a dying Southern soldier whose brother is Union:

> I have one brother in this wide world
> He's fighting for the Union
> But oh, dear love, I've lost my life
> And I shall die a Southern

For some, Southern-ness wasn't a matter of heritage or region, but a chosen allegiance. Men felt they ought to fight out of duty, but many later became disillusioned with a war to which they felt no connection. Some switched sides, and others simply left.

In many cases, though, Southern-ness was a matter of happenstance and being drafted at gunpoint. Many men and boys in western North Carolina were conscripted once the Confederacy established a draft in 1862.

~

I've found Rebel and Union branches in my family tree as I've started looking through records at the historical society in town. Abraham's granddaughter married Captain Robert Jones, who served as the leader of the local militia, or Home Guard, for five years. But he left the position as the war ensued because it legally held him under the command of the Confederacy. He found such a role trying, as his sons and a number of grandsons had joined, and in many cases were recruiting for, the Union army. He and Elizabeth tried to live quietly on their land between Flat Rock and Edneyville.

His son Hiram found no peace at home. One afternoon during the war, a Confederate detail rode onto Hiram's land in Big Hungry. They'd come to take Hiram's teenage sons into the Confederate army, they said. Hiram wasn't home; he had ridden into town. When his boys refused to join, the solders tied them up, threw them over horses, and led them bound and gagged toward war.

In town, Great-great-great-granddaddy Hiram got word that men had come for his boys. He pointed his horse back toward Big Hungry. On the way, he heard the unit marching up the road. Hiram and his horse crept into the forest to wait for the first sight of his sons. As the soldiers passed, guiding the horses bearing the tied-up boys, Hiram whacked his mount and fired his rifle as he burst from the woods. He somehow managed to hit and kill a Confederate soldier with his flying shot. Hiram's sons fell from the bucking horses in the excitement; they crawled under a downed tree off the road and waited. Upon hearing a

second shot, the soldiers hightailed it up the road, fearing more am-
bushers were on the edge of the forest, riding Hiram's shirttails. But
Hiram's second shot proved more symbolic than dangerous to the soldiers—he mistakenly shot his own horse, which he'd quickly dismount-
ed. The horse died, but Hiram led his boys back home safely. The next
week, they joined the Union army.

These are my people, I'm learning: caught between loyalties. More
complicated than Southern.

⌒

In the beginning, during the watch-and-wait period, mountain
Unionists and Confederates alike sang "The Compromise Song." Yet as
the fighting dragged on and fewer and fewer men returned home, songs
such as "The Battle of Shiloh Hill" began to document the horrors of
the war and the houses and farms left without fathers and sons:

> There were men from every nation
> Laid on them bloody plains,
> Fathers, sons and brothers
> Were numbered with the slain,
> That has caused so many homes
> With deep mourning to be filled,
> All from the bloody battle
> That was fought on Shiloh Hill.

It's impossible to know what songs, whether Union or Confederate, were sung the loudest up on Bearwallow, but I'm sure no one sang
anything like Alabama's (and Willie's) "Song of the South," as life was
hard, fearsome, and desperate. No matter the harsh conditions, these
mountains came to represent refuge for many during the Civil War.
Their geographical separation from the battles lured deserters, but so
did the mixed loyalties, the private nature of the people, and the vast
number of caves. Western North Carolina was called "a hiding place
of Tories and deserters"—a sanctuary for Unionists and defecting

soldiers. Like Abraham a hundred years before, the escaping soldiers saw the hazy mountains and hoped to slide seamlessly into them, to pass from sight.

As more and more men fled in the latter part of the war, the Confederacy engaged local conscript guards not only to draft men into war, but also to patrol possible hiding places and return deserters to battle or prison.

From Internet searching, I've learned of an anonymous grave at the foot of Bearwallow. A Confederate deserter is buried there, where he'd apparently been hiding with two other men in a ravine near Laurel Creek.

One morning, three Edneyville conscript guardsmen—a Whitaker (my great-grandmother's maiden name), a Lyda, and a Case—set out up a mountain trail looking for defectors. Maybe someone had tipped them off, or perhaps they regularly searched the nooks in Bearwallow's side. In any case, the three men hiding in the gap heard the guards and tore off into the trees. The guards shot at the blurs. Two of the defectors kept on blurring up Bearwallow. The other fell still, dead. The guards buried his body next to the trail and gave him a headstone on that day in 1865, mere months from the end of the war. They never found the other two turncoats, who forever disappeared into Bearwallow Mountain.

Sitting behind my newly planted desk and looking out the window, I imagine the scene down in Bearwallow's shadow. I try out something of my own on the banjo. It's simple, a couple chords, but I hammer on until it sounds old and dangerous and dissonant.

I wonder which side I would have been on, had I been forced to choose. Am I a Rebel or a loyalist? A hider or a fighter? I put my cripple finger to work, rapping on while I trace Bearwallow's lines up to its soon-to-be-developed peak. I try to imagine that shadow stretching across its side as a line demarcating Confederate and Union. But it's hard to see exactly where the shadow starts and stops. It's hard to find the line. I keep on, trying to make everything black and white, speeding up my song until it falls apart entirely.

4

I admittedly didn't invest in my costume as fully as Debbie and some other teachers. They're clad in traditional Mexican dresses of bright red, all flowy and flowery. I bought a green T-shirt and wrote *"¡Viva México!"* across the chest in red Sharpie. Luckily, it's not up to me to reveal the signs that today is September 16; students have prepared Mexican flags of construction paper, the gym has been plastered in reds and greens and whites, and kids jitter with the excitement of an off-schedule day. Mexican Independence Day.

This isn't normal, of course. I'm sure no other elementary schools in this mountain county have shifted schedules and prepared a program for a gym full of white and brown kids to celebrate Miguel Hidalgo shouting his "Cry of Dolores" to begin a war of independence against Spain. This celebration, though, has been happening at Edneyville for a few years now, ever since Debbie took over as ESL teacher. So I'm toting my guitar and wearing my homemade shirt to lead a group of fifth-grade students in the singing of "De Colores" in front of the school.

Already, the trailer smells of tamales. Mothers of students have been delivering giant soup pots filled with the corn-husk-wrapped, chicken-and-cheese-filled food all morning, along with candy and tacos and punch and *tres leches*. Convincing myself not to get handsy with the steaming food waiting unguarded, I take my guitar

to Mrs. Miller's classroom for one more practice run before the show.
Manuel and the other fifth-graders—some Mexican, some American, some both—sing in Spanish:

> And that is why I love
> the great loves of many colors.

Debbie and Sherri seem happy with the final practice run, so we line up to leave. I'm happy, too, for not instinctively arranging myself with the children, following the instructions of two women who had given me orders fifteen years prior.

In the gym, the smallest kids sit, legs crossed, in straight lines on the floor. Parents and teachers and big kids fill the bleachers. I wave to Carlos sitting quietly among his classmates in the corner. The inclusion classes—those intentionally made of an equal mix of Latino and white students—mill about along the wall, listening to last-minute instructions from teachers before their performances. The fourth-grade boys wear red, white, and green ponchos and giant sombreros. The first-graders have made their own wide hats of papier-mâché and paint.

The festivities begin with the third-grade class performing a traditional *campesino* dance, the boys stiff and upright, red bandanas tied around their necks, the girls twirling their long white dresses alongside. The dance ends with the boys on one knee and the girls sheepishly throwing a foot upon the boys' bent legs. They're nearly all blushing and twitchy as the applause begins. The kindergartners form a circle and manage to mostly stay there while they make hand gestures to music. And we sing "De Colores" without much of a hitch. The native-English-speaking students even remember the appropriate Spanish sound effects for the animals: *pío pío* for the chick, *cara cara* for the hen, *quiri quiri* for the rooster. Decked out in the colors of the Mexican flag, the principal, Mrs. Smith, thanks everyone for coming.

As the gym begins to clear, I'm thinking only of the tamales until I spot one of my friends, Freddy, a Mexican-American whose daughter is apparently in kindergarten. As we chat, I can't help wondering what high school might bring for these students, for his daughter. While

Freddy and I have been friends since middle school, high school meant clear lines between the immigrant and the native. Different lunch tables. Different halls. Different languages. But this morning, students from thousands of miles away and students coming down from the mountain above the school have waved flags and danced in costume to celebrate the start of a decade-long war for independence in some other place. Something has happened here.

~

After school and my fill of traditional Mexican food, I head out in search of "the Lonely Grave" at the foot of Bearwallow, chasing after an anonymous Civil War deserter's resting place. I don't know where it lies exactly, but before I leave school, I read in an archived newspaper article that it stands on private land, a rock headstone and a short fence making its presence known in the otherwise empty forest.

I don't know entirely what's driving me but feel I ought to have a look at the grave site, since one of my kin may have killed the escaping boy. I am also curious to put my feet on the ground, to see and smell what the defecting men may have while living a life on the run in our thick mountains. I've imagined the scene in my head: men hiding for their lives, hearing a rustle behind them, then charging toward Bearwallow—their only hope of salvation—as gunshots rang out.

Often on my rides, I've cycled past the dirt road leading to the property. Wash Freeman Road trails off Old Clear Creek a few miles beyond the road climbing to the peak of Bearwallow. Its loose gravel keeps me from pointing my bike down it, but I know where to turn once my car takes the sharp curve dipping through a cool, covered tract of forest. As soon as I'm off the pavement, gravel spits and dust rises beside a No Outlet sign.

The dirt road winds in the direction of Bearwallow, twisting past apple orchards and small clumps of forest. I pass only one house, which I gather from a sign belongs to a Freeman. The orchards are also likely Freeman's, but the newspaper story claimed that the grave rests on the property of a man named Lowell Jarrett, so I meander past the lone house, hoping to find another place or some sign of ownership. Dirt paths sporadically split off from the road, only to end at the edge of the forest. After following a few of these dead ends and hopping out to look around, I decide I have a ways yet to go, and push onward and upward.

Eventually, the gravel transforms into a neatly paved road. The dust settles behind me, all other paths end, and only the asphalt remains, straight ahead. Guarding its way are two rock pillars with American flags flying atop. The pillars seem to be waiting for a gate, something sturdy and iron, but there is no sign of such, only markers affixed to the rock reading, "Lace Falls Property." Beyond them, I spot two large houses, one farther ahead and another perched on a hill. I turn my vehicle around again to survey the apple orchards and winding road but finally figure that, as odd as it seems, the grave likely waits within the not-yet-gated development. As I enter Lace Falls, I note a smaller sign reading, "Lowell Jarrett Proprietor," and know I'm on the right path.

The road forks immediately; I instinctively turn left, up the mountain. Driving past expansive newly built houses and shiny SUVs and luxury cars, I have trouble picturing men hiding desperately on this land. It is cleared and clean—trimmed green yards with raked leaves and islands of mulch. Nothing of it seems reminiscent of the story I've heard or history I've envisioned. There's no place to disappear.

The road veers arbitrarily up Bearwallow until the pavement eventually stubs out at the edge of the forest spreading up the mountain. I hop out and walk to the end of the road, where the asphalt fades to gravel, then to dirt and plants, leading deeper into the woods. I wade in as though a clear line splits wild from residential. Crossing this line throws me into a world crowded with trees and mountain laurel. I search the ravine below, where I figure to see the grave. The forest is untouched, the bustle of the development deadened and distant.

I think of hiding in these woods with the deserters. I imagine feeling free of the battles farther north and east, the severed limbs and dried blood and nagging ringing of ears. But this freedom is tinged, on edge. Every snapped twig and mountain breeze must be the conscript guard or bushwhackers or soldiers working their way across the

Blue Ridge. Maybe we stop here for a quick drink before hiking the final few miles home. Or perhaps we're close to home, close enough to taste the other side of the ridge, but we're lying low on the periphery until the moment is right to surprise wives and children and mothers. Waiting for a clear coast. Maybe we're scared out of our minds, turned around, wholly lost, wondering if we're not in another country, in foreign mountains.

Standing here above the gap, I can see them. There. They sit around a small campfire, talking quietly, leaning against a fallen tree. I even smell the smoke of burning oak and maple, drifting up the mountainside.

I venture farther and deeper into the forest, keeping an eye on my dreamy scene down in the gap, but I find no sign of any grave or fence. Finally, I climb back into my car to leave my reverie and continue my search for the Lonely Grave.

On my way back down the mountain, a smooth-skinned, pretty woman in a silver Lexus stops beside a large rock house. Two schoolchildren pop from her backseat and spring through the yard, backpacks bouncing. I stop alongside her car, hoping to get some direction. Two other kids, I assume hers, sit in the car, the younger in the backseat. I'm not sure what to ask, so I try to speak generally, imagining she'll think me crazy for asking about an old, anonymous grave on a sunny, nearly fall day of clear air and cut grass.

"Do you know anything about an old Civil War grave back in here anywhere?"

She smiles. "The Confederate grave, sure. Just go right back down this road and turn left at the fork." She points in the direction I've come, a wide silver bracelet dangling from her arm. "You'll see after a mile or so. You can't miss it."

I thank her and, recognizing the young girl in the backseat from the elementary school, wave as the Lexus heads farther up Bearwallow.

I find the grave exactly where she said—frighteningly close to the road, with only a foot-tall wood fence standing guard. But despite the paved road only a few feet from the headstone and the houses farther up the mountain and down the road ahead of me, the grave site rests alone in the woods, mostly enclosed by thick rhododendron and tall trees. The sun streams thinly through the woods. Hiding now feels possible.

Once I park and kneel by the miniature fence, I find the original, worn headstone at the foot of an oak and a newer, chiseled granite stone rising from the other end of the plot. It reads,

> Unknown Soldier
> Infantry
> CSA
> 1865

I hear the softness of a thin stream that I assume to be Laurel Creek running unseen behind the plot. A tattered Confederate flag flies, tied to a stick stuck in the ground.

The Sons of the Confederacy donated the new headstone, a small sign tells me. While no one knows the dead boy's story, he likely was a Confederate deserter who abandoned the war and his loyalty to the South, whether genuine or forced, and was cut down by Edneyville men appointed to seek out and arrest Rebel deserters. So it's strange that his resting place is now adorned courtesy of groups fervently attached to the history and sacrifice of men and women to the Confederate cause. He fled the Confederacy, and the Confederacy killed him for it. But here he lies in the woods with a fresh headstone and a Rebel flag.

I'm not delusional enough to forget that I'm in the midst of a housing development, but the smell of a campfire still finds its way to my nose and into the imagined scenes floating around my gray matter. Since I know the boy was buried alongside the trail up the mountain, it seems likely that the paved road running toward more houses was laid upon the centuries-past path. Maybe the path was originally dug into the earth by buffalo or the Cherokees or my mythical bear on his way to the peak. I envision the men wildly running up this road, the babbling of Laurel Creek covered up by screams and shots and fear. My head erases the asphalt. The men don't dare look back. I wonder if the guards pursued them or simply dropped their weapons to bury the body of the boy they'd killed.

I step deeper into the forest behind the grave. As I make my way toward the creek, I find a square block of wood labeled with the number 9, nailed to a tree. It is impossible to know exactly how wide lot 9 reaches, but it seems to stretch to the grave. Back across the road, I clear a line of pines, and a house with a green yard and a sprinkler is revealed. The trees had hidden it from my historical visions. But as my actual surroundings begin to come more clearly into focus, I realize the grave isn't alone at all. It has neighbors a quick sprint across the road, peering through the thinning leaves. Likely, folks will be living directly next door soon.

A few hundred yards up the road, I come upon a house being built. Its skeleton stands, not yet filled in or painted. Downed trees burn in a pile. I recognize their smoke as the scent of my imagined campfire.

~

On Friday, I sit with Dr. George Jones in the historical society on Main Street downtown, at a long table among records of landholdings and grave sites and census data. George, the society's president, was a second cousin of my granddaddy Ray. Now, at eighty-six, his mind is still sharp and far-reaching. He can list family trees going back generations and tap into history and stories from all corners of the county. I've been coming to see him most weeks.

He's telling me of his recent struggles with Confederate groups in the area. The old courthouse is being renovated, and he's working to add to the rock monuments outside that list the names of fallen soldiers. There are memorials with names from the American Revolution to the current campaign in Iraq. But there is no rock or etching for the Union and its local soldiers. George and the historical society plan to install a memorial to those nearly 150 county men who wore blue during the Civil War. But Confederate groups are fighting them with fervor. They want no record that any local men fought for the North, and they certainly don't want to find any dissenting branches in their family trees. They prefer it all forgotten, buried, a Confederate flag and headstone atop it all.

George and I share a number of Union-fighting relatives—Captain

Robert and his sons, among others. George is nothing if not dedicated to the full, detailed chronicle of history. He has little sympathy for bent facts or ignored records for the sake of story or argument or pride. I have unwavering faith he'll have his memorial when the dust settles.

"I rode out to that grave off Laurel Creek this week," I tell him.

"Sir?" He cups a hand to his ear.

"I say, I rode out to that anonymous grave at the foot of Bearwallow this week."

As he's wont to do, he sits for a minute—smiling, gathering his thoughts, perhaps—and finally pulls out a piece of paper and begins drawing boxes. I lean in and watch, waiting for any hint of explanation.

He eventually says, "Anonymous no more," sticking his pointer finger into the air.

His rectangles and lines show me my connection to a man named Robert Jones Stepp, a Confederate deserter. Last week, after years of research, George was finally able to determine the identity of the anonymous deserter who lies beside lot 9. He combed through rolls and rolls of microfilm to find a short superior-court trial of the murder of this relative, Robert Jones Stepp. The records placed the murder along Laurel Creek in 1865. The captain of the Home Guard, Ambrose Featherstone, was charged with ordering the shots fired by Burgan Whitaker and the others that dropped the man into the earth. The court never made any ruling, as the case was said to be covered by the Amnesty Act. But the trial at least gave the boy a name.

I take notes, trying to get down the lines leading back generations, but the historical society is closing, and Sarah will likely be home soon, so I set out for Fruitland, thinking that somewhere in my blood run the lines of Robert Jones Stepp and Burgan Whitaker. Within my blood runs a man disillusioned with war and regional loyalty and another who followed orders earnestly and surely. A man who shot and a man who was shot.

5

Late in the Civil War, Union scouts donned Confederate uniforms to slide through enemy lines seamlessly, ghosting through the woods, trying to gather information. Most Southern soldiers were dressed raggedly by that point in the war, so the scouts intentionally dirtied the uniforms to make their appearance more believable.

I think of them when I pull out the passed-down flannel shirts I'd packed away before leaving the country. I toss on a tattered mesh hat to venture into Edneyville on Saturdays, dressed in the clothes of my grandfathers.

For those Union scouts, looking the part was only half the battle. They also worked at perfecting a Southern drawl. It was part espionage—they believed they'd be able to infiltrate enemy camps more easily with the right twang and regional lexicon—but also part self-preservation—they figured a Southern accent would invite sympathy if they were captured creeping through the woods and slipping into Confederate camps.

I imagine the men practicing their new accents, looking into rivers and lakes as their companies rested. I can see them working out the kinks, watching their rippling reflections adopt a foreign-sounding tongue, opening their mouths wider to soften their long *i*'s, slowing the rhythm of their sentences. I wonder if some of them became so invested in this character, so enamored with the sound of their new voices, that they began speaking to Union comrades with a Southern tongue.

There are mornings when I wake up and wonder if I'm dressing in these old clothes and this accent to fade easily into the world around me. Even though it at times feels intentional, I've started dropping regional words back into my speech, started bending my tongue back toward home. A *reckon* here and a *plumb* there. Otherwise, I know the men at the general store or the women in the gas station might look at me, hear my voice, and think, *He ain't from around here.* They may see the Union in me, hear the outsider on my tongue, and know.

In elementary school, we had folk teachers. Mrs. Brown and Mrs. Whitfield came to our class monthly to teach us about our region's traditions. We learned to make candles and candy. We learned old-timey games and ghost stories. The women sometimes wore long dresses and played music or churned butter.

I don't remember either of them playing a banjo. Actually, I don't remember anything specific about their lessons, except for a day when we made some chocolate desserts called Martha Washington Jets. But the classes intrigue me now. They existed to teach us of our place, of the world around and behind us. They said, *This is important; be proud.*

Appalachia is supposed to be a region of backwardness. We're toothless, gun-toting, moonshine-drinking hillbillies. We're Ernest T. Bass, Hatfields and McCoys, inbred, banjo-wielding figures lurking in the woods. It seems the question in education ought not be where we come from but rather how we can get away.

In many ways, that question of escape and change did shape pieces of the curriculum of my boyhood. Most of the teachers at Edneyville then were from the area and had last names drifting back hundreds of years in the county. But they were taught in college how to clean up their accents—"Ain't ain't a word, so I ain't a-gonna say it"—because those were the sounds of ignorance, the sounds of benightedness.

My accent thinned through elementary and middle school, but in high school, I took control of it because I didn't want to sound like the good ol' boys who wore camouflage and drove big trucks and carried Mountain Dew bottles in the back pockets of their jeans, spitting tobacco into the empty plastic when the soda was gone. Boys like Willie Griffin, who spent their days in auto mechanic and carpentry classes. I didn't think specifically about how to make my tongue sound different from theirs, but it happened.

It happened because I knew that, in many ways, the thickness of an accent could determine one's hall. Accent was predestination. Y-Hall meant Willie and other boys in shop classes, nearly all of them from Edneyville. X-Hall meant girls with equally thick accents in vocational classes, preparing for nursing and hospitality careers. Lesser accents placed students on the science-and-math hall. Those of us in English and art and foreign language classes built an academic voice. We had college plans, and we talked like it.

Late in my high-school career, an older friend who had moved away for college returned home.

"What are you doing tomorrow night?" he asked me.

"I've got a soccer match at Poke."

"Polk?" he asked, emphasizing the *l* I'd disregarded.

Polk, I repeated softly inside my mouth. I'd never thought of the *l* before; I'd always said what everyone else said, what seemed right. Even though I'd thinned my accent for classes, I realized that afternoon with the help of my college-going friend that my mouth was still full of words tinged with Appalachia.

After that, I made a conscious choice to pronounce words phonetically. I slipped the *l* in and felt I had inside information. The Polk incident started me questioning the pronunciation of other words that came instinctually from my mouth: *arrenge* for *orange* and *dawg* for *dog*.

The small, private university to which I eventually moved was full of Northern students from New Jersey and D.C., most from private and prestigious high schools.

My freshman year, a girl from Philadelphia living across the hall asked me why I said *mash* when I meant *press*. "Mash the button?" she echoed as we played Nintendo. "And why do you keep saying 'used to could'? That sounds funny."

What she meant was that it sounded stupid. I agreed. I stepped outside myself and quickly decided I still sounded like a hillbilly: a long, buck-toothed dunce from a movie. I blushed but was secretly glad for her pointing out my language's quirks.

I searched out any other words that might cast me as ignorant and tried to remove them. I took extra moments before speaking to review and dust off the words on their way to my tongue. I made sure I didn't say *innerstin* for *interesting*. I made sure to use *those* when I might have said *them*. ~~Them~~ *Those books are heavy.*

I'd always been a good student, so I knew the parts of speech and their roles, but I had mostly applied that knowledge to writing and academic work. Spoken language was something else, something overheard and taken on. In college, I began to think through my daily and colloquial speech as well, always using an adverb to modify an adjective: "really cold in here" instead of "real." My speech became upright, more grammatically correct than that of many of the privately schooled Northerners around me, and I liked it.

Once I moved to Honduras, I became English in the flesh. Daily, I represented an entire language for the students sitting in front of me. I had to decide what English I would be. What words and sounds would I give my students? Should I leave a room of Honduran nine-year-olds saying *y'all* or *you'uns*?

Outside the school's walls, my tongue was unwieldy. While my English was bookish and "standard," I strived to make my Spanish regional and colloquial. My tongue shortened words—*va* for *verdad*. I started ending sentences with the quick rise of *va*, as people did when talking about weather or pigs or money in the cobblestone streets of western Honduras—the quick sound of a question softening a statement. "*¿Ayer me vio, va?*" ("Yesterday you saw me, right?") *Verdad* literally means *truth*, but my tongue freely chopped it up.

I dropped letters from common words, *más* (more) becoming *má*, *usted* (you) becoming *uste*. This Central American accent and rhetoric obviously didn't find their way into my mouth from my genes. My tongue created them from the world around me. I passed through my days tapering words, speaking in a voice recently invented.

When I traveled to other countries, my tongue again reacted. In Costa Rica, I stopped rolling my *r*'s and spoke more clearly because that was the world around me. In Ecuador and Mexico, I found new words and tempered the formality of Honduran Spanish, freely using the informal second-person *tú*.

These shiftings mostly happened of my tongue's volition. It wanted to fit in—an aural chameleon. But while it spent the evenings and weekends pulling in bits of Honduran slang and dropping letters, from eight to three Monday through Friday, it shaped up. It hit every diphthong and smattering of consonants clearly. Then the bell would ring again, and I'd walk into the street to buy homemade bread, my tongue again loosening.

And here I am, back on the land of my boyhood, walking the halls of the elementary school where my tongue first began to shed its Appalachian tics, and my voice is now wholly confused, my tongue often stilled.

More and more, I don't know how the words coming from my mouth ought to sound. After traveling among myriad accents and grammars, I'm charmed by the ring of my mother tongue, allured by my grandma calling a *fight* a *racket* or Mom saying last night's rain was a *gully-washer*. The sounds around me are mine; they're from my place. But I don't know that I can take them on entirely. I can certainly create the accent and find regional words to line my sentences, but that would feel constructed and modeled. It might feel like a British accent taken on at a party—an affectation.

Chopping up words and blurring sounds to create a Honduran voice felt fair. I had no connection to the language, so inventing an accent for its words seemed necessary. But the language of home shouldn't be something to take on like an enemy's uniform. Rather, it should be something to remember, something to slide back inside.

The weight of this feels stronger some days. Days when I picture the students at Edneyville in five years, beginning high school. I hear their voices now and know their futures. I wonder about my responsibility to them, to their accents and vocations. I find myself thinking about my hypothetical children. How I want them to have natural access to the sound of the mountains, but how I know that such a sound has to be tempered or buried or lost to escape stereotypes.

Plus, I'm not sure I could provide the sound box of Appalachia to these ghost sons and daughters, since I can't find my own voice.

⌇

Today, I'm lugging the Saga to school. It's Heritage Week, and I'm glad. A month has passed since Mexican Independence Day, and I notice that I enjoy changes in my daily schedule; elementary school is nothing if not monotonous. My students will learn about their adopted homeland at every turn this week. Yesterday, a man played the bagpipes below the basketball goal outside. Fred Pittillo lined the blacktop with antique tractors from the sod farm and former dairy. Students are learning to clog. A storyteller came to tell Jack Tales, a genre of stories (Jack and the Beanstalk, etc.) that likely began in Britain in the fifteenth or sixteenth century and has managed to persist and grow in Appalachia for over three hundred years.

I'm supposed to play my banjo in the cafeteria while the students eat pizza and broccoli (I translate the menu into Spanish every month, so I'm intimate with the daily offerings). From a Doc Watson recording, I've managed to piece together the chords and a few moments of melody from "My Home's Across the Blue Ridge Mountains." The song seems apt for the week. Its history is unclear; it wasn't recorded until the early twentieth century, but it seems to reach as far back as the Civil War. It was likely sung by men pulled away from the mountains by war. A song of escape and return all at once. I like that.

I did some research into the history of the banjo for today. I figured I ought to know something to share, since I'm a "Mister" and all. I checked out books from the library in town; one was called *America's*

Instrument. What I quickly found was a history I didn't expect. While *America's Instrument* contended that the banjo was likely one of the few instruments—if not the only instrument—created and shaped in the United States, it admitted that its roots reached into West Africa, likely what is now Nigeria, where Olaitan's forefathers may have pieced together the instrument centuries ago. Slavery brought the lutelike contraptions to America. Africans played them throughout the South, sometimes building them from gourds. Older slaves often taught young white men to build and play what we call the banjo (or *banjer*, as most old-timers say).

What I grabbed hold of as a direct link to my history and region is actually an African instrument transformed by slavery. Something taken and remade. Suddenly, my banjo's name—Saga—feels loaded. Slaves who played the banjo were worth more money and often were forced to showcase their musical abilities when auctioned off.

The banjo's entrance into Appalachia is vague, since slaves weren't distributed uniformly throughout the region. Likely, it found its way in through vacationing Southerners' slaves, minstrel shows, soldiers, and explorers. Its history is a blurry jumble of lives, but once it found a home, it settled in. Like the Jack Tales, it persisted in the isolated mountains while the rest of the world moved on. Eventually, the African lute was stretched out, given an extra string, and played in English and Scots-Irish ballads. A century ago, a fiddle and a banjo made a band.

Living in Central America, I came across a man on the Caribbean coast of Costa Rica playing a banjo to calypso music. At the time, I found the instrument's presence eccentric, albeit interesting. But blacks living on Costa Rica's coast were brought from Jamaica to build a railroad in the nineteenth century, their descendants having been transported from Africa to Jamaica as slaves. It makes sense, now, to picture the man wildly strumming the banjo in a town of dreadlocks and displaced history.

I try to see my tongue in this banjo I carry to school. In it, I hear bits of a wholly confused history. The slave and slave owner. The North and the South, the Rebel and the loyalist, and everything in between. I carry both my shooter and my victim in this hybrid of an instrument.

And yet it somehow works. The slender neck and lone short string blend sweetly with the faux skin and open back. The near-fist of my hand manages to carve out notes. My smashed finger slides along and works out the melody. The thing is a mishmash, its form something of Africa, its twang something of the British Isles, its forging something of my mountains. It's an ambivalent instrument in an ambivalent land.

I wonder if I can do to my tongue as has been done to the banjo. I wonder if I can take pieces here and there—reclaim echoes of a lost voice—and flesh them out into one smoothly singing instrument. If I can make a home of two minds.

I'm taken aback by the sound of the cafeteria as I lug my banjo inside. Perhaps Heritage Week has everyone excited, but it's likely always this loud. I suddenly miss my hideout in the teachers' lounge, where the only sounds are gossip and the whirring of the copier. The lunchroom is a static roar.

There's no microphone or stage, so I sit near the water fountain thumping the beginning of my song. It takes only a few chords for me to realize no one can hear me here on the outskirts of the room with my old instrument. So I stand to walk up and down the rows of tables filled with hungry children. As I pass, they turn with mouths of half-chewed food to reach out and touch the Saga. I tiptoe around spilled milk and strewn lunchboxes while rapping the strings and picking out,

> My home's across the Blue Ridge Mountains
> My home's across the Blue Ridge Mountains
> My home's across the Blue Ridge Mountains
> And I never expect to see you anymore

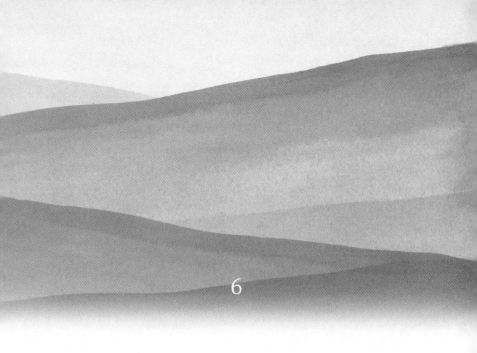

6

As Abraham and Bathsheba left the world behind, the land first rose easily, softly. Haze hung in the air, coloring the distance blue, as if the sky seeped from the peaks of the mountains themselves. But Abraham couldn't yet see the ominous gray of the Smoky Mountains or the shadowy dark of the Black Mountains. He couldn't know that the soft blue in front of him blurred the lines, hid the truth.

Beneath and behind and within this aura were mountains climbing to six thousand feet. Inside them, life was harsh; temperatures dropped below zero, snow fell in sheets, trees on high peaks rarely grew tops because of the whipping, persistent wind. Even though the mountains by then had been worn into comfortable, rolling forms by wind and snow and time, they had once risen higher and sharper than the Himalayas. Even though they birthed water and nurtured habitats from arctic to temperate, these mountains were hard and uncaring.

Abraham saw only empty land, so he and his new bride steadily disappeared deeper into the wild. Finally, they stopped on a wide plateau, the mountains rising at its edges. He likely didn't know the Cherokees had never settled there, forever setting it aside as hunting and resting grounds. He didn't know the plateau was purposed.

When he came upon the Wilderness, he found empty trails tracing what had come before him. Like tributaries, the trails converged at a wide table rock rising from the soil. He may have marveled at the grandness, at the flatness of the rock, but all that surrounded it now were the worn traces of history.

He likely found the land oddly quiet, knowing that men had lived and breathed and shouted and killed before the government pushed them away, before the land was his. But beneath its soil lived a history he could never know. He could only interpret the signs.

7

Before I came into the world, Granddaddy divided his land among his four sons. They each set out to mark a spot and settle in, imagining what the land would become at their hands.

Dad snatched a plot off in the forest, and when he married Mama and she left her family's land across the creek, they moved into a house they built in the woods. But for a dirt road leading up a hill and back toward the cornfields and the rest of the world, it stood entirely surrounded by forest.

Dad's brothers, too, took their land—Steve built on a slope out near the hayfields and apple orchard, Tim settled down by the creek, and Danny built on a bare hill overlooking Grandma and Granddaddy's place. Together, they surrounded the house of their parents, leaving us to be born immediately in the orbit of the rock house.

On summer mornings, we grandchildren drifted from our homes and toward the house of Grandma and Granddaddy, toward the middle, where we must have sensed we started. We wore trails into the ground. By pressing the earth in, we left signs like empty streams spreading across the land. We named these pathways—the Yellow Brick Road started near an old stump and cut through a cave of rhododendron before eventually arriving at the beagle pens and tractor shed; the Arrowhead began farther up the road and passed an old wooden target my uncle Tim had once used to practice his bow and arrow. Eventually, it reached a large stone sticking strangely from the ground. We felt sure it was a Cherokee grave. We returned over and over to it, stepped around it, and looked closely for any trace of etchings, any sign of life.

For all our hours of boyhood searching, we found only a few arrowheads on our land. But we knew in our bones that there were more, buried, and that we could surely unearth them if we only had the time.

~

After school today, I grab a coat, set out from the house, and fling open the gate. Our big dogs bound out, rushing toward the horse pasture and the hill down to the creek. Blue, our Great Dane puppy who seems to believe she is a horse, throws her giant front paws on the fence to stand upright like a floppy-eared man. The old mare ambles over, and they nearly touch noses while Blue's tail whacks my leg. The other dog, Banjer, is unsure of horses, unsure of everything. He whines and sniffs and pees until I finally whistle them on.

We follow Clear Creek downstream, edging the sod fields and pushing through a pocket of forest speckled in the browns and oranges of autumn to watch the land I know best open up before us. There, just across the dusty path that is Townsend Road, stretches the pastureland of my people. Up the hill, my great-great-grandparents' empty house stands guard over the slow-moving creek. Tucked in the woods reaching up the steep slope behind the barn waits my great-grandparents' boxy house. Deeper into the forest, out of sight, waits my grandparents' house, and burrowed even farther in stands my parents' house.

While I can't be sure about my tongue, I can trust my legs. They walk this patch of earth by instinct, passing the bridge to drop into the field. From here, I could make my way home with my eyes closed, entering by sense those old logging trails and dried riverbanks cut through the tangled wood.

But the dogs and I stop down in the bottom land, flanked by the creek and the barn. My daddy and his brothers spent their boyhoods in that barn, tossing themselves from the hayloft to land on the backs of the cattle milling unaware below, yelling "Yee-haw!" and imagining themselves in a John Wayne Western. It's a wonder Dad could make children after those free-falls onto the stout backs of cows, but I made my way into the world somehow.

The creek's waters running to our right are birthed on top of Bearwallow, in a seemingly hidden rock, the water leaking from the land itself. It drops down the mountain's steep grade, picking up thinner branches and digging out a way into the valleys, splitting our land. It empties into the French Broad River, where its waters run north, taking on more and more streams through the mountains before curling west into the Tennessee River and smacking into a Tennessee Valley Authority dam. Some of the water manages to trickle its way into the Mississippi and eventually escape into the Gulf of Mexico.

Clear Creek separates my father's and mother's families. This side has been tilled by the people of my paternal grandmother, the Prestwoods, but the soil just across the water is the land of the Maxwells, the hearty people of my mama's mama. Daddy grew up over here, rough and untamed; when Uncle Tim joined the army after high school, the barber found a map of boyhood violence on the newly shaven scalp—dents from rocks and elbows, scars from falls and sled crashes. Mama, though, grew more tamely on the other side of the creek. Her family had no cows on which to jump, but it did have horses. Her daddy helped run a stable up on Bearwallow, taking tourists on strolling promenades along ridge lines. She was raised with a sister amid the Maxwell fields— beans and corn, beans and corn.

All the land laid out before me spanning both sides of the creek has been put to work ever since the branches of my family tree established themselves here two hundred years ago. Both sides are now leased to Fred Pittillo, who owns the sod business and rents us our house.

The sod business used to be a dairy run by Fred's father. My great-grandfather Albert raised his dairy cows in this field. On Fridays, he would roll a small herd of metal milk vats out Townsend Road to Highway 64, where he'd sit and wait until Pittillo Dairy's truck drove by later in the day to pick them up. These days, Pittillo's trucks pull down into these fields to harvest the grass in squares that are tightly rolled up like rugs. Later, they are opened up in front of new houses and upon golf-course fairways many miles away to take hold as if they had never been uprooted.

As I stroll along the soon-to-be-transplanted grass, the dogs sniff out unseen histories: whiffs of rabbits now bunkered in the brambles up the hill, residues from the tires of the giant mowers now parked elsewhere, traces of gunpowder left from my cousin's rifles now standing upright in my grandfather's gun case. I wonder if the dogs might somehow catch faint hints of all that touched the land farther back: my grandfather's arrival as an orphaned teenager, my parents' courtship, my constant rock-skipping from the creek bank.

My great-grandfather Albert grew up on this land. He married a fiery woman from Mills River named Azalee; they had a daughter and settled into the house above the barn as a cozy family of three. But after a decade of working his acres upon acres of corn and cows alone, he and Azalee agreed to take in a boy whose mother had passed and whose father had vanished into alcoholism. Informal adoptions were common in the mountains, where there were no social services; my mother's father can't recall how many children his mother adopted but reckons the number close to eight.

So it was that a sixteen-year-old boy moved in with Albert, Azalee, and their daughter, Betty, and set to work in these fields that spring. He dug posts and picked beans and raised calves. He settled into a routine, became part of the family. Then Pearl Harbor. The boy joined the infantry, leaving the mountains and landing at a base in San Antonio before flying to England, where he repaired planes during the war.

Albert again worked his bottom land alone. He began delivering the mail on the side to make money. Betty started high school at Edneyville. Their family of three hummed along. But the boy stayed connected. He sent money to Azalee and wrote letters. He wrote of knocking out his teeth with a wrench while he repaired a plane. He sent occasional pictures. The Prestwoods reciprocated. The war churned along; Betty went to prom, dancing to the music supplied by the one-armed librarian playing piano. She readied to graduate. To become an adult.

One morning, she walked into her bedroom to find a box waiting on the dresser. She didn't ask who it was from or what it was; she set to tearing it open. Inside, she found a watch—a Bulova. She marveled at how it held the light; she tried it on, rotating her wrist to catch sun traipsing in the window.

She skipped into the kitchen to thank Azalee.

"That ain't from me. That come from across the ocean," Azalee told her.

Betty twisted it around on her wrist, smiling. "From England?"

Azalee nodded and returned to her cooking.

Betty had already graduated when the war ended and the boy returned to the mountains. She was still living at home, and the boy moved back in with Albert and Azalee after years of life abroad. The family returned to an even four.

But Betty had become a woman in the boy's absence. Casual exchanges and looks at family meals carried a new, odd shiver. Something had cropped up in Betty ever since she opened the watch. She gazed at the now twenty-eight-year-old man and felt nothing sisterly. The pinched breaths and quickened heartbeats felt like something else entirely. Something best ignored. He was no longer a boy but Ray, a man come home from across the sea. She pushed her thoughts away and went on dates with a boy or two from nearby families.

Ray worked the land, picking up the brunt of the chores while Albert delivered mail. He settled into the quiet life off Townsend Road—no houses in sight, only fields and forests and the never-ending push of Clear Creek.

I've pressed Grandma about the spark. When did she know? When did it happen?

She doesn't know or won't say, but before either she or Ray knew it, they were courting on their patch of family land. I imagine the relationship fell into place like the gradual roll of the creek. A joke. Brushed hands. Long nights sitting on the porch overlooking the bottom land where I now stand.

Albert and Azalee must have known. They may have known before Betty. They'd come to know Ray as family, and they liked the idea of his settling in full-time as a husband. He'd taken to the land, and they saw Betty's sparkle when he came back home. It seemed natural somehow.

So he proposed, Betty said yes, and soon the four of them drove like a family to Fruitland Methodist Church, which Albert's daddy had built by hand. The young couple made the *I do*s official on Christmas Eve and climbed into a car to head to Florida for a honeymoon.

Last week when I landed at Grandma's on one of these walks, she pulled out pictures and scraps from beneath the TV. Amid them, I found a photo of her and Ray in front of the car before leaving. They looked more glamorous than I expected, Ray in sunglasses and a trim suit and Betty holding her dress, hair caught in the wind. They didn't look like two adoptive hillbilly siblings quickly hitched back in the mountains.

After the ceremony, Albert and Azalee drove to Ray's best friend's house to tell him the news. He'd not even known the couple was dating. Betty and Ray Jones had kept their curious relationship hemmed inside the forests and fields of the Prestwood land. They grew their love here, not giving it away to the outside. But once they made the deal and exchanged the rings, they set to telling everyone and moved right back in where they'd left.

Now as a married couple, they slept and ate and worked in their parents' house. I sometimes imagine the strangeness of sharing Betty's childhood room. I wonder if she'd rid it of childhood reminders—dolls and trinkets. I wonder if Ray, my granddaddy, ever managed to get comfortable in that room, in his new role. I sometimes wonder if anything really changed.

They soon started building their rock house that would draw me into the forest as a child. Horses dug out the foundation by pulling a giant spoon-like tool over the land until room enough was made for a home. The place took shape like a bird's nest as they piled up and attached bits from the land—rocks, trees. They left Albert and Azalee's house and built their own life, barely out of sight of Betty's parents and grandparents. Ray worked pockets of the land but took a full-time job delivering mail in town. Betty had four boys. When they were old enough, Ray gave each of those wild sons a calf to raise as a chore—a lesson in how things grew, a lesson in loyalty. They fed and cared for the calves in this flat field, confined by a mix of wood and barbed-wire fences. Even though it is now deep green and fenceless, and even though cows no longer wander or boys drop onto their backs, Uncle Tim still stuffs hay into the barn loft year after year.

When both my dad and his calf had grown big enough, Dad sold it. With the money he collected, he bought Mom, the girl from across the creek, a ring. Just behind me on the bridge across Clear Creek, he knelt and proposed. Cattle ambled about the field. Albert and Azalee's place, where Betty and Ray had forged their love, rested easily on the hill. She said yes.

Standing in this field, I'm suddenly aware that I share something with the narrow bridge on Townsend Road stretching across Clear Creek. I'm the bridge between the cows of Daddy's land and the horses of Mama's, the bovine and equine, the lives and histories of the Maxwells and Harrells and Joneses and Prestwoods all coalescing in my blood.

Surely, that's why, after days of ushering newly arrived children into this language and land, I often walk toward the bridge like I stumbled toward Grandma's rock house on my boyhood summer mornings. I gather the dogs, and we sleepwalk to this field between the barn and the creek, below the cemetery where hundreds of years of my blood runs.

And then, once I feel settled, I whistle us all home.

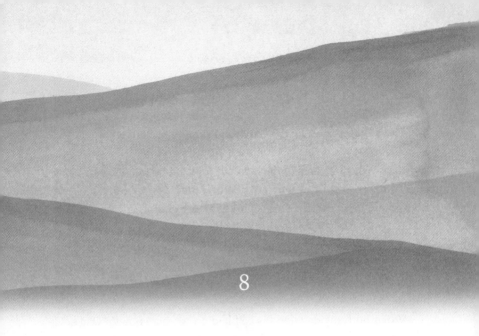

8

Field trip!

The fourth grade is busing into the gray mist of the Great Smoky Mountains to visit the Cherokee reservation today. A major perk of teaching "newcomers" is that I am sometimes recruited to accompany classes on field trips, giving me an entire day free of my trailer. I am a familiar face for my students, and I can communicate any important information when English doesn't work. So far this year, I've been to the zoo and to an apple-packing house where many of my students' parents work.

I've prepared my brown-bag lunch and grabbed a warm jacket, and I'm leaving home early this morning because we're supposed to head out at eight o'clock on the dime. I don't want to miss my bus.

In Honduras, I led my fourth-graders on field trips whenever I felt the urge. We padded through the dusty playground and swung open the ten-foot wooden door to the outside world. Beyond the school's court-yard waited Gracias, whose buildings were colonial and thus shared walls, making the town feel like a tightly constructed maze, roads pro-viding the only breaks in the adobe.

We interviewed a ninety-eight-year-old woman living beside the school for one of our impromptu field trips. When students kicked a ball over one set of classrooms within the school, it landed in her dirt yard. They yelled at her gate, hoping she'd finally hear—or more likely see—them bouncing up and down out front. In our interview, it was difficult to get my students to yell loudly enough for her to hear through her nearly century-old ears. Still, she told us of the Gracias of her youth—the same colonial maze of short buildings, but nothing except thick forest and a few dirt trails beyond the cobblestone streets.

On other trips, I led us single-file up the road past the four-hundred-year-old church, on our way to history. We'd climb the old Spanish fort built to defend against the Lenca warriors, dig around in the botanical gardens, tramp along the rocky river that provided the town's water. On a whim, I'd line them up and take off.

At Edneyville, the students have returned signed forms and the administration has allotted money and we've arranged lunches and contracted Mr. Cody to drive the bus to the Cherokee reservation. But when I climb aboard, I'm suddenly back in Honduras, where retired American school buses fuel public transportation. Finding myself amid diesel fumes and seats too small for my bent legs sets me back there, on my way to obscure corners of Central America. Those buses were older than I, but somehow Honduran ingenuity made them run, albeit loudly, gears grinding up and down mountains. The buses were painted bright colors and given names: Toro and Graciano. On weekends, Sarah and I crowded into seats with mothers and babies and chickens and farmers and students and, once, a pig to slowly climb off the plateau that was Gracias.

Today, I have a seat to myself, with plenty of room to spread out, just behind the driver. The windows are up, as it's below freezing, heavy frost sparkling on the tops of Bearwallow and Sugarloaf as we start up. I blow on my hands to make warmth. Debbie and Angie—my third- and fifth-grade teachers, respectively—are riding up front, too. In Angie's class, I once misspelled my middle name on a paper I turned in, *Brian* becoming *Brain*. Thus, Brain became my nickname. When my grandma, who taught reading down the hall, came into my classroom one afternoon and overheard someone call me Brain, I convinced her the name referred to my great intellect.

But today I'm Mr. Jones, and we're off, leaving the apple orchards of Edneyville for the interstate west into the Smoky Mountains. As the skyline opens, I understand why, for centuries, men have come here to vanish. From a distance, I feel as if I could sit down in these hazy and nebulous mountains and fall entirely out of view, be vapored over in blue mist.

Before Abraham and Bathsheba loaded up and drifted into the Wilderness, a young man named William Mills already lay inside a cave on Sugarloaf Mountain, healing from a gunshot wound and bayonet laceration that had nearly killed him. This was my land's first European settler—a man who came to hide. And in hiding, he found restoration.

In his twenties and loyal to the Crown, William Mills joined the Tory militia with his father. Not long after he joined, his unit moved to reinforce a group of British soldiers near Kings Mountain. Grossly outnumbered, they retreated but were easily surrounded and captured atop the mountain on October 7, 1780.

That evening, when darkness fell, the wounded William snuck into the bushes away from his captors and didn't look back for days, until he was deep into the Blue Ridge. He bled his way through forests, thinking of a cave on the side of a mountain that he'd explored as a boy, when he and his father had hunted in Cherokee country. He surely remembered the cave for its strangeness. Beyond its narrow entrance, a large room opened coolly, and a funnel of a hole grew from the room's ceiling to the top of the mountain, creating a natural flue for fire. He likely remembered the feeling of safety during nights of sitting balled-up by the fire, knowing he and his father couldn't be seen or heard as they trespassed on Cherokee land, knowing he was inside a mountain—in the earth, covered up by the very thing he walked upon.

So, as a man, he dragged his body through the mountains to finally crawl inside that boyhood safety, hunkering down to survive in what later came to be called the Devil's Smoke House, the only sign of his existence a spiral of smoke pouring from the earth.

Weeks later, William Mills emerged as if from a sweat lodge, convalesced. He set out for his family's home farther south in the flatlands. But after trekking down the mountains into South Carolina, he learned that his father had been captured and hanged and that the new government had taken his land. He briskly swore allegiance to America to become a citizen, gathered what was left of his family, and led them back to the empty plateau in Indian country where he'd escaped and mended. They bushwhacked their way north, blazing a path that eventually became a well-traveled route from South Carolina, intersecting the path running through Abraham's land. Today, that route is a road called Mills Gap, which runs behind Fruitland Baptist, the route I ride to reach Bearwallow. He and his family became the first white people to settle (albeit illegally) on the plateau. William built his homestead and planted fruit trees across the hills and meadows.

Later, when the Hopewell Treaty was signed and the land was officially opened to settlement, Abraham and Bathsheba tramped in. The state allowed William to retain his land and officially named his area full of fruit trees Fruitland, where our house on Gilliam Road now sits. He put names to the land my people would dig into and rise up from. He named (or renamed, as the Cherokees surely had their own names) these mountains—among them Sugarloaf, Pilot, and Bearwallow—surrounding our small house and muddy Clear Creek.

~

As our bus rattles along, I'm thinking not only about the way on to this land, but also about the path away. As handfuls of treaties pushed the Cherokees from corner to corner of southern Appalachia in the eighteenth century, they may have abandoned the plateau by traveling the winding paths that eventually became wagon trails and paved roads and now this four-lane interstate. But our route, while rolling and winding, doesn't climb over every peak it encounters. It cuts straight through. Dynamite-blown rock bluffs flank our journey. Rock slides shut down this section of interstate every month or so; boulders crash into the asphalt, trying to refill the mountain's breach. If the Cherokees took this route to leave the Blue Ridge and enter the Great Smokies, they had many peaks to conquer, a harsh up-and-down escape over pieces of mountains that no longer exist.

Leaving the discipline to Angie and Debbie, I sit quietly and watch Interstate 40 fade into Highway 74, with its outdated tourist traps.

We pass places where one can try a hand at gold pan-mining. What is meant to be a mountaineer—a giant wooden man with a corncob pipe and overalls—is planted on a hill's knob. "Gold in them thar hills," he says by way of a cartoon speech-bubble. The building below the sign looks like a wooden version of a strip mall—a wide, one-story shack running parallel to the road. Three cars are parked outside.

We come upon Ghost Town in the Sky, a hybrid amusement park and outdoor drama. A ski lift takes visitors up to the Western-themed town on top of the mountain. There are staged shootouts and a few shops and one rickety rollercoaster with no flips, only sharp turns on the edge of the mountain's peak. I visited Ghost Town a few times as a boy, when my family was on our way to Dollywood, Dolly Parton's country-music theme park in East Tennessee. The chairlift doesn't seem to be moving this frosty morning.

Many shops advertise folk art and crafts, canned fruits and vegetables, and even the chance to see a caged black bear. They're marked by signs that look handwritten—crooked with misspelled words. They're meant to read and look thoroughly hillbilly, attesting to each shop's regional and cultural authenticity. *We've got the real McCoy!* their *fokes* and backward letters scream. Beyond the attractions and stores are mountains and forests without noticeable sign of houses or roads or humans.

"I hain't been back up this a-way in years," Mr. Cody tells us as he drives. I lean in to hear him. "Years and years. I's raised back in here, you know, near Cherokee." He waves a hand toward the windshield and the dark mountains drawing closer.

Mr. Cody, in his seventies, drives a school bus for Edneyville in the mornings and afternoons—a long journey back in the mountains, lasting two hours, cresting Bearwallow. His wife, Ann, is a teacher assistant for a kindergarten class.

"How come you were to leave?" I ask him.

"The lake—"

"Johnny, put your rear in a seat!" Angie hollers.

"You know Fontana Lake?" he asks me.

I catch his eye in the mirror to nod that I do, while Angie threatens to get up and go back there. A narrowing of the brow, a quick hush among the students. " 'At's where we lived. I's a boy—eight, I reckon—when they come by telling us they's gonna flood it all. So we sold and moved out chonder to Edneyville."

After learning early in the year that Mr. and Mrs. Cody live at the edge of Grand Highlands on Bearwallow, I searched for their plot during a bike ride. I found *Cody* on a mailbox beside a pocket of forest and their trailer in a shaded gap off the road before the fence and sign marking the coming development. When I subsequently inquired about changes on the mountain, Mrs. Cody told me that the developer hadn't approached them directly with specifics, but that they'd gotten word that Grand Highlands wanted to buy their piece of land. She told me surely and quickly that they wouldn't sell. "It's our home. We're old, and it's what we have," she said.

I wondered how much they expected to be offered, but I held my tongue. I imagined it would be quite a bit, and I questioned if they'd really reject a large chunk of money just because it meant they'd have to find a new spot to settle down.

Today, as we drive toward Fonatana Lake, I want to ask Mr. Cody about the possibility—the irony, or the tragedy, perhaps—of being dislodged as a boy and now as an old man for the sake of development. But I'm not sure how to word it over the loud bus and the rumble of the children. Still, it makes sense to me now that Mrs. Cody could be so firm in her promise not to sell their piece of Bearwallow.

Mr. Cody is around my grandfather's age and has a thoroughly Appalachian voice—*thar*s and *you'uns*. So instead of asking about displacement and how he feels steering this bus back toward his drowned home, I talk about my grandfather.

"My mom's daddy was born out this way, too," I say. "Down in the Cataloochee Valley."

He moved to Henderson County, on to the Maxwell land of my grandmother, when they married and had their daughters. But his family left Cataloochee when the government claimed the valley as part of Great Smoky Mountains National Park. The region had been so heavily timbered in the early twentieth century that the government finally stepped in using eminent domain and claimed it from mills and timber trains. And the families living there.

Mr. Cody nods that he has heard me over the fourth grade but doesn't reply, only aims the bus farther west toward signs for whitewater rafting.

The formation of Fontana Lake flooded a number of small communities, including Proctor and Judson. The lake was one of many dammed by Roosevelt's Tennessee Valley Authority in the 1930s and 1940s. FDR sent the TVA to bring electricity and economic development to the region. Southern Appalachia had been timbered, mined, burnt, and overfarmed. The prospect of electricity was not only supposed to raise it out of the Great Depression but was meant to, at the very least, bring the isolated region to the brink of the modern world and allay its utter dependence on the land.

I know Fontana by its icy waters. I worked for a few summers at an outdoor camp, where I spent my days guiding children down the Nantahala River in large rafts, the water eventually dumping into Fontana. That river sits between two dammed-up lakes: Fontana at the mouth and Nantahala Lake at the head. Flipping a switch above the river transforms the Nantahala from a gentle, rocky stream into a whitewater roar of Class III and IV rapids. The release of that held-back water every morning makes the Nantahala a whitewater destination and a training site for Olympic paddlers by high noon. *Nantahala*, from the Cherokee language, means "Land of the Noonday Sun."

The United States exported the TVA model to developing countries like Honduras a few decades after stopping up rivers in southern Appalachia. "The TVA idea," it was called then. Our sporadic electricity in Gracias came from a hydropower dam on a reservoir named El

Cajón—"The Crate" or "The Coffin." A government-formed organization, ENEE, shaped El Cajón in the mid-1980s by stopping the Comayagua River in the center of the country. Like the TVA, ENEE devised and carried out the project to bring electricity to the impoverished and dark corners of the mountains.

We park outside Oconaluftee, a model Cherokee village meant to represent life in 1750, a few years before treaties and flight and the entrance of William Mills and Abraham. I spot the woven, bark-covered roof of what must be a traditional dwelling. Once the teachers manage to collect and sort the students, we file in small groups for our tour through the working village. A round woman who looks to be in her twenties welcomes us warmly but without a smile as we cross the threshold between the twenty-first and eighteenth centuries.

I'm excited, but I try not to show it. I haven't been to Cherokee since high school, when I played in a basketball tournament. The crowd whacked big drums and occasionally chanted. The local high school was a stressful, intimidating place to perform. My family came to Cherokee a few times when I was a boy. We stopped in shops and watched the outdoor drama about the Trail of Tears. I saw a caged bear in front of a store and bought a coonskin cap because I wanted to be Daniel Boone. I used to wear the cap, spending whole days in our woods, the raccoon tail brushing my neck as I fled invisible enemies through the logging trails and dried creek beds of our forest, not knowing the land had once been the hunting grounds of the Cherokees. I hid in stretches of rhododendron, perching on branches long enough to assure the squirrels and rabbits and birds that the coast was clear.

The model village sits within the Qualla Boundary. The Qualla land trust reaches across nearly a hundred square miles of three separate counties in western North Carolina and is home to around nine thousand members of the Eastern Band of the Cherokee Nation. The first part of the reservation we saw when the bus left the highway was Harrah's Casino and its giant sign shining with falling gold coins.

~

Gold was discovered in North Carolina around 1799. The Hopewell Treaty opened a path for Abraham and officially allowed William Mills and his fruit to stay put. But the unearthing of gold (North Carolina was the only gold-producing state until 1828) initiated treaty upon treaty to push the Cherokees (and others) farther west, away from profitable land and into small, slanted pockets of the hazy mountains, sequestering them in the Smokies. In 1838, once the United States no longer sought Cherokee assistance against the British and French, the natives were forced out of western North Carolina completely.

Recently, I've discovered the diary of my great-great-great-great-grandfather Prestwood. In it, he tracks fifty years' worth of mundane details—"plow'd corn, hunted mare, kill'd hog." But he left eighteen days in June 1838 empty. Those were the days he took part in the Cherokee Removal, a name that makes the whole process seem like the handling of infestation. The blankness following his June 6 entry—"Start army"—represents my line's dirty hands in the more aptly named Trail of Tears.

The Trail of Tears sent seventeen thousand Cherokees twelve hundred miles to Oklahoma. One person of every four died along the path, the fortunate ones resting in shallow graves instead of lying exposed to the frontier elements. The route of the Trail of Tears is well documented. Highway 74—the gold-mining, Ghost Town–advertising, y'all-come-back-now-sign-laden stretch we drove into Cherokee this morning—served as the passage out of the mountains and toward Oklahoma. The opening of a cruel pilgrimage.

During the forced march, a number of Cherokees managed to hide out in the mountains, evading the military and my kin. They burrowed into caves and hunkered down in gaps, walking quietly, sleeping in shifts. They lived a secretive life, ever-fearing they'd be found and pushed west. They lived undetected for decades.

Some descendants of that line of hiders make up the Eastern Band living on this reservation in western North Carolina. But most others on the Qualla Boundary come from a people who stayed put out of sheer determinedness, out of political savvy and hard-fought alliances. It is a lineage of wily persistence and survival.

In 1819, nearly twenty years before the Trail of Tears, the Eastern Band gave up their land, ceding control to the US Government. Ironically, it was this letting go of ownership that positioned these Cherokee to take back that land when Jackson forced everyone else to march. With the land handed over, many North Carolina Cherokee become US citizens, and so when the Treaty of New Echota was signed years later, they claimed exception to its order to move west. They were Americans, after all, and this was their land.

The central figure in the Eastern Band's story of abiding is a white man named William Holland Thomas. As a boy, he worked among the Cherokee, learning the language and making a life. Wil-Usdi, Little Will, the people called him, and soon, he owned his own store and was eating meals with the principal chief, Yonaguska. He made a home on that given-over land and started studying law. Before long, he was ready to fight.

The Eastern Band's secret weapon in the eternal battle against the United States was bureaucracy. William Thomas created a plan of government, which allowed the tribe to respond efficiently to each new policy thrown at them, each treaty and shifty offer. Armed with paper and legalese, the tribe stood their ground when the Trail of Tears began. They sent Thomas to Washington, DC, on their behalf, and for nearly a decade, he fought for Cherokee land and sovereignty: "The Indians are as much entitled to their rights as I am to mine," he said. On his death bed, Chief Yonaguska named Thomas the tribe's next leader. And so Chief William Holland Thomas, a white man born in Haywood County, purchased fifty thousand acres himself (the Cherokee weren't allowed to sign contracts), and today these kids and I stand on that same land, now forever protected. In 1848, after years of lobbying and arguing, he won: the United States officially recognized the Eastern Band of the Cherokee.

But like everything I'm unearthing in the past, the made-for-TV goodness of William Holland Thomas is messy. While he personally bought food and clothing for suffering Cherokee in 1838, he also helped the government track down Cherokee escaping from other states. While fighting for the Eastern Band's right to remain in their homes, he also speculated in lands freed up by their removal. Perhaps this duplicitousness only added to his credibility among the white politicians of Washington, DC; perhaps that's why he was able to save the Eastern Band in the end. But it's hard, on this side of history, to align many of his actions into a seamless narrative.

What's more, his ahead-of-his-time belief that everyone—"white man or red man"—carries inalienable rights doesn't line up with his fervent support of the Confederacy a few decades later. When North Carolina seceded, he rode home and persuaded the Cherokee to fight for the South, eventually leading a group into battle in east Tennessee to scalp wounded Union soldiers. He refused to lay down his weapons until May 1865—one of the last rebels in the country to surrender.

⁓

Our guide takes us into a world of bearskins and arrow making, tribal dances and blowgun demonstrations. During the rehearsed explanations, her accent sounds strangely Australian—an odd mix of mountain twang and Cherokee remnants. Something foreign with hints of home.

Women sit outside the squat dwellings weaving belts and shaping pots, talking among themselves occasionally. Men chip away at flint with deer antlers, shaping arrowheads to fix to the ends of straight pieces of cane, not making eye contact as we stand and watch. The eight children in my group seem genuinely interested. The boys especially enjoy the blowgun demonstrations. They all like that I have to duck to enter the houses.

The buildings—logs stacked and filled with a plaster made of natural scraps like cones, leaves, and grass—seem like sturdy bird's nests. I want to sit in one until its darkness settles upon my eyes. I want to imagine life within, but we keep moving from sweat houses to meeting lodges to canoes being dug out by smoldering ashes.

Our host reminds us that the Cherokees were a settled tribe, living in constructed, stable buildings, not a transient group like the natives of the plains, who lived in teepees and tents. The Cherokees planted roots along water—a stream runs through the village—and traveled by canoe along rivers including the Nantahala and the Ocoee. They stayed put, venturing out but always returning.

After the tour, Mr. Cody drives our bus to a picnic area, where we have our bag lunches beneath tall trees and beside a thin stream. After we eat, we will drive back past the faux gold mines and mock-but-real ghost towns. We will wave to the lake sitting atop Mr. Cody's childhood home. We'll hop on the interstate and take our exit, 64E/Bat Cave, to arrive back at Edneyville just before the bell rings. The students will head home, have a snack, play video games, finish math homework.

But I wonder if it would be better to have Mr. Cody drive the bus through the entire reservation before we roll back to the apple orchards of home. I'm thinking of Willie and our history lessons. The blacks and whites, blues and grays. Today, we learned of a surviving, distinct, proud people—people fully aware of their past—as we walked through a moving museum. But I wonder if such boxed-up history lessons are a disservice, a semi-truth. The whole truth is that the Qualla Boundary, like many reservations, is inundated with substance abuse and unemployment. Depression, alcoholism, and the violence that the two can create pervade the hundred square miles. There are few jobs, but residents don't want to leave the land and the protection of the boundary.

In my adult mind, the place is always gray and dreary. I partly wish I could be in fourth grade and have my bag lunch and ride home remembering canoes and arrows and bright garb lined with feathers, none the wiser to the complicated devastation of history. I wish I could find my coonskin cap and dig up arrowheads and disappear into a happy version of the past.

And maybe I should because the truth, like so many truths I'm finding, lies in the messy middle. This is a proud people who fought and bent, in miraculous fashion, to keep what was theirs. But that fighting and bending comes with wounds that are slow to heal and easy to scar.

As we eat, some boys run around pretending to shoot blowguns at each other as they duck and dodge behind trees. When their imaginations wear thin, they resort to throwing rocks, one of them claiming to be chief.

"Uh-uh." I stand, finally deciding to be teacherly. "Drop. The. Rocks."

～

The next day, I force myself to brave the cold on my bike. I haven't been riding much because December has sucked all warmth from the air. But this morning, I gather warm gear—gloves, long sleeves, ear covers—and formulate a plan: I'll let my bike wait on top of my vehicle while I'm teaching in my trailer.

Once I've finished my "Mister" responsibilities, I pull it down and leave from school on a straighter shot to Sugarloaf Mountain than I could get from home. I've been avoiding Bearwallow; I climb its sides occasionally, often spotting trucks with earthmovers in tow winding upward, but I don't follow them to the peak. I steer back down to find another climb.

This is a ride for pent-up energy. I've been feeling antsy since the excitement of the field trip. After following the same path Debbie and I took on the first day of school and riding gingerly across the gravel of Clark Road, I push off up Lamb Mountain. Then I rush down the switchbacks of Gilliam Mountain, leaning into my brakes to keep the bike from taking its own course into the frigid woods. I rise and fall toward the old high school but turn around as it comes into view to grind up Bald Ridge, on the way to the top of Sugarloaf.

The rockface that spreads across the mountain is marked with faint numbers and lines. Driving down Route 64 toward Bat Cave, one can make out paint and etchings as the mountain towers in the distance.

They seem hazy; it's hard to know what they mean. But I know. I know because the markings used to be clearer. I know because Dad made many of them.

Mom and Dad went to Edneyville High School. Grandma Betty worked as the librarian there for a long while. I spent most of my boyhood days, and many nights, in its gym while my dad was the basketball coach. But by the time I left elementary school, new, larger middle and high schools had been built in Fruitland, and Edneyville was left empty.

When he was in high school, Dad and others used to climb to the bluff on Sugarloaf to mark the mountain. They painted the year they graduated; they shaped symbols to stand for important wins; they recorded names. The rockface stood as a natural marquee, an evolving sign.

As I stand on the pedals, slowly pushing alongside bluffs and crags toward the top of Sugarloaf, cycling into the hazy puffs of air I'm exhaling, I think of the high-school version of my father scampering up the granite with paintbrushes in his back pockets. He's got bell-bottoms, maybe a letter jacket, certainly more hair. I superimpose this teenage Dad over a weak and shabbily uniformed William Mills. He trails blood across the pallid rock, pawing at holds and crevices. He searches for the opening. As Dad announces his presence to the world around him, leaving black and yellow markings to glint across the valleys and roads of Edneyville, William Mills digs deeper into the mountain. He shrinks himself, burrowing into darkness.

It strikes me that these two approaches to the mountain crop up again and again in the history I am uncovering. Men came to lay claim, to stake out the earth. Others came to pass from sight, to lie low within the folds of land. As I climb the snaking road higher, I wonder which impulse sends me into this mountain.

William Mills's lair has since closed up, but I wonder if the room in which he lay still stands hollow somewhere inside the mountain. A place without an entrance. There's no way in for a man because the rocks above slide like liquid, filling in and softening over time.

These mountains used to be full of ocean. They used to be upside down, concave. I don't entirely understand how concave becomes convex, the land a flat line that somehow dips into the earth, forming a *U*, shaping a valley that then fills with water. Around 750 million years ago, the Ocoee Basin dug itself out on the margin of what used to be a supercontinent, and seawater and rivers filled the wide crevice. This upside-down arc and its waters piled up sediment over millions of years, returning the land to a straight x-axis, again flat. But in the distance, volcanoes spilled over. Some violently opened; others leaked lava onto the earth. Something shifted. The continents lined up and faced off in a million-year game of chicken. They finally collided, sending islands and rocks and ocean floor inland. They heaped sediment and hardened lava, heated it all again, melted some rocks and cracked others. They bent and broke the land, pushing the straight line into the air, making it convex.

The durable bits of the ocean's history—sand and pebbles—rose with the mutating earth. Today, they rest as the peaks of these mountains. Clay and other fine-grained bits sank into the forming land. Marine fossils and ancient sediment are buried beneath these mountains.

Now, the mountains rise and fall like a slow-breathing man's chest. Bits wear away; things pile up. But there's more wearing than piling, as the mountains have softened from their sharp and heavens-reaching peaks. Bits fall away and are caught by Clear Creek and the French Broad and are eventually dumped again into the ocean, recycled. As wind and snow and feet pack the mountain down, I wonder if it is now on its way back to the x-axis, to again lie flat across the earth.

Just up the road from our house, at Fruitland Baptist, my sweet, silver-haired Sunday-school teachers—Minnie and Millie, then Evelyn and Norma—gave me the images I carry of Old Testament stories: Joshua at Jericho, Jonah in a whale, Moses in the split sea, Abraham over Isaac, David beside Bathsheba. Those songs and drawings and stories colored the biblical characters and events in my brain so that even now, they're moving around, fighting battles, escaping harm in my head.

So, too, I always carry with me Adam and Eve coming up out of the dust by magic. I sometimes imagine God spitting into the dirt to stick Adam together, rolling up the new man's arms and legs, fiddling with all the pieces until Adam held tight.

But it was only after God prepared the place that he pulled Adam and Eve out of the earth. Like the drawings made by my Honduran first-graders hunched over their wobbly desks, people didn't exist until the place existed, until the green stretched across the whole white page. It is as if God announced in the very beginning that place comes first, that we're secondary—we come from our land, our land doesn't come from us.

The rising and crashing of these mountains—their birth—literally shaped the movements of those of us sprouting on the land. The fault lines and ridges predestined the paths and roads leading into and through the land. They fashioned our futures.

The lava bedrocking the Blue Ridge made my people their mountain farm. Had my grandfathers not given it up, I'd likely be down in those bottoms turning the soil this afternoon, not on this bike, sweating my way to the rocky top of Sugarloaf. As nostalgic as I may find myself some days in the historical society or on field trips, I don't long for the farm. I don't wish to work the land for long, sweaty days. I have no illusions about the toil of sustenance. I'm glad to make money teaching, my hands dirty only with glue or chalk.

Yet I know that my granddaddies' opting for steady careers carrying the mail and driving a forklift has left their land quiet and has separated me from the soil in a way I can't get hold of. I have trouble knowing what to do in these mountains. I find myself fighting a constant battle between escaping and settling. So I do both.

But the shapes and lines of the mountains are so quickly changing that I find myself turned around, looking into the past more than the land. Mountains are reshaped for houses and golf courses. They're blown open for coal and minerals, cut straight through for roads. Bearwallow's bald peak won't stand empty much longer. And so I dig around in my family tree and land grants and centuries-old music to search out what the land has done to us, what it may have done to me. I figure an answer must be there because the earth around me is shifting. Everything is quickly becoming man-made, and I don't know what swaths of homes across the mountaintops—places called Wolfpen and Fox Run and Grand Highlands—reveal about me and the mountains' hold on me.

As I ride, I imagine I'm working my way higher as the mountain seeps slowly back into the earth. The rocks are stirring, the soil is fragmenting, and I'm riding a dissolving world.

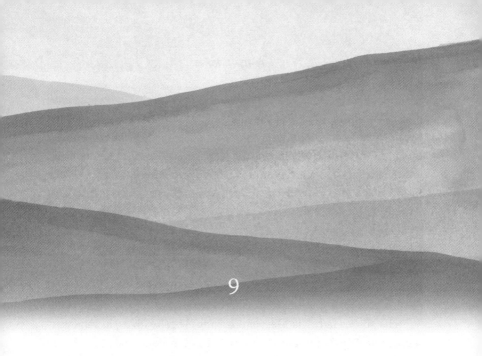

9

I'm frightened of the kindergartners. I worry about one disappearing under the crack of the door or running me in circles until smoke seeps from my joints. Ana and Maricruz formed a timid, tiny duo during the first month of school. They dutifully followed me up the ramp to the trailer and sat quietly as I danced around and used strange voices and tried just about anything to get them to speak or sing. Now, they're out of control.

I'm not Mister Rogers; I'm not their teacher. I'm the guy who frees them from the rules of a classroom. Maricruz breaks from the line and runs down the hall. Ana follows, skipping. They laugh and argue while a newer student, Angel, trudges along at my side. No matter my calls to walk, they burst from the building's door to race to the trailer. Even Angel takes off, leaving me as the only one following directions.

I'm sure one of my old teachers will burst from her classroom one day and see me race-walking after loose five-year-olds who are pulling paper Christmas trees and reindeer from the bulletin board, laughing all the way. We'll all get in trouble, but I'll be secretly glad to have someone take control.

Once in the trailer, they explode, leaping from their seats to dance around the room, picking up everything as they go—"*¿Qué es eso? ¿Qué es eso?*" I call them back to the table and pull out new books, but the condo isn't a classroom; it's a playground. I dread their forty-minute block on my schedule and breathe easy when I've successfully delivered them back to their classrooms without anything broken or anyone fired.

~

Angel joined our group after the first month of school. His teacher complained that he seemed behind, that he didn't speak much. But Angel doesn't speak Spanish. He is Cherokee.

His absent father is Mexican, leaving Angel with a Hispanic surname, but Angel's mother is from the Eastern Band and moved here from the reservation before Angel was born. She pronounces his name with the soft English version of a *g*, not as the Spanish *Ahn-hale*, as I called him until he finally corrected me last week. He has drooping, sad eyes, but when he gets tickled about something, his face morphs into a smile that closes his eyes and smushes his cheeks. He radiates.

We didn't suspect he'd need my class, but Mrs. Lunsford figured that extra language help wouldn't hurt, even if English is technically his only language. He's uncomfortable with it, even though it's his. He mumbles, often whispers, and keeps his eyes low. I imagine that bits of Cherokee language sail around in his head like ghosts he doesn't know or understand.

I can't imagine myself an ambassador to Angel. His line of people was in these mountains long before mine, and they persisted despite my people. My Scots-Irish kin came here swinging, hitting anything in their way. If Abraham was my genesis, my other forefathers were what followed: the holy wars.

~

While my Dutch Abraham, like many Swiss and Germans in the late seventeenth century, worked his way south bit by bit, drifting past the Quakers to eventually tiptoe into the fog with Bathsheba, the rest of my people crashed into these mountains and conquered as clans.

The Joneses originally hailed from Wales and the Whitakers from England, but they, like the Maxwells and Gilliams and Harrells and most of my other forefolk, came to America from Northern Ireland. My ancestors were Scots-Irish, a people never quite at home. In Ireland, they were strangers by blood and belief, persecuted and isolated. They eventually found a natural home across the sea, back in these hazy mountains.

Before smashing into the New World, my people were planted in Ireland by James I. After seeing wars and revolutions and massacres over the sparsely populated region of Ulster, James I set my people down as a buffer against the angry Irish. They were meant to keep the region in check, to prevent the blood from spilling into England. Plus, they were mostly Presbyterians, so they were positioned to convert the Catholic Irish to Protestantism and further unite Britain.

Despite the promises of fertile land and virgin forest the Scots were given, Ulster proved largely a boggy and infertile land. They thus found themselves in a new world without means. And beyond surviving the stubbornness of the land, the Scots were thrown immediately into the ever-turbulent battles between the Anglican English and the Catholic Irish. They lived constantly aware of borders and violence, fighting and farming simultaneously. They grew hard.

In the eighteenth century, many set out for America. Now hyphenated, a people with two homes, the Protestant Scots-Irish pushed into Pennsylvania and Virginia. Soon, the land grew crowded—the Quakers had dug in already—so many Scots-Irish pressed south, into Appalachia. Of the four hundred thousand immigrants who left Ireland leading up to the Revolutionary War, 95 percent are believed to have settled along and within the Appalachians. Here, they disappeared.

Life in the mountains must have felt normal and natural. Anointed. Again they fought unfruitful land, and again they found themselves amid borders and violence. They set to fighting with the Cherokees, toeing the line between the natives' land and their own. This land was theirs, as if divinely ordained. Like the Hebrew people, the Scots-Irish saw themselves as God's justice. His instrument.

Nineteenth-century historian Justin Winsor described the Scots-Irish as having "all that excitable character which goes with a keenminded adherence to original sin, total depravity, and election . . . [seeing] no use in an Indian but to be a target for their bullets." Horace Kephart claimed in 1913, "If any race was ordained to exterminate the Indians, that race was the Scotch-Irish."

Were these my people? Clearing land and natives in one fell swoop? The indigenous groups had lived and hunted for centuries in the Blue Ridge, but the Scots-Irish showed up and quickly picked up where they had left off back home—killing, then proselytizing.

Today, people speak of the Scots-Irish with pride. Their reckless, ceaseless brutality is lauded—James Webb has called them the "backbone" of the American military. They were fearless and tenacious, soldierly and solid. They were American before America.

But I can't help wondering how my kin felt after leaving violence behind in Ireland, only to be leading the charge in America. Did they regret their decisions? Did they deplore another violent role? Why, in a brand-new world, did they move into a hostile land, into a place they felt the need to subdue? Were they genetically shaped for violence? Was it in their skin? Is it in mine?

~

Every week, I'm assigned a new duty at school. Some weeks, I'm ordered to show up early for breakfast patrol. I pace among the tables, opening milks and warning finicky eaters to hurry. Then I wipe down their mess with a wet rag from the kitchen, chat with the lunchroom ladies, and head to class. Other weeks, I stand tall in the gym before school. The children are to sit in rows, grouped by grade level, and I'm the enforcer. No standing, no cutting in line, no running.

I have learned several lines of defense after taking on gym duty. I always begin with the teacherly stare. I drop my head and fix my eyes on the student. I glare a bit too long; I act as though I may come that way.

That is the first step. In fact, if the stare fails, I often feel I'm floundering, slowly drowning in weakness. I've learned that if I can't accomplish what I need to with my stare, I'm fighting a lost battle. In addition to the stare, I'll squat to have a stern chat. Occasionally, I'll take a student into the hall for a face-to-face.

But should those steps fail, I always have at my fingertips the last resort—the Switch. If the ricocheting noise, the chatting and laughing of a few hundred kids in a boxy gym, grows too loud, I can cut the lights. With the flick of a finger, I can hush the crowd. They look straight ahead or down at their loosely tied shoes, conditioned to know that the absence of electricity is abnormal and serious. But I try never to go to the Switch. I rely on my preliminary tactics.

However, I'm often grouped with another teacher or assistant, many of whom are trigger-happy. They cut the lights ten minutes into our half-hour duty, and then I know we're defeated. Once the darkness is used, there's no other weapon in the arsenal, no fail-safe, no cavalry. And once students know this, they see right through our adult uniforms and voices. They know we can't control them any more than we can grab them. And we can't grab them.

I hate gym duty the most. It seems inhumane to expect hundreds of elementary-school children to sit still, staring at the back of someone's head, for thirty minutes in a gym, of all places. I wish I could close the doors, give them a few balls, and say, "Don't hurt anyone."

My duties often remind me of the distinct shift in moving from an adobe Honduran school to a brick American institution. In Honduras, I was responsible for all of these duties on a daily basis. I showed up to welcome kids to school, cleaned up after their lunches, monitored and organized their post-school play and pickup. Yet my various, divided-up roles at Edneyville feel like work.

This week, I have afternoon duty—bus watch, which is my favorite. Afternoon duties—bus and car—mean keeping kids in lines, telling them when and where to go, and making sure no one escapes unless with a parent.

Most students don't have to wait long. The buses rumble up to the

front doors, and we usher the children into lines. Edneyville must have
the longest bus routes among the twelve county elementary schools.
Many buses, like the one Mr. Cody drives over Bearwallow, must climb
winding mountain roads and inch their way down switchbacks. The
buses leave with a first load right after the bell. After they've climbed a
mountain or two, a few of them return to take a second load.

This means that most of bus duty is walking the hall and chatting
with the thirty to forty students waiting for the second bus. Today, I
squat and tell Julio, a second-grader, that I have a blue dog. He doesn't
believe me. He demands I bring a picture tomorrow or, better yet, the
dog herself.

"What its name?" he asks.

"Blue," I say.

Now, he really doesn't believe me.

~

In Honduras, after the bell rang, I would plop down on a wooden
bench on the school's porch, overlooking the playground. Nearly all the
teachers sat or stood there every day, watching the children explode
with bottled energy and waiting for mothers and caretakers to walk
through the giant *portón* and yell, *"¡Carlos, vámonos!"* ("Carlos, let's
go!") or *"¡Luz, vengo por usted!"* ("Luz, I'm here for you!").

My fourth-graders, the oldest and biggest in the small school,
played soccer or some newly invented version of tag. The girls and boys
usually separated, and the third-graders joined in. The second- and
first-graders stuck to the swings or the monkey bars or the short palm
trees that protected and hid them from the others. They stayed on the
edges. During the day, we gave the younger students their chance with
the playground while the third- and fourth-graders were in class. Then
they became kings, playing their own versions of tag, which often involved roaring and screaming. They kicked balls and ran wild.

After school, the playground was fair game, so many of the younger
children floated around the porch with the teachers, bouncing balls or

jumping rope. Because the playground was dirt, it was easy for the girls to scratch hopscotch squares on the ground with sticks. They bounced along just below us, steering clear of the big-kid play.

These younger students were clingy. I understood not wanting to fling oneself into the ruckus of the playground at three in the afternoon. Many days, I didn't want to run that gauntlet myself, for fear of being struck by a dodge ball or an eighty-pound kid. So the first-graders stayed nearby and liked to hang on me after school. As I sat on the bench, kids climbed on my back or tried to perch on my lap. Usually, they latched on to the features that seemed the most foreign. It was the same with Sarah. Young girls leaned into her on the bench and pawed and petted her hair. They appeared entranced, as though they couldn't help themselves and had to touch. With me, they stroked my forearms, usually without noticing, as I monitored the playground activity. They asked me questions or tried to play games or made jokes, all the while brushing their small hands along the hair on my arms like I was a puppy.

I don't know why they didn't play jungle gym with the Honduran teachers like they did with Sarah and me. I suspect the Hondurans had more clearly defined the lines between student and teacher. I also suspect that everything about us seemed otherworldly to the children.

At first, it made me uncomfortable. I tried to distract Wilmer or Mario by standing to tell a story or throwing a ball. I wasn't sure how to instruct them not to pet me or sit on me. They weren't mal-intentioned; they were simply curious. What they knew of Americans came from TV and magazines, so they researched us with glue-and-marker-covered hands. They touched our skin and foreign features; they wanted to get on my shoulders to be the highest thing around. These after-school interactions felt more like playing with nephews or nieces than students. So I embraced them as such.

At Edneyville, during our first teachers' meeting, we were required to watch a video from the nineties called *Teaching and Touching*. We chatted about what physical contact was and wasn't appropriate. I'm not an especially touchy person. I don't feel the need to hug a student or rest my hand on a shoulder. I will occasionally pat a back or give a high-five, actions that are okay, according to the cheesy, dated video.

Today, as I am talking to Julio during bus duty, I suddenly feel that familiar pat and have to look around to remind myself I'm in America. He's touching my arm, curiously running his hand along my forearm's hair while we chat.

"Sky blue?" he asks, still wondering about my dog while petting my arm like I am one. We've been practicing colors in class.

"Kind of like gray. I'll bring a picture. How was your math test to-day?" I ask.

He gives me a thumbs-up. "Ninety-one."

I pull my arm away from his hand to give him a high-five, then stand to walk farther down the hall.

~

Here in my homeland, my arms aren't especially hairy. The hair is fairly fair and not easily noticeable, but it's certainly fuller than men's in Central America.

In Honduras, I envied what it was that attracted everyone to Sarah. I heard whispers from adults about her hair. They watched her on the street, pointing. She even felt her hair stroked by strangers on buses, adults embracing their inner-child curiosity. She grew tired of the touching and attention, but it was also charming. Her hair, while thick and long and shiny, isn't out of the ordinary back home. Here, she has thick brown hair, but in Honduras, the girls believed her a princess, saying her hair looked like a doll's. Perhaps that was because many of the dolls the girls grew up with came from America and were fashioned after American women—or unrealistic versions of American women. Nonetheless, Sarah was *bonita*—pretty—while I was simply *peludo*—hairy.

One morning in Honduras, I carried a batch of exams from the porch to my classroom, across the playground. School hadn't begun, and the children were charging around, dust flying behind their stubby legs. I was still trying to wake up, and the careening little people were helping. The shirt I wore was red plaid and didn't button; it snapped.

Its edges were fraying, but I wore it often because it was thin enough to keep me cool on baking Honduran days.

As I passed the swing set, thinking about my first lesson—a review on arthropods—I hung on tightly to my papers in fear that the children might send them fluttering up into the mango tree, where two plastic balls were already stuck. From my left, a tall first-grade girl named Luna came bouncing by, giggling, and I watched her dart toward the palms. As I turned back, I noticed Edgardo, a funny first-grader who ran as though the world was off its axis. He swung one arm higher than the other and tilted his body to the right, like he couldn't quite gain his balance. His face always wore something between a smile and a grimace. As he charged toward me, raking his arms through the air and howling, channeling his inner lion, I stopped. I decided to let him pass in front of me and my fat stack of papers in his pursuit of Luna. But as Edgardo came at me with his animal battle cry, he grabbed me, intending to swing his weight around me and charge straight into the palms behind me, cutting Luna off. As he grabbed and spun, he got a handful of the frayed edge of my shirt; he kept hold and ran past, unsnapping the entire plaid getup.

I stood, chest bare and hands full, in the middle of a playground of children and animals disguised as children. And somehow, despite their disparate games and the fire with which they were playing them, they all stopped at once, balls dropping, jump ropes falling. As if one organism in slow motion, they turned to see me, *Meester*, bare-chested on a sunny, new morning.

In the silence, Edgardo stumbled back to me, momentarily free of his animal persona. He pointed up at me, finally yelling, "*¡Peludo!*"

Everyone laughed, and I faltered for a minute, not sure if I should set the exams on the ground to resnap my shirt or if I should rush on my way. Deciding to make a break for it, I held the papers to my chest, covering up like a teenage girl at a pool party as I scampered into my classroom.

〜

This hair of mine—the thickness that covers my chest and belly and draws children to my forearms—must be a feature from my ancestors sequestered in the Blue Ridge Mountains for 250 years. I'm built to survive chilly winds and icy winters. I'm of a surviving people, predestined to abide.

Perhaps I should have left my shirt wide open that morning, hopped up on the big rock by the swings, and shouted, "Yes, look at me! I am the upshot of Scots-Irish digging into the Appalachian Mountains. Their blood has sown in me this thickness, this layer of hair. Come and touch. These are my people fighting through my skin!"

I wonder if I should have been the one roaring.

Instead, I flipped on the lights of my classroom, snapped up my shirt, and wrote the word of the day, *scurry*, on the blackboard before the bell rang.

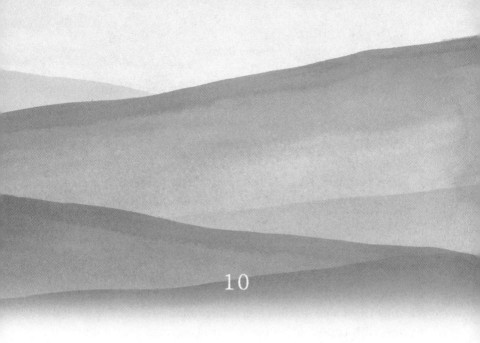

10

We've been sliding back into American life—gradually accumulating more stuff, easing into TV. We've sparsely filled the top floor of this house, mostly with used furniture, but two rooms downstairs stand entirely empty. The dogs have claimed one, where we close them in at night so they don't wake us in the mornings with their whining and wrestling. The other room we've found no use for.

Upstairs in the living room, beside the couch that Sarah's parents passed on to us, stands a cheap floor lamp Sarah bought in college. Its shade, a light burgundy, looks like a mix between a section of stained glass and translucent leather. The light that works through the shade fills the room with a subdued orange. At night, when we find something of interest on our four television channels, we cut the overhead light and let the lamp do all the work.

At school, others have noticed our lamp as well.

"Seen your lamp last night, Jeremy," Jayne says as I heat my lunch in the microwave.

"Oh yeah?" I don't turn, just stir my beans before sticking them back in.

"Yeah, the red-light district," Terry says.

From their joint laughter, I know this was a setup. I turn to humor them.

"Yep, me and Terry always look in when we pass to see if Jeremy's got the red light on tonight," Jayne says.

"Oh yeah?"

"And last night was a red-light night," Terry snickers.

These are women I called *Mrs.* and *ma'am* until this year.

Sarah has grown uncomfortable with the closeness of our Fruitland community. The road beyond our pasture isn't busy by any means. We might spot a car passing every thirty minutes or so. But the traffic stays fairly consistent because our road connects Fruitland Road to Highway 64.

On Sundays, though, as everyone heads to Fruitland Baptist or Fruitland Methodist, the road holds a steady stream of cars. These passersby—people I've known my whole life—tend to notice if we're home. They know if we've skipped church. They know if the shades are still drawn and we're sleeping. They know what we're thinking. They know when the red light's on.

Family and friends may stop by at any moment on a whim. To me, this is normal and natural, but Sarah says she feels like she's on an episode of *Everybody Loves Raymond* (we get that channel).

She should have known it would be this way. After our wedding, we returned to Fruitland for a night before our honeymoon. At seven the next morning, we awoke to a car horn seemingly coming from the paneling of the house. I hopped up and looked out the window to see John Henderson (our neighbor and my former classmate) circling our house in his green Honda, blaring the horn at one-second intervals. As I threw on a shirt and Sarah sank deeper under the covers, John made a few more circles and then pulled away, heading back home, the horn's pitch bending. *Welcome to Fruitland, dear.*

"Heard anything new about Bearwallow?" I ask Jayne.

"They're bringing up water," she says.

I raise an eyebrow as I eat. "Oh?"

"City water," Terry adds, giving me one serious nod and brushing lint off the arm of her sweater.

"They say they're gonna pipe it all the way out, run it along Bear-wallow Road and then up the mountain," Jayne fills in.

"Yep," Terry says. "People buying them houses say they won't live up there 'less there's city water."

"Hmm," I say. "That's a long way to run water, must be ten or fifteen miles."

"Well, they can't dig enough wells for all them houses across the peak," Jayne says. "They gotta get water somehow."

"I guess so," I say, but this seems pretty strange. Jayne's land borders my family's, and we, like most of the people in Edneyville and Fruitland, have wells reaching into the water table, which is fed by streams and creeks running down from Bearwallow. Yet the people who are soon to build directly upon the source itself have to draw in water from miles away.

I decide to look into this. Rumors fly at Edneyville Elementary—news about family feuds, teachers' diets, cheating parents. As a boy, I never knew that the portal into the teachers' lounge opened up a world of gossip, of information and misinformation.

Once I finish eating, I head back to the trailer to check my e-mail before picking up my next batch of kids.

As I go, Terry calls out, "Don't bother pulling the shades, Jeremy. That red light comes right through."

"Will do," I say as I let the door close, their laughter spilling into the hall of confused, aligned children.

After school, I drive into town. The Grand Highlands' office stands at the end of Main Street, a couple blocks north of the historical society. I've walked by a few times before and peered in the dark windows, once curiously touching the wooden exterior installed upon the brick. Grand Highlands isn't the only developer on the block. Across the street, Vista has a large-screen TV in the window, scrolling through pictures of waterfalls and panoramic views. Looking inside, I spot a three-dimensional model of the development standing on a table alone in a room. Farther south on Main Street, near the old hardware store, Pinnacle Falls boasts miraculous views and comfortable life. Main Street is a winding stretch of road with one- and two-story buildings all connected. There's no space for new construction, so these offices have filled old diners and shops. Just above Grand Highlands used to be the Skyland Hotel, where F. Scott Fitzgerald stayed for a spell while Zelda received treatment in Asheville.

As I walk by the Grand Highlands office, I snag a brochure from the wooden box beside the door. The front is covered in light blues and greens. At the top, soft gold letters on a flat aqua blue read, "Discover Living. Elevated in Every Way." I sit on a bench farther up the block, just in front of the old barbershop, to discover.

A photo of the meadow on the peak fills the most space on the brochure's cover. Green grass spreads evenly like a golf course, and mountains and clouds mesh in varying shades of blue and gray in the distance. The trees left on the meadow are changing into autumn's colors: rusty oranges, yellowed ochers, fiery reds. The edges of the mountains in the distance are flecked with these colors, as if fall has fallen only lightly upon the Blue Ridge. The road winds through the center of the meadow, and I can see the spot where I first stopped on Bearwallow's peak. I walked my bike up a soft hill off the road and stood beside an outcrop of rock to peer down at the farmland of Fruitland and Edneyville after that first draining ride years ago.

When I bring the brochure close and squint, I can make out the signs marking the house lots. They're tiny yellow dabs in the photo, but once I spot one, I see them everywhere. I try to envision the meadow not empty and smooth like in the picture but full of tall houses. Imagining a house for each tiny sign quickly covers the photo so fully that I have to picture them standing one on top of another, looking something like a Richard Scarry *Busytown* book I read as a child.

Below the meadow are two smaller photos. One shows two older couples eating at a wooden table outside; they're raising their wineglasses in a toast, sleeves rolled up, smiling. In the other, two thirty-something day-hikers, a man and woman, are grinning their way through the woods, sweaters tied around their waists. Mid-laugh, they look past the camera.

The development's logo—"The Grand Highlands at Bearwallow Mountain" standing below an outline of the mountain—covers the bottom portion of the front of the brochure. Splashed along the top of this outline is a blobby blue that appears to be dripping from the peak and down Bearwallow.

The inside is full of words like *lush, spacious, breathtaking, pristine,* and *authentic.* The biggest sentence stretches in cursive along the top: "Life from this height looks different."

The euphoria driving the language reminds me of my first encounter with the mountain. As I stood in the silence of the peak, seeing land stretch in all directions, hearing nothing but the life of the mountain, I felt in Eden, transported to another time, another way.

The development's vision is outlined in a paragraph alongside another panorama of the fall-colored mountains:

> Grand Highlands at Bearwallow Mountain is a new kind of Carolina community inspired by an old kind of mountain escape: the high country estates of the Blue Ridge Mountains. These high country family retreats were luxurious yet livable, and established an elevated sense of what a mountain getaway should be.

The themes of elevation and escape are repeated throughout the brochure. The rhetoric presents the mountain as an old sanctuary, a place where one might return to a simpler life. A list on the last page documents the ageless simplicity Grand Highlands offers: "Gated community, resort-style swimming pool and hot tub, billiards room, carefully preserved forests, and fitness facilities."

Additionally, standing "in the heart of this 289-acre gated community" is a members' clubhouse. A colored drawing shows the giant, soon-to-be structure surrounded by rock walls and a man-made pond. Pastel people lounge in beach chairs by the water. The brochure promises that Bearwallow Mountain will "change your perspective" and that this experience will be "shared by a few fortunate families and friends."

The office is empty when I enter. A leather couch stretches out to my left, positioned in front of a fireplace. A wooden table, which seems to be the front desk, stands to the right with more information about the development and Bearwallow sprinkled on top. The walls and the floor are dark wood. The space immediately feels like a TV version of a ski lodge in the Rockies. The lighting is controlled to appear natural and dim, as though snow is falling, the sun is setting, and this space is the only place where one would want to be.

I peer around corners and pick up pamphlets from the desk. Eventually, from a room behind the rock fireplace, comes a smiling man.

"Hi there," he says, approaching me.

"Hey." I close the brochure.

He seems to be about my age, mid-twenties. A big fellow, well over six feet and heavyset. He wears a pair of loose khakis and a white polo shirt with Grand Highlands' logo embroidered on the chest. We shake hands beside the fireless fireplace.

"Jason," he says, stepping back and smiling.

"Jeremy."

"Welcome, Jeremy. I see you've gotten some of our materials already. Can I answer any questions?"

I hadn't really thought about what I would say once inside. I don't have a plan. I'm not sure how to present myself, how to explain my motives, so I don't. I let him assume I'm a potential buyer, although I'm not sure why he would believe such—I'm young, not expensively dressed, and bumbling about like I'm in a library.

"Uh, yeah, sure. I was wondering how many lots you-all have up there."

"Currently, we have ninety lots across the peak, and all but one of those has sold. But we have plans to expand to well over three hundred lots in the next year—that's Phase 2."

"Really? On the peak?"

"No, most of these new lots would be on the edge, many of them Swiss-style cottages, offering amazing views. So even though they won't be right on top of the mountain, you'd have that great vista because you're right there on the ridge. Here, let me show you."

I follow him into the room from which he came. It's a square space with a long table in the center. On the table rests a broad map of Bearwallow, the lots marked by bold yellow lines. They take odd geometrical forms—misshapen rectangles, slender trapezoids. The map is a computer-created drawing with soft colors noting the trees and meadows and rocks.

"Here's our original site—Phase 1." He draws a circle around the mountain's peak with his finger. "Here, we'll have our clubhouse with resort-style pool, hot tub, billiards, fitness—everything you could want. Over here, we have our horse stables. We'll have community horses, with plenty of pastureland for riding. This area here is already fenced, and it's an amazing thing to ride a horse in these meadows while looking out from the highest peak around. Miles of hiking trails lead off from here and circle the peak, into the forest. We'll have community bikes so that you can bike these trails, too."

I nod, leaning in to try to remember each of the spots from my visits up the mountain.

"And the new sites?"

"Well, they'd likely be here and here." He points to woods on the east and west sides of the mountain. "We haven't surveyed and plotted out those lots yet, but they'd have trails to the clubhouse and stables and pools and fitness facilities—all the amenities that the other residents have access to."

The Barnwells own some of the land he just pointed to. Nancy Lyda, née Barnwell, is at Edneyville Elementary; she worked in my kindergarten class when I was five, opening my milks and cleaning my spills. She told me last week that her family won't sell its land, despite offers from the developers. But Jason is running his finger along it, telling me where my next house could stand.

I follow with interest as he explains what will be on Bearwallow. I try to imagine it but have trouble picturing the meadow on top of the mountain full of ninety houses, much less hundreds more standing on stilts on the ridge.

"The community will have city amenities but with the rustic nature that Bearwallow offers. Plus, you're a short drive from Hendersonville and Asheville, so you can stay on the mountain and enjoy the trails and views, or drive down for dinner and dancing."

The only dancing that happens in Hendersonville are shag classes at the senior center.

"And where are most of your buyers coming from?"

"Some from D.C., some from New York, some from Florida, a few from out west. Really from all over. We've had people visit the mountain, and they immediately know they've found a second home. You should take a drive up to see for yourself."

I decide to ease Jason's performance by letting him know I'm not a buyer. He's working so hard to sell me that I feel I'm missing information that I want. I tell him I've been up there a lot, and that I'm writing about the mountain.

"Let me grab Bill." He seems excited. "He knows more about the mountain than I do."

He disappears down the hall; I wait, fingering the lines of homesites on the map. Soon, Jason's back with a middle-aged, mustached man. We shake hands and share introductions.

I ask when they'll start building, if they plan to buy more acreage.

Jason jumps in, telling me they'll have over five hundred acres when all is said and done in the next year.

"And you'll cut all those trees on the edge to make room for these new sites?" I ask, pointing at the map.

"The great thing about Grand Highlands is that we're building along the natural contours of the mountain. We don't want to change the mountain; we want to build with it. For example, we're leaving a quarter of the original meadow untouched on the peak. We'll have to cut some trees, but we want to leave as many as possible, too."

"And I hear you have plans to get water up there."

"Well," Jason, barely taking a breath, goes on, "we have an agreement with the city. We're going to run pipes to the bottom of the mountain, and the city's going to extend their water line to the base of the mountain."

"That's an awful long way, isn't it?"

"Really, just a few miles. They already have water running out 64 to the old high school—"

"Let me ask you," Bill interrupts, finally entering the conversation as I scribble notes, "are you planning to portray us in a negative light?"

I still my pen and look up from my notebook. He's looking straight into my eyes, not with the salesmanship of Jason but rather with the let's-cut-the-crap look of a back-room dealer. I am taken off-guard.

"Uh, no, well, not really. I mean, I'm looking at Bearwallow's history, not just this development."

"I see," he says.

"I'm interested in the mountain and how it's developing, changing," I add. "Documenting, I would say."

I'm not sure how to read his still-straight face, so I go on. "Tell me about the Grand Highlands," I say, hoping to set him at ease. "Where did the idea for this development come from?"

"We prefer *community*," Bill says.

I must look confused.

"Not *development*," he continues. "We're creating a place—a *community*—for families to experience all that Bearwallow offers."

I nod, hoping he'll still answer my original question. "Community,"

I say as I make a note for Bill's sake.

"Well, I'll tell you, it's a story of serendipity. Dean, the president of our company, was driving up from Gerton, past Chimney Rock, one morning, and he'd heard a piece of land was for sale on the peak. So he drove up to the top of Bearwallow, and he climbed out on the peak and was unimpressed. It was foggy out; you couldn't see anything from the peak. The field hadn't been cut; there was cow shit everywhere. He walked around and actually passed on buying the land."

Bill's accent rings of the Midwest. He pronounces Bearwallow fully and phonetically—*Bear-wal-loh*. Most locals call the mountain *Bear-wal-lah*, if not *Bahr-wal-lah*.

"But Dean happened to come back through on another day," Bill continues, "and that day was clear. Someone had cut the fields. And this time when he climbed out of his car, he was just awe-struck by the view, by the character of the mountain. I assume you've been up there?"

I nod.

"Well, he bought it after that second visit. But it took him two years just to clean it up. He had to pull out rocks, clean up and grade the land to make it walkable and buildable. Took a long time before he could even think about building anything up there."

"And when did the devel . . . the community officially open for houses?"

"Earlier this year, and we sold nearly all of the first lots quickly. What I love about the community is that the central amenity it offers— and this is how Dean imagined it when he decided to buy it—the central amenity is the mountain itself. There's no golf course or outside thing that brings people here; it's the character of the mountain. And that's why we're maintaining the integrity of the mountain in our building practices."

"How do you mean?" I ask as flatly as possible.

"Well, we have communities in the Rockies, in Colorado." This explains the feel of this ski-lodge office. "And we have a lake community in South Carolina. In each of these, we have been careful to build along the contours of the landscape and change or cut only what's needed.

We're good at it and have some of the best builders in the country. We want to be part of the community, not change it."

I don't ask about the language of exclusivity throughout the brochures. We chat for a bit longer; they tell me they have collected many old photos in the barn on the mountain that they'll eventually put in the clubhouse, and I say I'll stop by up there sometime to see them. After we shake hands, I grab the brochures and materials I've accumulated and head outside, back to Main Street.

As I drive away, I'm thinking of the smoothly paved roads that the development will likely bring up the mountain, how they'll make for easier bike rides. I'm thinking of the city water piped to residents in Fruitland, the money to be made by farmers selling their land—farmers who can no longer sustain themselves with cattle and corn.

But I'm also thinking of the crowded peak of houses, the animals scurrying down the mountain and the birds looking for new roosts, the vacationers bringing more development to cover up the farmland and mountain peaks of Edneyville. I'm thinking about how nothing is simple or clear. The Latin root of the word *ambiguity* is *ambi-agere*—to wander uncertainly. As I drop down the hill from Main Street, I decide to embrace this ambiguity and wander.

I turn arbitrarily, crisscrossing the streets surrounding downtown, passing the old, tall houses with wraparound porches. I drift away from the blocks extending from the town's center until I'm weaving along the curvy county roads, squat houses and trailers and new modular homes sprinkled along the way. I try to drive until I don't recognize where I am. But it's not long before I find myself on Highway 64 again, as if by accident, pulled toward Bearwallow.

Ambiguity's origin conjures up thoughts of rambling. Roaming. No set path, no true way. I wonder about my ambiguous afternoon journeys up mountains and to obscure grave sites. Is wandering the same as searching? I've never been a good rambler. I hike the woods and cycle over the mountains and drift down the streams, but I like direction. I'm not a real rambler. I'm something more of a pilgrim.

I traveled through Latin America, skipping from town to town, walking up and down streets looking for places to stay, hopping on and off random buses. But I liked a home, a base. I remember the solace of riding down the mountain into Gracias as the sky grew dark.

In this memory, I'm sitting near the back of the bus, the sun has just set—the deep green of Celaque fades into black—and a misty rain seems to hang, not fall, in the air. It's six o'clock—the last bus. The mustached driver lets the squeaky old bus build speed.

Usually when descending into the valley, the drivers downshift their way slowly down the mountain in order to save the brakes of the decades-old buses. They creep along, RPMs rising, and occasionally stop completely at worn paths and dirt trails leading to tiny villages, where they pick up and drop off passengers and packages and pigs.

But the driver of this six o'clock bus abandons the loud downshifting, uses the brakes sparingly as the bus begins to pick up speed, and often skips the worn-path stops altogether. At times, the old bus seemingly lifts off the ground taking tight turns. It occasionally lurches to miss large rocks loosed by rain up on the mountain, shivering on its shocks.

I can call up that ride easily in my mind—the bus pouring smoke and roaring like a lion galloping downhill. As we drop dangerously down the mountain, I'm not thinking of wet roads or mud slides or the bridge missing its guardrail from a wreck last week. As the passengers slide in their seats around tight turns, I am thinking of fried chicken and tortillas. I'm glad to be returning from a weekend of travel; I'm glad *don* Marco and *la profesora* Celeste will know what I want to eat as soon as I walk into their restaurant; I'm glad to have a cement apartment off a cobblestone street, a place to return.

And today, leaving Grand Highlands, I'm happy to know Sarah's home and the dogs are waiting for me to turn them loose into the bottom land. I'm happy to have a place.

⌒

As I leave behind the string of fast-food restaurants in town, I watch Bearwallow as it slides nearer. The mountain is something like a *U*. Its bareness lies in the middle—in its dip. Trees stand on the peaks flanking this meadow. As if the mountain is torn, as if it's of two minds, separate peaks rise on either side of the softly drooping crux. The mountains around it rise and fall as expected. They climb to clear, albeit worn, peaks. But Bearwallow is confused, ambivalent. It peaks, then drops, then rises again.

I get the clearest shot crossing the bridge over the interstate, just before reaching the new Walmart Supercenter. The mountain floats behind Walmart and the strip mall of shops and restaurants that grew up alongside it while we were in Honduras. When Sarah and I left the country, this land was wooded and swampy. Now, it's asphalt and sidewalks, groceries and electronics, Bearwallow watching over.

Grandma says "the Walmart," as if it's the only one in the whole country. As in, "We got gas at the Walmart on the way back from town." She says the same for the chain grocery stores—"the Ingles," "the Bi-Lo"—and restaurants—"the McDonald's," "the Hardee's." Walmart isn't new to our county. We had a Walmart for years, located behind all the fast-food restaurants on the way to town. But last year, while I was away, a larger version moved into the low-lying land nearer to Fruitland. Before I left, crossing this bridge over the interstate meant sparseness—a gas station and a church. The highway dropped to two lanes. The commercial property was apple houses and a general store. Now, a wide-reaching housing development stands beyond the Walmart. Wolfpen, it's called. Houses all seemingly cut from the same plastic cloth stretch across the hill, pressing against the Barnwell apple orchards. When I was a boy, a general store called Uno was across the road from where Wolfpen has grown. The small wooden shop sold a random assortment including live crickets and night crawlers from large bins in the back beside the cold drinks. The new four-lane road took out the Uno.

Wolfpen sprang up last year, but this year it has new neighbors. Another development, Brittany Place, has filled a former cow pasture with apartments and townhouses, and there are plans to line the hills beside this development with another stretch of quick family homes.

I find the Walmart a strange creature because it brought with it ambiguous sidewalks. From its parking lots extend sidewalks to nowhere. They stretch in both directions—toward town and toward Edneyville—but promptly stop after a hundred yards. They are dried up, dammed sidewalks: routes without purpose.

But today, as I drift beyond Walmart and reach Wolfpen and Brittany Place, I understand the pointless sidewalks. While I was in town this afternoon chatting with Bill and Jason, a few squares of cement were poured extending from Brittany Place. I imagine tomorrow this newly forming sidewalk will stretch longer and longer, each sectioned square hardening over time until the string of them eventually gives purpose to the stalled sidewalk of the Walmart.

As the developments fade and the road again shrinks to two lanes, Bearwallow slides directly in front of my drive, and it seems to rise taller from the earth as I get closer. I superimpose the Grand Highlands' logo on to the mountain—the outline of the peak with the blue shadowy paint that seems to be dripping. I try to picture Grand Highlands itself; soon, I see it trickling, like the paint, farther down the mountain, coloring it and spilling into the valleys below.

I have been wondering why William Mills named this mountain Bearwallow. I imagine him constructing a creation story for the two-peaked, meadowed creature—the young William and his father hunting in late summer; his father creeping quietly, ears raised, eyes ahead, peripheral vision alert to any movement. William, though, follows indiscriminately. His eyes are fixed on Bearwallow. He's thinking about the force required to scoop out the top of a mountain. A hand reaching in and scooping. No, not scooping, but something different. The mountain must have been worn down, pressed in, he thinks.

His father stops, crouches, raises his rifle. William follows suit robotically, but he's not watching rustling leaves or waiting for the right moment; he's imagining a giant bear sitting on the peak, then rolling on to its back. It twists and worms. It shakes the mountain as it flails and thrashes. It wallows deeper, as William has seen his itchy-backed dog do in the dirt behind the cabin. For days, years, the bear must have climbed the peak to roll and scratch until it wore down the trees and then the earth itself, removing the original crest. The bear wallowed until it left rocks jutting from the ground like bones worked through thin skin.

Years later, when William returned to his boyhood hunting ground looking for resurrection, he buried himself inside the mountains. Then he gathered his family, planted his trees, and put a name to his creation myth: Bearwallow.

I like those beginnings. Two hundred years ago, my bear was William's bear. His wallowed and burrowed. Mine patrols and protects.

11

Deeper into the Wilderness, beyond the flat rock, Abraham discovered the route he'd heard of before he set out—an old native trail
recently converted to a passage through the Blue Ridge, now the main
road from Tennessee to the lowlands and coast. Pioneer men drove
livestock along it, across and down the mountains, to and from markets
in Charleston and Savannah. As Abraham surveyed the Wilderness and
the road before him, he saw more than fertile land and opportunity
for sustenance. He saw a chance for more—for wealth, for fortune. For
purpose.

There, off the ancient road that split his property, he and Bathsheba
began pulling down bits of virgin forest. They started building. As if he
could somehow feel the coming world in the soil beneath his feet, he
fashioned a place to draw pioneers. First came a tavern, then an inn,
and finally animal holding pens behind it all. News of the inn spread
quickly among traveling men, not only for its comforts and for the raw
whiskey from Abraham's still, but also because of the practicality of eating and sleeping and drinking while knowing one's livestock and livelihood waited securely out back.

Once the buildings stood upright, Abraham leaned back upon his
new land and watched the world come to him. And come it did.

12

I shouldn't look forward to Friday lunches as much as I do, but any break in the routine sparkles lately. This morning, I stopped in the office to drop off money and give the secretary my order—Calabash chicken wrap and fries. By lunchtime, her son has delivered the food from his restaurant in town. After I return the first-graders to their classrooms, I dip into the office for the Styrofoam container awaiting me.

Jayne and Terry have already started eating when I enter the lounge. They're talking about a mess one of the kids made with glue in Terry's classroom, but I'm too distracted by eating something other than a peanut butter sandwich or reheated leftovers to listen. Soon, they're talking about a particularly bad second-grader with precocious powers of manipulation.

"You know this one, Jeremy?" Terry asks.

I shake my head, mouth full of chicken, and let them go on without me.

Before long, though, there's a lull and I've done a fair amount of damage to my lunch, so I hop in: "I drove out to the Grand Highlands' office last week."

"Oh yeah? How come?" Jayne asks.

"I don't know—just to ask some questions, I guess."

"You looking to buy you a house, Jeremy?" Terry says. "They must be paying you more than us."

"Yep, moving on up," I say.

One of the custodians comes in, dragging a vacuum cleaner behind her like a shy child. "Excuse me," she says, pulling it past me into the closet. She wheels it in, rearranges a cart of supplies inside.

"They tell you they's fixing to build a thousand houses up there?" Jayne asks.

"Well, close. He did say they hope to build nearly five hundred eventually."

"Lord," Terry says.

The custodian closes the closet and turns back to us.

"You have to clean up all that glue, Rose?" Jayne asks her.

"Glue? Where?"

"In my classroom," Terry says. "One of the girls spilled some, then a boy stepped in it. The stuff got spread near across the whole room."

"Ain't nobody told me. Maybe Theresa cleaned it. I been out cleaning the floors of the dance trailer. Them kids drug in every leaf in Edneyville this morning." She stands beside the couch looking at the empty seat for a long while, but then seems to think better of it. "Well, let me go check on this glue, then. The kids at lunch?"

"Yep," Terry says, looking at the clock above the sink. "For ten more minutes. Valerie may take them out to the playground, though—it's right warm today, must be near sixty in the sunshine."

"Yeah, yeah, it is," Rose says, looking out the window. Then she sighs and sets out after the mess.

I paw around at my remaining fries. "They did tell me about the water," I say after a moment. "They've got plans to bring up city water sometime."

"Yep, I told you," Jayne says, turning to the window to watch a line of fourth-graders climb the hill toward the cafeteria. "City's going to spend a lot of money to get water out to that mountain."

"Seems like a big project for some houses that aren't yet built."

"Got to have the water first," Jayne says.

"Yeah," Terry says. "They've got 'em a regular garden up there—gotta water the thing, get it growing." She turns toward the window; her class and the teacher are marching across the blacktop from the cafeteria. "Well, off to the playground," she says, slapping her leg and standing.

"I'd better go, too," Jayne says, looking up at the clock. "We've done had our recess, right here in the lounge."

"Yeah, I'll do a few jumping jacks after y'all leave," I say, and they vanish into the hall.

<hr/>

After lunch, I pick up Antonio and Carlos. Before I can get them to the door, they pull the tiny line toward the water fountain. Recently, I implemented a one-sip rule. I used to let them drink freely, but it became a back-and-forth, never-ending game—Antonio drank, Carlos drank, Antonio suddenly grew thirsty again, then Carlos, and onward. "May I have some water?" is an English expression they both deliver with fluency. Today, they take their turns, Carlos wiping his mouth with his sleeve before we walk outside to the condo to play bingo.

In Honduras, a green plastic cup waited by the sink outside for the kids. They rushed to the faucet to fill the cup, take a swig, and play on. Some of the wildest boys forewent the cup altogether, sticking their heads under the spigot. The custodians washed the communal cup between classes. I, however, walked to the corner store by the sixteenth-century ruined church to buy bottled water shipped in from somewhere else. My American organs could not handle the bacteria and whatever else floated in the water.

Gracias' water flowed freely from the river rushing down from Celaque. A plastic pipe ran above ground from a spot just at the edge of the cloud forest downward to town. There was no filtration system, no treatment station. Every few weeks, I had to unscrew the showerhead in the apartment to remove the slivers of wood and leaves that had backed up there.

Ironically, the heavier the rain, the less water we had at the foot of the mountain. When Celaque was drowned, the river climbed higher and faster, and as it swelled, leaves and branches swarmed the lone pipe leading to us. Soon, they filled its open mouth entirely, leaving the town without water. No matter the overflowing river, Gracias stayed dry. Until the boy on the mountain came running.

I saw him once or twice, always shoeless, wearing shorts and a T-shirt. After the monsoon-like rains, he scampered up Celaque to wade into the rushing water and dig out the natural fragments clogging the pipe. He stuck his hands fully in, our water surgeon, and soon the kitchen sinks and showers of Gracias spurted like they'd come alive. Needles and bits of wood poured out. We bathed in pieces of loosened mountain as the clouds receded.

Even though I couldn't drink from the river, bathing in the mountain's fragments made it impossible to forget the source supplying water to our town. I don't usually consider the wells drawing up the water to the fountains at school and my shower at home, but in Honduras, I couldn't escape my connection, my dependence on the mountain's river.

Before my people settled here, the Cherokees built along the rivers and streams of these mountains. In the land grants I uncover in the historical society, I find my kin working close to the water from the moment they arrived here. Surveying the Maxwell and Prestwood plots near my house, I easily see that what connects them, what sustains them, is Clear Creek.

On a recent walk along the creek to Grandma's, I found a newspaper article beneath her TV about her father, Albert, delivering the mail in the flood of 1916. The article also told of other postal adventures, including a trip down Bearwallow in a Model A without brakes. But central to the story was Albert's survival of the Great Flood.

When a hurricane hit Charleston, western North Carolina sank under heavy and continuous rains. Clear Creek filled to the brim, and eventually the French Broad jumped its banks, dumping more than five feet of water into streets. Albert was called on to deliver early in these rains, and the newspaper quoted his account of the trip:

> A patron had told me he had to get to a place some distance down the road but feared he couldn't make it because of high water. I told him to hop into my car but he protested he wouldn't be able to ride in a mail vehicle. I told him I would use him to push me out if I got stuck. Sure enough, the French Broad was flowing over the road and the Model T stalled. I climbed out on the hood and managed to reach in and drain the carburetor and we were able to back out of the floodwaters.

Southern Railways' 1917 report noted that "the water-soaked forest soil, with its large content of mica, was almost in a state of movement on the mountain sides." The land, the mountains themselves, began to shift at the water's power.

Water requires frustrating moderation: too much sends us belly up, too little withers us into nothingness. It moves mountains, civilizations. It brought my people to this creek to grow the corn and cattle that sustained them. In like manner, Grand Highlands has gone searching for enough of it to sustain itself, to develop.

Last week when I entered the Grand Highlands' office, I knew the negative connotations of the word *development*, but I was still taken aback by Bill's quick reaction: "We prefer *community*." When I surveyed the materials I collected, I discovered that nowhere did *development* expose itself. The company has rejected the word wholesale.

Development ought to be a positive notion, attached to improvement. But the trend among the developers in Henderson County appears to be a reliance on ideas of *community*, rather than a push to *develop*. None of the other offices on Main Street makes use of the word in their pamphlets or signs. They're community builders, not land developers.

Develop comes from the Old French word *desveloper*—to un-enclose or, better translated, to unwrap or expose. The word *development* suggests unfolding or laying out. To develop is to bring out the possibilities, to mine a thing of latent promise.

And I gather from these brochures and my conversation on Main Street that Grand Highlands believes that, by literal definition, it is developing Bearwallow. It's pulling out possibility; it's reshaping the land for enjoyment and use. It has cleaned and cleared it up. Now, all it needs is water.

~

Terry was right: the day does warm up. It's barely March, but the sun is growing stronger. I suit up and climb on my bike once I'm home from school. I head back toward the school and then cycle into the small community of Dana, rolling slowly toward Abraham's Wilderness. There, traffic grows, buildings rise. I pass inns and bed-and-breakfasts; cars with license tags from faraway states weave along the roads. Giant houses stand in the woods, and gated developments, golf courses, and retirement communities with names such as Charleston Place and Kenmure line the narrow road.

After Abraham cut trees and opened the earth to spread his inn over the empty land, pioneers and traders came to know that the plateau in the Blue Ridge—the land of the flat rock—meant repose. But even before Abraham, the Cherokees had set the plateau aside for meetings and hunting and rest. And this purposing has continued. Abraham's Wilderness soon came to be called Flat Rock, and it persists today as a land of relief.

Less than a century after Abraham arrived, Flat Rock earned the nickname "Little Charleston in the Mountains." Wealthy plantation owners from the South Carolina lowlands made Flat Rock their second home. They built vacation homes to escape the balmy summers. Many lived their final days here.

Mitchell King, an influential Charleston judge, built a second home in 1829 on land formerly belonging to Abraham. He started work to bring a railroad from the lowlands to the Blue Ridge.

Joseph Marie Gabriel St. Xavier de Choiseul, a French count who settled in Charleston, built a large house near Flat Rock. "The Castle," as it came to be called, stood as a French-style chateau in the Wilderness until it was ransacked and left for dead by bushwhackers during the War Between the States.

Christopher Gustavus Memminger, the first secretary of the Confederacy, made a second home in Flat Rock before the war began. The German-born Charleston resident was buried in Flat Rock in 1888. Carl Sandburg moved to Flat Rock in 1945, buying Memminger's former estate, Connemara. "The Poet of the People" spent his final twenty-two years living on a hill above a small lake and his wife's goat farm.

As suggested by the language of the Grand Highlands' brochures, wealthy outsiders thronged to the hazy mountains for escape. But others such as William Mills flocked here for healing. Even before white men settled these mountains, the Cherokees brought their sick to Flat Rock for new life. And after they were gone, the mountain air was purported to aid the lungs and rejuvenate deteriorating bodies. This was a land of resurrection, people heard.

Once the railroad worked its way to nearby Asheville a few decades after the Civil War, physicians swooped in to set up tuberculosis clinics. Soon, over twenty tuberculosis specialists had set up camp. The temperature and barometric pressure of the mountains were said to be optimal for the treatment of TB. To bring patients to the area, the specialists published brochures with titles such as *Western North Carolina—Its Agricultural Resources, Mineral Wealth, Climate, Salubrity and Scenery*. Giant boardinghouses and sanitariums were opened as treatment centers for TB, the leading cause of death at the time. Ill outsiders hurried to the area for promised restoration. And strangely, this restoration also brought economic development.

George Vanderbilt, of the railroading and steamboating Vanderbilts, visited western North Carolina at the end of the nineteenth century with his ailing mother, who sought mountain mending. George began to buy pieces of land on his visits. A few years later, he started building his estate near Asheville. The three-year project resulted in a 250-room French-style manor whose reach stretched across 125,000 acres. Architect Richard Morris Hunt designed the estate, and Fredrick Law Olmsted landscaped the grounds. Today, Biltmore House is still the largest private residence in the United States, attracting over a million tourists every year and sustaining a wide swath of hotels, restaurants, and shops.

Edwin Wiley Grove built the Grove Park Inn, a rock lodge sitting on a mountain ridge. The immense inn, whose sections rise and fall with the ridge line, has welcomed presidents (Woodrow Wilson, Bill Clinton), businessmen (Henry Ford, John Rockefeller), and celebrities (F. Scott Fitzgerald, William Shatner).

~

From Flat Rock, planned developments reach in all directions. Many of them have been here for decades, and they're hardly noticeable as I pass their entrances now; they've been part of the landscape since I was born. The economy of this land has been driven by tourism and second-home living for centuries. Fruitland, where my people eventually hunkered down, has been turned over to growing since William Mills planted his first fruit trees. As I shoot the bike back across Spartanburg Highway to work toward home, the houses thin and the land spreads.

In Fruitland, people shake their heads at the word *development*, as in "that development up on Bearwalla." Development is something encroaching, an outside force falling upon our land—a coming flood. But others, those climbing higher into the middle class with in-town jobs, slide proudly inside the gates of development. They've arrived, moved up. Some families gladly but quietly sell off bits of forests and fields for development, pieces of land their grandparents farmed but their daddies gave up because they couldn't make money. They sell and move away after jobs.

As uneasy as the Grand Highlands' project to cover Bearwallow makes me, wholly rejecting development, rhetorically and ideologically, is too easy, too naïve. We're living in a developed place. The men in the general store shaking their heads at the word pull out cell phones pinging off the towers on Bearwallow to arrange hunting trips. Centuries ago, our families developed this land through subsistence farming. They cut down trees and cleared brambles; they cultivated and laid out crops. They unfolded.

Even though my people ended up off-stage of the growth of Hendersonville and Flat Rock and Asheville, our land grows apples to sell to the tourists visiting those places. The two patches of land work symbiotically.

Since the entrances of William Mills and Abraham Kuykendall, the long lines of land purposing seem entrenched, buried in the soil from the residues of ancient lava—the flat rock within Abraham's Wilderness was a place of rest for the Cherokees and has remained a place for vacation since; the land of Williams Mills was Cherokee hunting ground and has remained a place for harvesting since. Flat Rock means rest, and Fruitland means creation. Flat Rock, the seventh day; Fruitland, the rest of the week.

Today, though, the lines blur, the purposing fades. Many of us in Fruitland have left the land alone; we don't need it as we always have. An Ingles grocery store waits a few miles up the road. It imports apples from Washington State; it has bananas year-round from Honduras; it sells boxed-up firewood from New York. We forget any dependence on the land because we don't see it, don't feel it daily.

Except for its sturdiness. We appreciate its staying underfoot, supporting our houses. So we use the land for its space, for its dirt, but not much more. It's as if we don't know what else to do. We've been sustained by the land since our people have been here, and now that we don't grow anything in it, we sell the land itself for sustenance. We section it off and stick signs up and watch the developments clear trees and grow more houses in ten acres than had stood in a square mile. We develop.

Back home, I track down online records of the city's water plans. It will run a water line nearly four miles from Highway 64, where pipe already stretches to a police training facility in the old Edneyville High School, to the foot of Bearwallow. Grand Highlands will send its own line another four miles down the mountain to the city's pipe just behind the trailer park where most of my students live. They will meet in the middle, like those coming sidewalks from the Walmart. The project, titled "East Side Improvement," will cost the city $2.5 million. But non–Grand Highlands residents on the mountain won't be able to use the water. The eight-inch pipe will be so highly pressurized to reach the forty-two-hundred-foot peak that there will be no way to tie into it. "Shared by a few fortunate families and friends" indeed.

As I shower before supper, I think of the water falling on my head being sucked up from somewhere deep beneath the house, a dark pool cupped by rock. I watch the water run down my skin and think of it rushing down the mountain into the streams that fill the creek below the house. This same water has been turned over and over and over and dumped on the heads of the Maxwells and Prestwoods and Gilliams and Joneses for centuries. I might not dig my hands into the dirt like those who came before me, but I cover myself in its recycled water. I imagine it seeping into my skin as it seeped through the soil to rest under this land. And when I step out, I let it sit there too long, dripping tiny pools onto the floor, before I finally snatch a towel and wipe it all away.

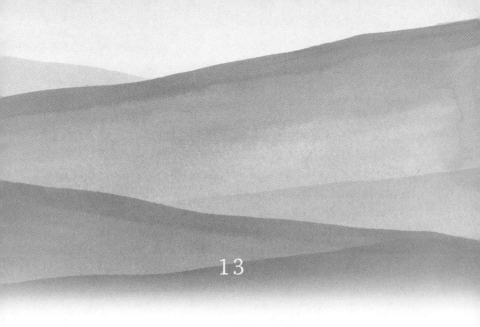

13

I haven't yet made it past the creek without stopping to skip a rock. Most days, I don't think; I'm suddenly bent over the edge of Clear Creek shuffling through rocks in search of the perfect skipping stone: softly rounded, not too heavy or too light. But I'm out of practice. My throws send the rocks knifing into the water or gliding like Frisbees into the field. Still, every walk, as the dogs wallow in the mud, I take a few throws before we're on our way again.

Today, I skip so many stones that the dogs seem to be urging me on. Banjer, the rambler, has already decided we're headed farther downstream and has disappeared, while Blue, the loyalist, waits by my rock-skipping side.

The sun stood unobstructed for most of the day today while I sat in my trailer at Edneyville, but along the creek and the shaded trail leading toward my family's land, the ground is sheer mud from yesterday's rain. I don't mind. I decided early on in this walk that I would come home messy. To prove it to myself, I'm standing ankle deep in the water skipping stones. And just to spite Banjer, I decide to cross the creek entirely and start our journey on another path.

The water feels chilly as it climbs above my knees, but winter's edge is drifting out of Clear Creek. The thick mud and the clear air and the warming water are signs that spring is coming to Fruitland. I stumble up the bank and turn to see Blue, the clumsy Great Dane, trying to follow my steep path. She looks at me helplessly as she begins to slide back toward the water, but she soon finds another way and meets me at the edge of the sod field. I whistle for Banjer. Minutes later, he comes sprinting, as if shot from a hidden cannon. He lurches to a stop beside me, just in time to shake the creek water from his dirty fur all over me.

Farther downstream, the creek deepens just enough for a slow tube ride, but here below our house, it barely reaches the knees in most spots. The dogs and I will follow the creek downstream for a mile or so until we reach the bridge on Townsend Road, where Dad proposed to Mom. Then we'll head up the Prestwood hill and through the woods— to Grandmother's house we go.

～

Before we reach the bridge, the trees squeeze in and stifle the sod field entirely; only a narrow trail lies ahead. Beyond the trail, I come upon another expanse of sod field stretching out wide again. Before it, a muddy, nearly dried-up spring gurgles to my right, and a grassy, shaded stretch of land runs along the creek.

I spent nearly every Fourth of July around a campfire in that grassy patch. My family and other Fruitland families camp out down in these bottoms every year; we've been flocking down here for over fifty years. As boys, we spent the afternoons frog-gigging at the springhead, and if we had any luck, Grandma would fry up frog legs in the evening.

We turned the sod into a baseball field before it grew dark. Back in the days when the bottoms would draw fifty to sixty people, we'd have music around the campfire at night. Fred Pittillo would bring giant inner tubes from his sod tractors for us to cling to as we drifted downstream the next morning. We'd race and flip each other, always watching for water snakes. These days, the clan has thinned, and many of the children have grown and moved away. No one tubes, but they still sit around the fire. I plan to be in the bottoms this Fourth of July, for the first time in a long time.

What sticks with me most about those days is a memory of an odd July decades ago when Clear Creek rose to its banks. We passed through days of consistent rain, and when it finally stopped and we tramped into the bottoms for the Fourth, we found the creek as loud as a river and high enough for a small boat. Mothers warned us about getting too close, but we shot downstream in tubes anyway. We ran the river until we grew tired.

Later that afternoon, we brought Uncle Steve's canoe down the hill. We piled in, filling it fuller than we should have, but the strength of the creek carried us downstream, under the Townsend bridge, past our family barn. We drifted around bends in the creek that had been greatly softened by the swelling water, and I watched smaller branches pour in along our journey. I remember worrying that we'd suddenly hit the French Broad and find ourselves on an unstoppable charge toward the Mississippi. I had visions of a waterfall, of tumbling slowly down. We were miles from the French Broad and states from the Mississippi, but we drifted for so long that the land surrounding us became unknown to me.

I spent much of my boyhood on and in and around this creek. We waded upstream and floated down. We fished and built dams. We climbed the banks and hid in the trees. I knew this stream inside and out. But that July day when we finally directed the canoe into a bank and climbed out, I stood up in what seemed another world.

For all I knew, we had landed in Tennessee or Germany. Nothing about the land seemed identifiable except that we stood in a flat field that grew the same grass as the fields upstream. It was surrounded by trees, and I didn't recognize any of the houses back in the woods. And even though I knew the land in front of us was a sod field, it, too, seemed wrong because much of it was inundated. I imagined we'd landed in a rice field in a foreign land; I worried our boyhood games of Vietnam may have actually sent us east.

We embraced the newfound land. At first, we used the wet field as a giant Slip 'N Slide. We ran and dove face-first into the thin water, blasting through the grass and sliding for what seemed forever.

Eventually, someone tackled someone into deeper water, and soon we were playing football with my cousin's shoe, trudging in slow motion through the standing water.

That Fourth sticks with me because of its foreignness. Suddenly, after merely a few days of rain and a short ride downstream, the world I knew was transformed entirely.

When the dogs and I reach the Townsend bridge, I decide against taking it. I'm already wet and muddy, so I descend the bank again and push myself across the stream. I'm now stepping into the waters I know best, the bank immediately in front of the barn. From here, we floated sticks and tried to sink them with perfectly tossed rocks as kids; we hollered at cars and quickly hid in the woods; we tempted the bulls and escaped through the fence. The water is deep; I'm up to my chest, but the dogs manage to beat me across. Soon, we're all shaking the water off us on the bank.

Once up the bank, we cut through the sod field. Uncle Tim says this field is growing the turf for Tiger Woods's new golf course near the South Carolina border—his first American course, billboards boast. I hope Tiger won't mind that Banjer has peed on it twice already. He runs from corner to corner while Blue trots by my side.

We plod up the hill to my great-great-grandparents' house, Albert's boyhood home, which stands empty above the barn. I sit on the side porch overlooking the creek and the Maxwell land while Banjer sniffs at the brambles and wild blackberry bushes stretching down the hill.

This house scared me as a boy. We'd ride down the dirt road in the back of Granddaddy's truck when he needed to work on the place. When he fixed pipes, we crawled with him under the house, where there seemed to always be some dead varmint rotting; even now, I imagine the underbelly of the house wearing the smell of decomposition. We charged up and down the wooden stairs while he worked on the sink or fixed a door. The nineteenth-century house's small rooms seemed full of mystery and hidden ways. The skeletons beneath the house and passages in the rooms ought to have been perfect for a young boy, but rumbling beneath those allures was the sinister story an older cousin told me as soon I was old enough to understand.

He said that the Prestwoods bought the house from the county in the nineteenth century. It had been seized by the authorities sometime before, after a farmer took an ax to his wife one evening following supper. He was said to have chopped off her head cleanly at the top of the stairs late one night. He was possessed, and when the sheriff showed, he was easily carted off to jail.

The Prestwoods bought the house and the hundred acres surrounding it from Henderson County for a good price. They also bought the phantom of a headless woman, whose ghostly skull thumps down the stairs when no one's around. The sounds serve as a constant reminder that the woman had lost her head and sought revenge. As a boy, every creak and pop in that old house sent me barreling out the front door.

When I started driving into town in the afternoons to look through records at the historical society, the Prestwood house's history was one of the first searches I undertook. Cousin George directed me to land deeds and census data and court records, and after an afternoon of digging, I found no record of murder. What's more, the house wasn't bought from the county at all. But Josh, my older cousin, didn't invent the story. He heard bits from his dad, who heard bits from his great-uncle, who grew up in the house. All of them swore there was a kernel of truth somewhere in the story. But the fine print of history revealed a past less mysterious and exciting.

Still, at twenty-four years old, sitting on the porch, I catch myself on edge when the house settles loudly with a crack.

~

Once we amble up the next hill, arriving at the woods leading to Grandma's, the dogs and I set off on a trail. Granddaddy's old truck still sits on this wide path back in the woods. It has rested here for nearly a decade, collecting leaves and moss. The passenger window is down, and I imagine critters live inside, burrowing into the cloth bench seat and hiding beneath Granddaddy's baseball cap, still sitting on the dash. The truck has been dying out here in the forest since Granddaddy passed. It's seeping into the earth like it was formed of the very soil beneath its tires. I hardly notice it anymore. A dark brown 1972 Ford seems as natural as the oak that shades it.

Eventually, I reach Grandma's yard and pull the back screen door, uselessly asking Banjer not to go far as Blue hovers around the back porch. I know I'll be able to keep an eye on them through the picture window as they sniff their way through the hayfield and apple orchards.

"How do?" Grandma calls from the living room. She doesn't know it's me. This back door is never locked; she reckons whoever has come has come in peace.

"Hidey," I call back as I snitch a cookie from the kitchen.

"What do you know good?" she asks as she swivels her recliner to see me and my half-eaten cookie.

"It's sunny," I say. I grab a handful of peppermints from her coffee table, grab an old towel from the closet, and sit my muddy body on the couch as I watch Banjer drifting toward the hayfield.

We chat about the weather, who she has seen today, where she has been. Soon, we're on to birds.

"Here comes Mr. Cardinal." She turns toward the picture window to watch a redbird light on the feeder. Birds are formal creatures for Grandma. They're always *sir* and *madam*, *Mr.* and *Mrs.*

"I've had a few hummingbirds at this front feeder today," she says. "One will come in, and pretty soon two or three are doing like they do—floating around." She dances her fingers in the air.

At this window, I learned the personalities of the birds: the bullying blue jays, the finicky finches. I watched them in the woods and from my bike. I learned to talk to them, too. I spoke most to the bobwhites, though they called from out of sight in a nearby field. The long, low note required dropping my chin and lips. The note felt slow, like the start of a deep, chilly wind. After starting it, I'd pause briefly and raise my lips slightly, pushing the air quickly up. The second, short note needed tightly pursed lips, the sound rising like a slide whistle. The call rang like the name, the low *bob* and the quick-rising *white*.

"Now, Jay-ray-me," she says, "they's a bunch of old books on that bookcase by the back door. Go and see what you want. They just sit back there, and they may as well be put to use."

Grandma knows I'm digging around in the past. From albums beneath the TV, she has begun pulling out old photographs and newspaper clippings, like the pre-honeymoon picture of her and her adoptive-brother husband. She often hands me pictures when I walk in, expecting me to recognize second and third cousins I've never met. "Oh, you know," she'll say, "that's your granddaddy's brother, Leonard's nephew."

I'm happy to poke through the books, but I get uncomfortable when she starts giving things away. She's nearly eighty, becoming more and more sedentary, and I fear she knows something I don't.

Most of the books on the two shelves are Bibles and bird books. I want to grab a few bird books, but they seem as much a part of the house as Granddaddy's truck is part of the woods. I'd like to have them to broaden my bird knowledge. I can spot the birds that I learned as a boy, but there are sparrows and finches and warblers I don't know from Adam.

I sometimes wonder if I got my shifty tongue from whistling to birds. I learned as a boy to make sounds foreign to me to get a response. When the calls coming back at me changed, I adapted, repeating the new calls. Traveling to new countries and sinking into various forms of Spanish, I repeated the tics and sounds I heard. I did the same in college. I mimicked; I aped.

When I studied in Costa Rica during college, I arranged my daily route to get a peek at the Montezuma oropendolas. I followed the abandoned railroad tracks from classes at the Universidad de Costa Rica to the small office where I worked, paralleling a line of palms. From the branches of many of the trees hung what looked like deep, woven baskets. Despite the size of the large, black, gold-tipped birds, they wove intricate hanging nests. Only certain sturdy trees could support the nests because they hung nearly two feet and were occupied by a few big birds.

Once I found the nests along the railroad tracks, I tried to walk by every day, just on the edge of the giant American-style mall. The trek was truly a walk along an ecotone, the mall and traffic pushed against the quiet stretch of grass and trees where the birds nested. I tightroped the empty railroad tracks as I watched the birds burrow into their nests and shoot out to glide over the busy city roads.

I wasn't only fascinated by the strangeness of the nests but drawn to the birds' calls as well. I was convinced that bells lined their throats. They called out to each other in a metallic song, something unlike any bird I'd ever heard. Their song contained a series of jingling clucks, described by ornithologist Dan Mennill as "overlapping bubbly syllables." The sound ascended and climaxed at a unified high note, sometimes backed by scratchy pops similar to a "fizzling firecracker or the ripping of thick fabric."

The oropendolas' song was one I could never echo; my vocal chords had no access to it. I felt a sadness in watching the birds daily and rearranging my routes to be near them but never being able to call to them. I felt distant and disconnected. I could only look. There was no plane upon which I could touch the birds or imagine any sort of interaction. In a dirty capital city, the oropendolas served as a reminder of a natural world at times covered in cement and soot. In my inability to imitate the birds' call, I felt closer to the manufactured world than to the seamless, natural realm of the birds.

⌘

"You findin' anything that suits you?" Grandma calls from the other room.

"Can't say just yet."

I grab a white book. Its spine reads, in red and blue letters, *USA Holiday in Poetry.* I'm curious about a book of poetry on these shelves. Everything else tells of birds or food or God. Maybe the poems speak about all three. Inside the front cover, I find scrawling longhand: "Presented to Albert Prestwood, Aug. 31/67, by the Mr. Himself." I assume the writing to be that of my grandma's mother, Azalee, or Nanny, as I knew her. The "Mr. Himself," I determine, is the poet, Irving P. Zieman. As I flip through the pages, I see pen underlines within many of the poems. The book is separated into sections—regions of the United States. "The Smokie [*sic*] Mountains" is the first of the four sections. Within that portion, I find Nanny's marks noting familiar characters in poems with titles such as "Clear Creek Road" and "Fruitland."

I find a poem, "The Habits of Rabbits," about Jack Jones, who was no relation to me but who delivered the mail to our community when my parents were young. Great-granddaddy Albert and Granddaddy both worked with Jack at the post office. Mom has told me about Jack leaving gum in the mailbox for her and her sister. When they were out of stamps, they'd leave change in the box, and Jack would provide the postage.

> To neighbors around the bend
> Jack is everyone's friend.

After leafing through a few poems and reading the biographical information about the poet, I learn that Zieman was a Bostonian who got rich young and then puttered about writing rhymes. Zieman gets a bit saccharine, his verse elementary and forced. But in these poems, he has freeze-framed the community of my great-grandparents.

I leave the bird books on the shelf for another time but decide to take *USA Holiday in Poetry*. I ask Grandma about it when I head back into the living room. She picks through the pages and confirms that the handwriting is Nanny's, but she has no idea how Albert, her daddy, knew Irving P. Zieman. I snag another peppermint, say goodbye, and walk out the front door, hollering for the dogs to take me home.

~

On many of these walks, I feel right at home back on this land. I walk in back doors and hop into streams and know where and why I am. I speak the language and call out to familiar birds. Other days, though, I get itchy feet. This has been happening more and more often. I think of faraway places and languages, of oropendolas and cloud forests. Some days I'm Blue; others I'm Banjer.

Today, I know I'm part of this land and it is part of me. These trees hid and held me as a boy. I dug in and wore this dirt on summer days. My people have walked these trails and crossed these streams for generations.

I head down the hill to the Prestwood house without looking, flipping through the book of poetry as I go. In the poem "Harper's Creek," I find this stanza:

> Willie fell from his apple tree on a sack
> Of apples he hand picked—and broke his back
> The earth is parched, the farmers look for rain,
> But Willie feels only a constant pain.

I stop on the hill beside the Prestwood house and look out toward Bearwallow. It stands tall and bald and empty and confused. Banjer is thinking of inching his way into the rabbit- and briar-filled slope in search of adventure, while Blue seems worn out and ready to get back. I think I hear the call of a bobwhite up the hill. I whistle back and wait as I imagine Willie up there on the mountain. I think about a bird-themed banjo song I recently learned, "The Coo Coo Bird." One of the verses is about Willie:

> Gonna build me a log cabin
> On a mountain so high
> So I can see Willie
> As he goes on by

I wonder if my old friend Willie laments the South from his perch on top of the mountain, if he laments change, or if he's happy as a lark living every day in his place.

The bobwhite calls back, and I whistle to Banjer, thinking maybe we'll take a new route home.

14

Spring break. And not a moment too soon. The slow march of January and February left us with no breathers, save a stray snow day. Now lying in front of me is a week with no permission slips to translate, no calls of "Sit down, please," no repeat (and repeat) performances of songs about animals. If I had my druthers, we'd pack a bag and vanish, but Sarah gets no spring break at her dad's law firm in town, so I'm here above Clear Creek with idle time.

After the dogs tear around the sod field, I push out for a short loop, skirting the foot of Bearwallow and riding Mills Gap back home. Before I jump in the shower, the phone rings.

"Jeremy?"

"Hey," I say to the voice of my grandma, my mom's mom.

"Listen, I'm fixing some vegetables for me and Papaw for dinner. You want to come eat?"

"Sure," I say, looking at the time on the microwave: 11:27.

"Okay, well, come on now. It'll be ready before long."

Dinner is a word I had to unlearn in college and have relearned now. To my grandparents, as to many from their generation growing up on farms in these mountains, *dinner* means *lunch*, the substantial meal of the day. Breakfast, dinner, and supper. I've done some similar unlearning in regard to many of the Mexican parents and students at Edneyville. Unlike Hondurans, many of them have borrowed the traditional word for lunch, *almuerzo*, to mean breakfast. They have adopted an Anglicized word, *lonche*, to mean lunch. As with my grandparents now, I often have to pause for a moment at these words to process just which place, which culture, which time I'm in.

"Okay, I'm going to rinse off and then come on."

⌁

Most of the land I cycled this morning, along with the land I pass now driving down Gilliam Road to my grandparents' place on Fruitland Road, used to be covered in my grandmother's people, the Maxwells. My great-great-great-great-great-grandfather Andrew Maxwell came first, a Scot from Ireland. In the eighteenth century, he received a land grant stretching across Fruitland. Over time, his children sprawled across the earth, planting seeds and putting the soil to work in the shade of the mountains I climb. In land records from the mid-nineteenth century, I found Maxwell land reaching along nearly all the bottom land beside Clear Creek, acres upon acres stretching into the valleys below Sugarloaf and Gilliam. I found Maxwells living at the foot of Bearwallow and saw records of their buying and trading sections of the mountain itself. As a clan, they entirely surrounded William Mills's small plot when he named these peaks.

But as time passed and the soil was used up, sections of land were sold or traded as Maxwells moved on. But my line stayed put, even after my great-great-grandfather was killed in the Civil War. It dug in deeper alongside Clear Creek, just across from the land of the Prestwoods.

Before the Maxwells arrived, the tribes of Cherokees in the Blue Ridge were known as "the mountaineers." Unlike the Iroquois, the Cherokees lived in autonomous clans, refusing to form a cohesive nation. Already, it seems, the mountains were shaping people into inward, tight-knit communities.

By the nineteenth century, once treaties and deception and guns had pushed out most of "the mountaineers," my people dug in deeper. They were no longer newcomers, no longer Scots-Irish or Dutch or any other ethnicity connecting them to another homeland. They were all one: "the mountain whites."

In his 1913 book, *Our Southern Highlanders*, Horace Kephart claimed that the term *mountain whites* wasn't imposed upon my people to distinguish them from mountain blacks; there were few slaves or freed blacks in these mountains. Instead, *mountain whites* linked these mountaineers to the poor whites of the South. The mountain whites, like the poor whites, were something unfamiliar, something other; they were a people from the bottom stratum of Southern society.

The mountain whites were akin to the poor whites in their poverty and subsistence farming. The poor whites of the South were also called "corn crackers" and, later, simply "crackers." They, like most mountaineers, survived on anything the land would produce—mostly corn. Both groups were seen as incapable of economic or societal evolution, forever at the mercy of hard ground and slow minds.

But while the term *mountain whites* connected us to the poor whites, it also meant to separate us. Poor whites accepted slavery easily because they were ever aware that without such an institution, they would be field hands, their backs catching the whip. Their paleness was all that kept them from the bottom of the pile. Generally, poor whites had arrived in America under some form of servitude. Many hoped to escape poverty through emigration, while others were criminals serving their time in the fields of the New World. They came with nothing and lived with less.

The mountain whites, though, took their plight intentionally. They chose these mountains; they staked out their land and survived on it. They conquered. They came of free will and fiery blood, and while they were thought to be backward and strange, they weren't for pushing around or putting to work.

I've been pulling stories from Grandma and Papaw during my visits. Today, as I sit at the small kitchen table and watch Grandma season the collards and stir the mashed potatoes and hear Papaw fiddling with something and whistling in another room, I ask Grandma to tell me about her childhood. As soon as I ask it, I fear the question is too broad, but she just slaps her thigh and turns toward me to say, "Jeremy, all I ever did was hoe corn."

She went to work as soon as she could. The youngest of five, she dug potatoes and strung beans alongside the Maxwell men, her uncles and cousins and brothers, and then set to helping her mom serve noon dinner, cooking the same vegetables she's fixing me today.

She also worked alongside migrant workers. Her family, like some other mountain whites at the beginning of the twentieth century, could afford to hire cheap labor. But like her siblings, Grandma still worked the fields as a child, alongside the hired help, field hand and sodbuster all at once.

These days, nearly all the migrant workers in Henderson County are Latino, primarily from Mexico and Central America—they're the parents of my students, tending and packing apples. But in Grandma's day, most migrant workers were black, often whole families working any farmland that needed hands. As the mountains grew cold, the workers would travel south, following a harvest line toward Florida, trying to make ends meet by chasing hard labor and amenable climate.

Those workers were mostly Southern, descendants of slaves and then sharecroppers. And so Grandma, a mountain white 150 years removed from Scotland, worked the fields of her childhood alongside black families barely fifty years removed from slavery.

But in the 1940s, she found herself, not yet a teenager, down in those bottoms pulling corn and picking beans with funny-sounding white men. As she tells it, the men were all blond and tall and tongue-tied and handsome. "We just worked down there with everybody. It didn't matter who you were. In the field, you worked."

As we sit to eat, she tells me of one hot day when she was a girl. She left the field to help her mama start dinner, and on the way to the house, she spotted one of those men—a boy, really, maybe twenty—creeping from the Maxwell cellar. In his arms, he cradled a jar of canned peaches. She stopped and spied him around the corner of the house. There, he paused, stuck his whole hand in the jar, and swallowed down a slimy handful of peaches. Grandma watched him swiftly tighten the lid and stuff the jar in his pants after wiping his mouth clean.

She leaned there against the edge of the house and only watched. While she did, her older sister, Carolyn, trudged up the hill to the house. The boy drifted back to the field, peaches in his pants.

"What are you doing?" Carolyn, born into bossiness, asked.

"Walking," Grandma snapped, turning briskly back to the house and aiming for the front door.

And she went about her day. She didn't tell her daddy about the boy thieving their preserves, never shared the story. "I reckon he needed something sweet," she says. "Plus, he was kindly cute."

She worked the fields with the corners of her eyes aimed at that boy. He was tall and strong, mysterious and silent. She may have been too young to know who he was then, but it might not have mattered. Her crush and the other men sweating in the Maxwell field that summer were Germans, World War II prisoners. They would show up in the mornings heaped in the back of a truck; some would hop off at the Maxwell farm, and the truck would head up the road, delivering the foreign labor to other farms.

Some of the men were carted to the top of Bearwallow day after day. The truck snaked them higher and higher until they finally set to work above everything else in the county, digging holes and eventually erecting a tower. I imagine them struggling to communicate with the bosses and landowners—building Babel's tower with babbled language. After weeks of working on the peak, the prisoners left the mountain with a narrow structure rising from it like a flag claiming territory. This fire tower raised by the prison labor watched over Edneyville and Fruitland, looking for the first glint of change, the first flicker of danger. It, like my bear, protected.

The Germans were held on the other side of town, near Long John

Mountain, in a POW camp that officially opened on Independence Day in 1944. Established to relieve the crowding of a camp in Tennessee, the internment camp held 263 men off a road leading to Pisgah Forest.

Those men fell to the bottom of the social ladder—below the mountain whites, below the black migrants. They bent their backs to till our soil, pulling our food from the land. They allowed farmers like my great-grandfather to sell extra produce at the curb market. They brought an economic boost to our soil during war on theirs.

The stability of the Maxwell farm helped Grandma and her sister attend college in Brevard and then Cullowhee. They graduated, started teaching, married, and built sturdy, comfortable lives: brick homes with yards. Grandma didn't manage to land a German man. But she did marry my grandfather after he returned from a long stint of duty in Germany during the Korean War. She'd seen him in Waynesville before he left, where he was running Queen's Dairy: "I saw him riding up and down the road on his little pinto pony, and I thought he was right cute."

✦

Just across the road from their ranch-style house is a newly situated mobile home on the edge of the former Maxwell farm. An old car and a fishing boat stand guard in the trailer's yard. Farther up the road, nearing Bearwallow, trailer parks house migrant families who have left their former lives to bring our apple trees to fruition. They all make homes on this land given to Andrew Maxwell after it was taken from the Cherokees.

This class division—trailers and houses—is palpable across Edneyville and Fruitland. Beyond the pasture in front of our boxy brown house on Gilliam stand two trailers. One family lives in them simultaneously. Surrounding the trailers are scraps of machines, wheelless cars, kids' toys. The yard is littered with brokenness. Yesterday, I watched the mom mow the grass while holding a diapered baby with one arm and the steering wheel with the other.

I've never met these people, even though I can see their trailers from the window and we've been here for months. When I let the dogs loose, Banjer often circumvents the horse pasture's fence to run up the road to these neighbors' plot. But I stand by the barn on our land and call him back, without getting too close.

Across the creek, on my daddy's family's land, I grew up ever aware of the lines between houses and trailers. We had houses, but the Wallaces, our neighbors near Highway 64, lived in mobile homes. As boys, my cousins and I would walk out the edge of the hayfield, near the end of our land, and yell. Eventually, a few Stepps (Jayne's sons) would burst through the apple orchard from their land on Townsend Road, and the Wallace boys would emerge from the end of our road, where they lived in a series of trailers above their apple house. We'd soon line up and start calling fake football plays and hitting each other up and down the hayfield.

Our games were friendly enough, but the Wallaces were the enemies of our boyhood imaginings. We set Tinkertoy traps for them in the woods; we plotted lines of defense—trip lines, hidden holes—to keep them away from our land. They never crossed on to our plot uninvited—probably never cared to—but we felt sure they would try to seize our territory or sneak into our hideouts. And they weren't welcome.

Even though we met up during summer vacation to clobber each other, I didn't associate with the Wallaces at school, don't even remember saying "Hey" in the hall. We never ventured on to their land for our games; we just hollered from our field, knowing where the line between us lay.

Even our dogs didn't get along with Wallace dogs. They'd sometimes circle, hair raised, in that same hayfield and fight to slobbery, bloody ends.

Our parents never stopped to chat with the Wallaces as we pulled on to Highway 64 from the driveway. We'd see the father—wild, thick beard and dirty T-shirt—picking up pallets of apples with the tractor or sitting in front of the apple house in a metal chair. We'd sometimes wave, but we didn't stop to ask about family or chat about the weather. The Wallaces' narrow stretch of land along 64 marked a boundary we didn't cross, physically or socially. It meant danger—the end of our land, the highway, the unknown.

When I was a boy, my uncle planted a line of pine trees along the hayfield to more clearly mark the boundary between Jones land and Wallace land. Today, the pines have grown tall enough to hide any trace of the Wallaces from our property. They form a natural wall. Behind the wall, the Wallaces sell apples and other produce from a brown garage-like building at the end of the road, beside our mailboxes. Farther down 64, they have a few rows of apple trees, but much of what they sell they buy from other orchards and farms. They're farmers and middlemen all at once. Outside the apple house and the trailers stand old trucks and broken-down cars, busted-up tractor parts and empty pallets. When one of the kids marries or reaches adulthood, they stick another trailer above the apple house. Four trailers now stand off 64, crammed within an acre and climbing the hill, backed by a row of immense pines. The Wallaces, like us, stick to their piece of earth, living in each other's backyards, perpetually staying put.

～

After lunch—dinner—I decide to drive across the creek to my parents' plot. As I turn off 64, I grow curious about the Wallace land. I've never been in or near a Wallace trailer, even though they stand just beside the hill we sledded as kids. I explored every bit of our family land as a boy—knew every climbable tree, every enveloping patch of rhododendron—but I never happened on to Wallace land, never crossed the line.

These days, I tip my cap or wave at them when we make eye contact. But most times, they don't look at me. I wonder if they even know who—or whose—I am after years of being away. Maybe it's obvious from the dress shirt I wear pulling in the driveway after a day at school. Maybe my newish SUV marks me, places me on the Jones land, sets me in a house instead of a trailer. Maybe they just don't care.

Even though we filled our woods with Wallace-aimed traps, and even though our parents shielded us from the Wallaces with trees and careful eyes, Grandma and Granddaddy maintained relations with them. Granddaddy used to stop his old truck at the end of the road to shoot the breeze outside the apple house in the afternoons. They would gift Grandma a bushel of apples from time to time, and she'd return thanks in the form of an apple pie. But we next-generation Joneses learned to push them away, to roll up our windows pulling out of the drive.

When I turn up the driveway past their plot and find myself uncomfortable, I try to trace what it is about them that keeps us at bay, noses upturned and eyes fearful. Of course, it's painfully obvious to me now as a twenty-four-year-old man coming home. We drive newer cars. We built a pool behind our house. Our parents work in town, wearing ties, not NASCAR T-shirts. We're better.

But we're all mountain whites. We're all Scots-Irish. We have the same homeland, here and abroad. We're the same.

In the generations from Grandma to me, something changed. We're no longer laborers, no longer dependent on those apple trees surrounding our land. We're no longer victims or stewards of the land. We don't need handwritten "Corn, Tomatoes, Half-Runners" signs along the road to make ends meet. We've moved on.

Despite my newfound idealism, I breathe easier on the other side of the pines, heading toward home, toward the sturdiness of a house. This afternoon, I find myself instinctively rushing past Wallace land, afraid of getting caught or stuck in our shared past.

15

During the rest of the week, I don't wait for Grandma to call. I find excuses to stop by around noon—"Oh yes, why, sure, I can stay for dinner." More than the food, though, I'm filling up on stories about my great-grandparents. For months now, I have been searching out these people in my skin, piecing together the lives of those who planted our mountain roots, parsing how my forefolk worked their way into my genes.

Lately, I find myself stretching for those out of reach—the great-grandparents who saw me born but have no real place in my memory. Jim and Cora, William and Clara, Leroy and Essie, Albert and Azalee. As I hear their stories, I see their ripples in my grandparents and parents, and I'm convinced they are buried in the bones and blood that keep me upright. These are the folks whittled by the geology of southern Appalachia. The traces of them that I discern in and around me ought to yield some outline of a mountaineer, of those ways in which I'm part and product of the Blue Ridge.

And I can find them. Their bodies aren't far. I walk down the creek to the Fruitland Cemetery and find Azalee and Albert Prestwood. A few feet away lie William and Clara Maxwell, alongside generations of Maxwells. A bike ride toward Flat Rock drops me in front of the bodies of Leroy and Essie Jones. They're all resting in the very soil I've settled upon. But my grandfather Baby Ray comes from the Smoky Mountains near Tennessee. His clan, the Harrells, is still in the Cataloochee Valley, farther west, deeper in. I've never seen where his parents rest; they're ghosts and stories.

Baby Ray and Grace lived on Harrell land after they married. They settled into a small place with a little garden out front: "We had lettuce and onions and all that stuff in it." Grace tells me of being intimidated as a nineteen-year-old wife living next door to her mother-in-law. Baby Ray's mama was a stern, sharp woman. To Grace, Cora seemed all-knowing and rough. The archetypal mountain wife.

Mrs. Harrell had chickens. One day, as Grace worked outside, an old hen of Mrs. Harrell's "got out and got in our garden, and it was just a-goin' down there pecking the lettuce, just a-eatin' it all the way down." So Grace did what any reasonable nineteen-year-old newlywed would: "I picked up a rock, and I threw it hard as I could. And I hit that chicken right in the head—which I couldn't do again in a million years. That chicken just fell over. I thought—I hadn't been married long—'Boy, Miz Harrell will kill me.' "

Grace stood for a moment before finally deciding she had to walk next door to her husband's mother to tell her she had just murdered a Harrell chicken. "So I go over to her and say, 'Miz Harrell, I think I killed one of your chickens. I hit it in the head with a rock.' And she said, 'Well, it shouldn't have been in your garden anyhow. That's all right.' " The two women walked over to the garden, but the chicken was gone—dust to dust. They decided it was either a ghost or Grace had just knocked it out; it woke up, figured something was wrong with that lettuce, and poked along on its way.

Baby Ray's mother was used to reckless behavior. By the time Grace married Baby Ray, he had wrecked thirteen cars, including the one he ran over with a stolen school bus.

I hadn't known about this wildness of Baby Ray. He worked long shifts at a textile mill when I was a boy and retired when I was in middle school. Now, he piddles around fixing anything that breaks or squeaks, while whistling a song he must have invented—his theme whistle. He likes to play cards and mow his yard. But before I came into the world, he was, as my mom always said of me as a child, a wild man.

Baby Ray's childhood was filled with death-defying acts, and my childhood was similar. I spent more time in the woods and creeks than I did inside a house. At times, I devolved into some form of animal. I remember riding with my grandma Grace one day after school. She turned and asked me if I ever thought before doing things. I said—without thinking—"Not usually." I don't remember what incident prompted this discussion. Something dumb I'd done—jumping off the giant oil tank and cutting a gash up my thigh or surfing on a sled, weaving down the snowy, wooded hill. I acted, reacted, ran on instinct. Baby Ray grew up the same.

When he and my grandmother moved back to Henderson County, he helped run a riding stable on Bearwallow. He took tourists up the mountain on horseback, riding the lead horse while the others tagged along behind him. It was easy work; the horses knew the mountain. But they also knew when they were getting close to the stables—close to losing a hundred-plus pounds and eating a meal. One trip, coming back down Bearwallow, a horse took off past Baby Ray, charging in the direction of the stables. The tourist waving and flopping around on the horse's back didn't know how to stop or slow the thing as it tore along the ridge line. Baby Ray took off after the runaway horse, hoping to catch it before the tourist tumbled off the mountain. Before they all slipped down into the valley, he snatched the horse's reins and stopped it—and the screaming tourist.

Grace is equally quick-acting but more intentional than reckless. The same grandma who asked me if I ever thought before I acted was the woman who defiantly wore pants to work when they weren't allowed for women. She taught at Edneyville Elementary in an age that assumed women ever lived in dresses and skirts. But one winter day,

the temperature below freezing and Bearwallow capped in snow, Grace
didn't want cold air blowing all over her legs as she walked between
the buildings and took kids to recess. So she wore the cute new pant-
suit she had bought. She strolled past the principal's office a few times,
making no effort to hide her attire. That Friday, her garment was one
of the items on the agenda at the faculty meeting. But before she could
be disciplined, a few other female teachers backed her. From then on,
teachers were allowed to wear pants on cold days.

    Today, the teachers patrolling the halls wear pants more often than
not. On cold Fridays, many walk in with jeans and Edneyville Elementary polos—an ongoing result of Grace's rebellion decades ago.

    She is blunt and fearless, the kind of lady who will throw a rock at
a chicken and hit it square between the eyes.

～

    I would like to have known Baby Ray's daddy. I've been pulling sto-
ries about him from my grandparents, and it hasn't taken me long to
know Jim Harrell was a crafty character.

    He started his own business out of anger one spring. He and one
of his sons walked from their land to a small general store owned by a
man named Messer. They lived twelve miles from town, so, like most
everyone on the mountain, they bought what they needed at Messer's.

    As they pulled cans and odds and ends off the shelves and stacked
them up to buy, Jim's boy's dog trailed in and managed to get behind the
counter. As Messer came around the corner, he saw the dog and kicked
it out of his way. It whimpered and scurried off.

    Calmly, Jim stopped what he was doing, removed the items he'd
stacked on the counter, and reshelved them all. He left the store empty-
handed, the dog skulking behind them back up the mountain. Once
home, Jim hitched the wagon to a few horses and drove them to town.
He filled his wagon, buying anything and everything—fruit preserves
and motor oil, cigarettes and butter. He had a few of his boys carry
boxes out to his wagon, then pointed it home. By the next day, he'd

started his own general store. Within a month, Jim's store put Messer, the dog kicker, out of business.

Although he was mostly a subsistence farmer back in the Smoky Mountains, Jim was also an entrepreneur, an opportunist, a trader. He'd come home with anything he could fit in his truck—hitchhikers, cows, pigs. Often, he'd be out, headed to town, and come back with a horse riding in the back of the truck as if it had simply fallen from the sky. He'd pull up and yell at the nearest boy to take it into the barn.

Jim especially liked to trade for calves. But often when he found a good deal, he was in his car. So he'd stick the animal in the backseat. It wasn't unusual to see Jim Harrell driving up the mountain with a calf back there, the windows wide open. Baby Ray tells me, "Lord, I washed the car many a time, gettin' ready to go out to town on a Saturdee night, and he'd yell, 'I'll be back in a minute, son!' And he'd come back in an hour with a calf in the backseat." Jim was never one to worry about looks or smells or whatever other implications could be drawn from having livestock in the car.

I sometimes imagine Jim driving the tight turns of the dirt roads back in Cataloochee, livestock and all, and I realize that this vision is a blurring of Honduras and home. I see his old truck churning up dust on the mountain roads circling Gracias, those roads I used to hitchhike.

In Gracias, no buses wound into the small mountain villages, but those who could afford a truck drove the narrow dirt roads. Climbing in the back of a truck was far quicker than walking ten miles to small *aldeas* like La Campa. "*Jalón*," I would say. The driver would nod or point his thumb toward the truck bed, and I'd hop in. *Jalón* literally means *a pull*, but in Honduras, it's a ride, a hitchhike, a lift.

I imagine Jim as one of those drivers in the mountains of Honduras, trails passing for roads, houses without electricity or plumbing pushed back in the hills. I know from stories I'm collecting that he would pick up anyone looking for a pull—anybody on the side of the road. *Come on home, son.*

Jim once picked up a man working his way toward Cherokee. He brought the fellow home for supper and told him he could stay and work the land a few days if he wanted. The man agreed, had his supper, and soon fell asleep. The next morning, he said he needed to go to Waynesville before he started working, so Jim lent him the truck. Only one real road ran from Cataloochee in those days. Today it is a four-lane stretch, but then it was dirt and twisted sharply up through the mountains. There weren't many cars back then, so when a man came by Jim's store and said he'd seen the truck headed toward Knoxville—the opposite direction from Waynesville—Jim knew something wasn't right. Jim closed the store, hollered for Baby Ray, and the two hopped in the car and took off down the road after the hitchhiker and their truck.

They caught up in a hurry. I don't know if the truck was that much slower than the car or if Jim simply knew those mountain curves better than the man, but they made up a thirty-minute head start in no time. They forced the truck over, the man climbed out, and the rest of the story amazes me. Not for its suspense but for the easygoingness. The fellow apologized, Jim took the car and Baby Ray the truck, and they headed back home. No arrests, no shots. They simply retrieved the truck.

Jim picked up another hitchhiker the next week on his way back from town.

⁓

I know how Jim's hastiness oozed into my grandfather's and my childhoods—we ran wide open—but I wonder how his other qualities trickled down the family tree. My granddaddy Baby Ray is an ordered man. He turns the money in his wallet all the same direction and keeps his truck clean, with no livestock inside. He's mostly quiet, doesn't like to cause a scene. He's different from his daddy in those ways. But Baby Ray doesn't care much about what people think. His life is in no way motivated by what others feel he ought and ought not do. I suppose I possess these qualities, but not as through and through as Jim—not enough to throw a cow in my backseat.

Mountain folk—the term that blanketed Sarah and me years ago when my car broke down—still intrigues me. As I dig up stories of my kin and trace their lines and land and peculiarities, I try to pin down the qualities and actions that make me a result of this place. But what I'm finding more than connections are teased-out differences. My chicken-killing, pants-wearing grandma who stroked my hair and rocked me to sleep as a boy. My great-grandfather who started a store out of vengeance, yet sent a car thief on his way without incident. In this family tree, I find my forefathers fighting on both sides of the Revolutionary and Civil wars. I see me as a child, learning dances that mixed Cherokee steps and Irish tunes. My people hid and ran; they fought and fled. This is a blurred land, and the more I learn of my people, the more leery I grow of easy stereotypes of my home. Stereotypes both good and bad—Andy Taylor and Ernest T. Bass, the simple wisdom and the backward violence. We're more complicated.

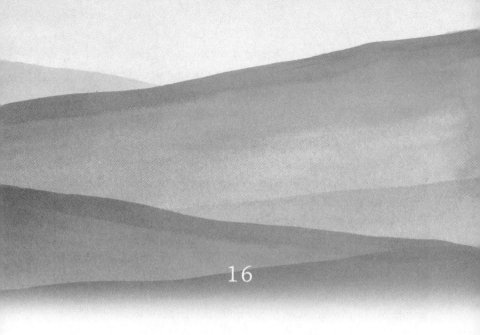

16

I am duty-free some weeks. This morning, I have no breakfast tables to clean or child-lined gyms to monitor, so I'm piling books and papers I'll need beside the table in my trailer before the bell rings.

"Mr. Jones." The wall is speaking to me.

When the office calls through our trailer-specific intercom, it's rarely a question. It comes out as more of a claim, a staticky announcement. *Yes*, I think, *this is me, Mr. Jones.* I move toward the sound.

I can't simply speak and be heard like in the classrooms in the main building; I have to grab the CB-like microphone from the wall to call back to the office. But before I can get across the room to the speaker, the statement turns to a question: "Mr. Jones?"

I nearly trip over a pile of books. "Yes?" I finally return, rattling the mic from its place, the cord eternally tangled.

"Could you come to the office, please? We have new students."

When I'm beckoned to the office, I try to remind myself of the pedestrian lifestyle I left in Honduras. In Gracias, when I needed photocopies, I had to walk across town to the Internet café. If I wanted lunch, I had to hoof it to a small restaurant near the park for a to-go plate. If I forgot something at home, I couldn't simply hop in the car at lunch and speed up Highway 64 on a two-minute drive home; I had to ascend and descend and sweat all over the mismatched sidewalks until I neared the entrance to town.

A walk through the lower building (past the teachers' lounge and the gym) and a short hike up the hill to the upper building (where the office and first to third grades live) ought to be an easy stroll compared to Honduras. But I've grown lazy in my return to America.

I made this climb a few weeks ago to welcome Alicia and Lupe, a third-grader and kindergartner recently arrived from Mexico. Their father had been here for nearly a year, I learned, and the girls and mother had just come to join him in a trailer at the foot of Bearwallow. The girls have added to the little lines leading to my condo. Lupe, the younger, has warmed quickly, jabbering away in Spanish with my kindergarten group. Alicia, though, stays pretty quiet alongside Antonio and Carlos.

~

Outside the office sits a small family—a young girl and an older boy sandwiched by two short parents. I smile as I head into the office, but they look flatly at me, then back to the hall, where a straight and curious line of second-graders passes.

The secretary, Catherine, hands me the paperwork and tells me that the family is new. "None of 'em speak English. Far as I can tell anyhow."

Catherine was the secretary when I was a boy. Her presence behind the front desk makes my trips to the office eerie. She looks the same as twenty years before, though she must be over seventy. As I enter, I sometimes feel myself shrinking to a seven-year-old boy on his way to the principal's office.

I take the papers from her.

"*Buenos días*," I say as I walk back into the hall.

The parents stand. "*Buenos días.*"

"*¿Como están? Soy profesor Jones.*"

I know I'm a strange sight—a young white man amid a school of older women, speaking Spanish tinged with Central America. Because my tongue worked to fit in while in Central America, my accent sounds mostly natural and normal. When I speak to parents on the phone, they rarely recognize me in person, expecting some hint of Latino in me.

But I know that the formality of my Central American Spanish and the expressions that come from a Honduran life color my language differently from Mexican Spanish. A parent once asked if I was Argentine, trying to match my paleness and noticeable nose with my voice.

"No, I'm from here," I replied.

"How is that?" she asked.

I smiled and shrugged instead of saying, "That's the question I'm trying to answer."

~

At first, parents usually speak with short words, unsure of me until they realize I have a firm grasp of the language. This morning is no different. These parents tilt their heads at me almost simultaneously and start slowly.

"José," the father says as we shake hands.

"*Mucho gusto,*" I say. "*Vamos por acá—a la biblioteca para rellenar algunos formularios.*"

We walk to a table in the library to fill out the forms and gather the information needed to enroll the students. I ask where they're from (Mexico), when they arrived (the father came months ago, the others last week), where they live (a trailer park at the foot of Bearwallow). I'm careful not to ask questions related to immigration. I don't ask how they came, where they crossed, if they have citizenship. The county schools' stance is that we don't care how students arrive, but that once they're here, it's our responsibility to teach and care.

We talk about bus routes and lunch prices and classroom materials. The children will be in kindergarten and fourth grade. Once the office has assigned them teachers, I offer to walk the family to each child's classroom. The parents are resistant at first, telling me it's not necessary. But after I assure them it's okay, they gladly follow me down the hill to the lower building.

Many parents of Latino students are highly trusting of teachers. The shared opinion seems to be, *You know best; I trust you.* I sense from the other teachers that this attitude is refreshing. These parents don't want to be in the way or cause problems, complaining about grades or discipline or curriculum. They simply want their children to *comportarse bien*—behave themselves.

But sometimes I wonder where this blind support ends. My Spanish isn't native or flawless by any means. Last week while speaking to the parents of a kindergarten student, I confused the words for *survey (encuesta)* and *kidnapping (secuestra)*. Despite this grave mix-up, the parents nodded as though I must have known what I was doing.

We sat at a tiny red table in the back of Mrs. Salatino's kindergarten classroom, caged hamsters, guinea pigs, and a rabbit lining the walls, blocks stacked along the floor. The exchange, roughly translated:

"We need you to answer a few questions because the teacher is having a kidnapping."

Nodding, slight confusion.

"She wants to get information from the students to have the kidnapping."

Nodding.

"I'll translate the questions of the kidnapping so that you can answer them at home on your own."

"Okay."

⌐

Susi, the daughter, goes first to her class. Mrs. Salatino, who was my kindergarten teacher, comes into the hall to shake hands with the parents. José says hello, and his wife, Ana, smiles and nods. I give Mrs. Salatino a few papers denoting Susi's bus number, lunch plan, and shot records. She hands them to Mrs. Lyda, the assistant.

Mrs. Salatino is as energetic and peppy as she was nineteen years ago. She wears loud colors and spends much of the day performing for the students. Her voice is often hoarse not from yelling but from reading and singing and laughing.

She turns back to the class from the doorway. "Everyone, welcome Susi! Peter, make room for her on the floor." A round, freckled boy scoots to his right.

Mrs. Lyda leads Susi to where the class sits cross-legged on a multicolored rug in front of the board and a trunk with costume pieces spilling out. They turn to look at the new student, some leaning in too close. I squat by Susi to tell her I'll be back in a few hours to take her to a class to practice English. I assure her other kids who speak Spanish will be there.

As I lead José, Ana, and their son, Mario, away from the kindergarten hall, Mrs. Salatino jogs back into the class: "Who's ready to sing?" The students cheer, Mrs. Salatino shoots her arms into the air, and Susi looks around like she has just awakened from a deep sleep.

As we walk past the gym, Mario bends his neck to see a third-grade class scooting around on their butts, kicking a giant bouncing ball. "Crab soccer," I try to tell him. But I don't know if my translation— "football of crabs"—makes sense. He halfway smiles.

Once we arrive at Mario's new class, Mrs. Queen—Beth—comes to shake hands with the parents. Beth doesn't have any other "newcomer" students. She looks as wide-eyed as Susi. She's a fairly new teacher and is understandably nervous about getting a new student in the last quarter of the school year, especially a student who doesn't speak a word of English and will be expected to pass standardized tests in a few months. She looks around for a desk, deciding where to put him. I suggest a spot near her desk, where she can help him more easily. He sits and hangs his backpack on his chair.

I will be back soon, I tell Mario and Beth. They both look worried.

Once we reach the office, I bid José and Ana *adiós*. I tell them they can call and ask for me when needed.

"*¿Y el bus va a parar en frente de la casa?*" Ana asks—"The bus will stop in front of our house?"

I assure her it will. Most of my students live in the same trailer park, on Koala Bear and Grizzly Bear lanes, and I know for certain the bus will stop in front of the stretch of trailers on Bearwallow Mountain Road.

~

I've missed most of my first class—a batch of five second-grade boys. Instead of fetching them from their respective classes and heading to the trailer for the remaining twenty minutes, I decide to check in on Mario and Beth.

When I peek in, Mario's desk is tightly aligned with Adam's. Adam's parents are Mexican, but he was born and raised in Henderson County. He's never been to Mexico. His parents both have a good hold on English, but they speak Spanish in the house. For Adam, though, English has become his first reaction, his predominant tongue. He and his older brother speak English to one another. Adam likes to draw sports cars and to wear his brother's hand-me-downs—giant T-shirts and FUBU jeans.

As he sits beside Mario, Adam's American-ness is palpable. Mario's jeans are pulled too high to be hip, and his button-up striped shirt is tucked tightly in above his waist.

"I put Mario beside Adam so he can translate. Does that seem good?" Beth asks.

"Yeah, that's good for instructions. And that way, he can feel more comfortable, too. I'll bring some materials for Mario, but basically the more visual you can make everything, the better. So you don't need Adam to translate everything; Mario will start to catch on. But he probably won't say much of anything for a while, and that's normal."

She and I compare schedules so I can find a time that works to pick up Mario. I decide to come by for him later with Antonio and Carlos.

As I turn to head back to the condo, the class begins to line up for PE. I hear Adam tell Mario, "*Vamos a* PE." He says the letters *PE* in English.

"*¿Qué es eso?*" Mario asks.

"*Es . . . pues, vamos a jugar*," Adam offers—"It's . . . just, we're going to play."

As Mario lines up, he watches Adam chat in English with Jason and Paul, two white students. They're wearing cargo shorts and tennis shoes. Jason wears an Atlanta Braves T-shirt, and Paul has a shirt with a deer and a bull's-eye on it. They talk about basketball.

Mario looks back at the room of empty desks, then looks down at himself at the back of the line. He untucks his button-up shirt and tugs at his high-rising pants as the children file out of the classroom to PE.

～

We have lots of Adams at Edneyville—second-generation immigrants. They begin kindergarten with a head of Spanish and English phrases and slowly dig out an American identity accented with blurs of their parents' home cultures.

There are fewer third-generation immigrants, but the lower grades have a growing number. Former high-school classmates of mine—second-generation immigrants—now have young children in the kindergarten classes at Edneyville. It's strange to see old soccer teammates and lab partners walking young versions of themselves down the hall, lunchboxes in hand. Their kids have American-sounding names and speak English at home.

And of course, we have many first-generation immigrants who show up at the office and wait for me to trudge up the hill to lead them to class, to America. My students are predominantly first- and second-generation, and it's strange to watch them interact. The second-generation students like to school the newcomers on all things American, all things Edneyville—popular music, food, cars. They make fun of the newcomers in English, laugh at their accents and mispronunciations. The newcomers take their cues from the second-generation students, who must seem wholly American, save for their still-Spanish-laden tongues. The newcomers adjust their dress, affect their mannerisms.

I don't serve any third-generation kids, but I see them interact with my students in the halls and cafeteria. While the first-generation students often take cues from the second generation, the second generation clearly looks up to the third. They try to make friends with these brown-but-American kids; they latch on to colloquialisms and slang popular among these English-speakers. *Dude*s and *like*s and *man*s abound.

But strangely, the third generation sometimes looks back to the first. They ask questions about Mexico, a place many have never been. They sometimes try out their Spanish on the freshly arrived students. They see in the newcomers their past. Playing out in the halls and classes is a phenomenon I've recently realized that I, too, am in the midst of: the process of shaping immigrant identity.

~~~~

In 1938, historian Marcus Lee Hansen gave a speech titled "The Problem of the Third-Generation Immigrant" to the Augustana Historical Society. In it, he briefly outlined a theory of "third generation return" that I feel inside me. Although I'm living on land my family has claimed for over two centuries, I realize that the world around me—my mountains—is a far different country from that of my grandparents. I'm on the same land but in a different world, and I'm taken with, gripped by, the notion of returning to the lost country of my grandparents. To the Appalachia of yore.

In his speech, Hansen argued that the American immigrant experience often follows a predictable pattern.

First-generation immigrants find comfort and connection in the culture they've left. They resist the push of American-ness, and thus create pockets of their native culture in their transplanted home. They maintain their language and traditions and customs, and they adapt to survive—out of necessity—not to fit in or assimilate.

The second generation, though, finds itself in the midst of a push and pull. At home, the members find a culture they've never known in its natural context. But in the world surrounding them, they encounter a pervasive lifestyle they've always known. The second generation, argued Hansen, inhabits "two worlds at the same time"—Adam chatting with Paul about basketball and trying to explain PE, in Spanish, to Mario. The response, once the second-generation member is independent, is an escape from the immigrant culture and an acceptance of the surrounding world. The second-generation immigrant "wanted to be away from all physical reminders of early days, in an environment so different, so American, that all associates naturally assumed he was as American as they," Hansen noted. The second generation has little interest in history—the past—and sinks deeper into American life—the future.

The third generation finds itself in a new world containing only wisps of the old. It starts looking back. "The principle of the third generation interest," Hansen called it. He illustrated the difference between the second and third generations with this oft-quoted line: "What the son wishes to forget, the grandson wishes to remember."

While the second generation hopes to escape the foreign homeland by Americanizing, the third is drawn by the idea of return. The third-generation immigrant faces no insecurity over his Americanness—he speaks the language; he was born American. He exists naturally and easily in the world surrounding him. Often, having reached a comfortable economic status, he looks around at what his line has accomplished and says, "This prosperity is our achievement, that of myself and my fathers. It is a sign of the hardy stock from which we sprung. Who are we, and why did we come?"

The third generation is curious, backward-looking. Me.

⌣

The Appalachia of my grandparents is something of a phantom to me. I can see its edges, its remnants, but I can't quite hold it.

My grandparents were raised in the mountains in a rolling period of transition, on the edge of two countries. In Appalachia after the Civil War, missionaries came in, schools were built, trains wound farther on. People arrived to help, to modernize, to integrate this region. The Tennessee Valley Authority dammed rivers. The Civilian Conservation Corps built roads. My grandparents lived on subsistence farms on the fringe of modernity. They didn't stay breakably rigid during this transition—they bent and adjusted. They took jobs off the farm, at a school and a factory. Grandma went to college and earned her master's. But they also held to the life, the country, they knew. Today, despite living a few miles from the Walmart, my grandparents can vegetables and piece quilts. They speak the language of another time. They're first-generation.

And I want to know this other time, the world of my great-grandparents. I'm trying to return to, to connect with, my homeland in the Blue Ridge. I'm a third-generation immigrant who still lives in his home country.

If my grandparents lived on the narrow brink of an opening world, I live in the result: a wide-open region. Four-lane interstates lead anywhere. Airports wait only miles away. Mrs. Salatino, my first teacher, is a Northerner who settled in our mountains. I attended school with a Nigerian and Mexicans. We learned foreign languages and watched space ships lift off on TV. Little about the world I grew up in was isolated.

I left and looked outward, but now that I'm back on this land, I'm looking inward. I'm concerned with what the region used to be—the customs, the words, the music of the motherland.

My parents mostly fit into Hansen's theory. They show little preoccupation with history. They don't like fiddle music or even country music. They wore bell-bottoms and listened to rock 'n' roll. They got jobs in town, built a comfortable life that sent my sister and me to college. They still live on family land, but they like buying the newest gadgets, eating out, going to the Flat Rock Playhouse, taking beach vacations.

My parents visited me for a week in Honduras and grew quickly tense from the surroundings—the rustic buildings, the crude infrastructure, the simple foods. Their discomfort didn't subside until we went to the city at the end of their visit. They booked a room at a Holiday Inn and took us to eat at an Applebee's. They appeared at ease for the first time all week.

I found their unease in Gracias curious, given that the houses and facilities and simplicity harked back to the world of their parents. The mountains looked like home; the stoves and livestock and markets were the stuff of my grandparents' stories. But my parents have Americanized, by Hansen's definition. They're happy looking ahead, following new trends and escaping the hardness and isolation of their parents' former country.

I'm of the lucky-but-discontented generation. I grew up comfortably. I got new school clothes and played video games. I traveled and explored without having to plow fields or butcher hogs. But now, barely an adult, I'm trying to return to a world that no longer exists.

17

On the Saturdays that Sarah and I stayed put in Gracias, not hitching a ride into El Salvador or toward the Honduran coast, we slept late and made baleadas. I hoofed it the three blocks up to the market—loud and bustling on a Saturday morning—and grabbed a couple of onions and a hunk of springy cheese, then dipped into a corner store to buy refried beans, Coke, and salsa.

Honduras doesn't boast much inventive cuisine—certainly not in the mountains. It's a poor man's diet: set plates of varying combinations of beans, tortillas, eggs, avocado, and sometimes meat. A baleada is merely refried beans and cheese melted inside a browned tortilla. We dressed ours up slightly, filling them with caramelized onions and garlic and then Americanizing them with canned salsa and a bottle of Coke on the side.

When I returned with the supplies, Sarah would set to cooking the onions and garlic and I'd slice the cheese. Before long, we were stuffed.

This Saturday morning in Fruitland, we sleep late and wake up craving the simple food of somewhere else. We tried making baleadas here once before, using the refried beans we bought at Ingles, but they weren't the same—not the right consistency, the flavor muted somehow. This morning, I volunteer to drive to the Mexican store beyond the elementary school in search of appropriate foreign beans while Sarah prepares the rest.

The tiny, square store stands off Highway 64 just beside an apple house belonging to the family of the PE teacher. The window is covered in stickers advertising calling cards—nine cents per minute to Nicaragua! Inside, the coolers hold Jarritos sodas—pineapple and orange and fruit punch—and the shelves reveal bags of dried spices and candy covered in chili powder. I stroll through, reading the Spanish labels on the cans and bags and taking in the smells of other countries.

I nearly bump into a little person as I round the first row. When I look down, I see the round face and bob cut of Lupe, who looks up at me with wide eyes. I am used to that face: the face of a student seeing a teacher out of context. I encounter this often in Ingles and Walmart. Teachers ought to live within the walls of the school, never put on T-shirts, certainly not shop for food.

"Hi, Lupe," I say to the face.

She stares back.

Farther up the short aisle, her mom, Rosa, turns to us as she pulls a can off the shelf.

"*Hola*," I say to her.

As she smiles and walks toward me and the still-stunned Lupe, I see Alicia, with her matching bob cut, come around the corner behind her mother.

"Hello, Alicia. How are you?"

She drifts closer to her mom, blushing.

I ask Rosa how they are settling in. She says well. She is happy to have everyone together again. She is looking for a job, maybe cleaning houses. When she asks how the girls are doing at school, the blushing returns. I say well; they are working hard.

"Alicia is always writing at home," Rosa says in Spanish.

I ask Alicia what she writes. She shrugs, sticking her ear to her shoulder to try to shrink herself.

"*Dile*, Alicia"—"Tell him, Alicia."

"*Cuentos*," Alicia finally says, looking down—"Stories."

"How great," I say, sticking to Spanish. "Would you bring some for me to see?"

"They are in Spanish," she whispers.

"That is fine—I want to read them. I will show you some stories I wrote at your age, too."

She smiles and looks at her mom. Lupe is reaching for the candy on the shelf.

"*No, señora*," Rosa says, snatching the hand. "We haven't eaten *lonche* yet."

"Me neither," I say to Lupe. "I need to buy some beans." She smiles like I just said a dragon landed on the roof. "*Nos vemos*," I say to them.

They wave and tote their items to the front to check out. I continue my search.

⌐∾

Not long after I arrived at Edneyville, Debbie dropped a stack of thin books on my desk. As I picked them up, I quickly recognized the dinosaur on the front of one as a creature from my third-grade brain.

"Remember these?" she asked.

"Sort of," I said, splaying them out.

"You wrote three more than you had to that year."

The other books recast stories of Pecos Bill and Paul Bunyan and told of a fight between a "sharkman" and a bear.

"Quite the collection I put together," I said, opening one.

As I flipped through my pencil etchings of Pecos Bill swinging a snake over his head like a lasso and the bear's blood spilling from the sharkman's bite, I noticed how faint the drawings were, some never colored in. I remembered blurring through the illustrations, wanting to move on to new stories, trying to get them out of my head as quickly as possible. I rushed, always ready to move on.

Debbie revealed to me later that she made two predictions about my life from my third-grade days: I would become a writer, and I would marry Juliet Pack. I am not sure those violent, undeveloped stories from third grade have proven the first, and I certainly didn't tie the knot with the elementary-school classmate I haven't seen for a decade. No matter Debbie's success rate in foretelling the future, it made me wonder about the predications I might make about my students. What glimmers do I see in these students trying to adjust to a new world? What do I hear in their voices that might predestine their paths, as Willie's accent sent him to Y-Hall and my hollowed-out voice sent me somewhere else?

Lately, I have been wondering what I hear fading from my students' voices. As they gain English, bits of Spanish wear away. I cringe to notice them losing reading ability in their native tongue when we open bilingual books. Maybe this is how it works: they need to trade in one language like I traded in my accent. But I wonder if Alicia will continue writing stories in her room once the voice filling her head speaks mostly English.

During the second half of the year, the students have been attending "enrichment" classes on Friday afternoons. All the teachers get to offer fun workshops of their choosing—watercolor painting, board games. In January, students picked what they wanted. I wish now that I had chosen to offer a class on reading in Spanish, giving these students a space to read and share stories in their native language. Instead, I spend my Friday afternoons teaching a roomful of Latino boys magic tricks. Showing them how to disappear.

꤮

I don't find the packets of refried beans we survived on in Honduras. Instead, I buy two different cans in hopes that one will be close enough to send our tongues back to Central America. I snatch some Pingüinos—packaged chocolate cupcakes we sometimes ate after school—to help the cause.

When I begin to pull on to Highway 64, I realize we're missing another important ingredient—Coke. I drive a stone's throw up the road to the general store. I park between two big Ford trucks and head in, the bell on the door clanging. A couple of old men drink coffee at a table beside the window; a man buys a can of Skoal and drops it to fit into the already worn-in ring in the back pocket of his jeans. I head past the candy bars and pine-tree air fresheners toward the drinks in the back.

On the way, I see Jayne Stepp's son, Ryan. We chat for a minute about people from high school, his new landscaping business. He tells me he has moved into his grandma's house, just up the road from me and from his family's plot of land on Townsend Road. As we talk, I feel my voice transforming, the *g*'s falling away, the long *i*'s stretching longer. I fetch the Coke and walk it to the counter.

"S'at it?" the woman asks.

"Yes, ma'am," I say, reaching for my wallet.

"See ya later, Mary," Ryan says to the cashier. "Jeremy, reckon I'll see you around."

I turn toward the door, my stomach growling for a Saturday-morning baleada, and say, "You never know."

                        ~

Back home, Sarah has everything laid out, waiting only for the beans. The preparations go quickly with more than one stovetop burner.

"Here's what they had," I say, displaying the cans.

"Mmm, these will do," she says, reaching past the cans for the Pingüinos.

We choose the beans randomly, and I let her spread them across the tortillas because I tend to slap them on unevenly, rushing as I once did with my third-grade drawings. After they're warmed, we sit to eat.

"Well?" I ask, pouring Coke and watching her take a bite.

"Good," she says. "Not the same, but still good."

I cut an uneven square and have my taste. "Yeah," I say after a moment. "Good enough, I guess."

18

After I turn off Highway 191, the road leading in rises quickly. My car slowly climbs the turns of the mountain, past the brick homes. After the first switchback, I have to pull off the edge of the road to let a UPS truck rush by. I drift back on to the pavement to continue ascending and spot a woman just up the road, walking her tiny, fuzzy dog. I'm bad with dog breeds; they're all either *big* or *small*. This one is of the yippy variety. As I pass the woman, she raises a hand holding a clear plastic bag carrying her dog's waste and waves it at me. The friendliest swinging shit I've ever seen. The dog yips by her heel.

This is it, as best I can tell: Long John Mountain. I swerve through a development of brick homes. They're all at least thirty years old, spreading up the mountain. But these places are more widely spaced than the new developments' houses. Many are tucked within small batches of trees, their yards in the side and back. The new developments across the county tend to set their houses close, raise them high, and clear the land around them. I suspect this brick development was one of the first in the county. But I'm not here looking for houses. I'm here in search of what used to be farmland, the flat stuff. Really, I'm looking for where we kept the Germans sixty years ago.

I manage to find a wide enough stretch of land to accommodate a three-point turn without sending me off the side of the mountain. I again pass the woman and her dog, which sets to bouncing and barking before I finally leave what I now see is called Long John Mountain Estates.

Back on Highway 191, I see the sign for a new, gated development ahead of me, more creatively but less aptly named—Carriage Park—but I turn first into an in-process community called Creekside. This place is flatter, evenly stretching across the land backing into Long John Mountain. Some houses are in progress; others are already lit and lived in. All the structures look like siblings—not identical but similar somehow. They're all large, multistory, cleanly pieced-together modular houses. Each rests on an acre or less. I feel sure this was the POW camp. The land sidles up to a creek; I know the camp was planned along a water source. Plus, I know the camp was farmland owned by a Bowen family, and the first street I turn on to is called Bowen Terra.

I didn't know what I'd find out here on the other side of the county at the foot of Long John Mountain. I half expected the land to still be fields, cattle grazing or long rows of tomatoes sprouting. Instead, I find packed-in houses, structures sitting nearly as close as they must have in 1944.

I wonder if any of the families breaking ground or moving in couches and desk lamps know about the former tenants. No signs or markers or memorials denote the former internment camp. Had I not spent a few hours trolling through microfiche of archived newspaper articles, I wouldn't have known the camp's location well enough to find this spot.

But why should the residents care, really? Why should a twenty-four-year-old man drive through a pleasantly cropped housing development wondering about the ghosts of Nazis? About a young German man his grandmother let filch a jar of peaches? About the never-still life of this land?

~

In the creation account in Genesis 2, God shapes the animals from the land. I can't help imagining God at work like a kid with Play-Doh. Snatching up hunks of land, rolling out a tail like a snake—rolling out a snake like a snake. After God breathes life into these bits—the birds and bees and yippy dogs—he sends them to Adam.

And then the naming of things. Why did Adam get this duty, this power to name the creatures? This was before Babel. Words weren't yet misleading. Those words were the only words; one might imagine they were God's words. Adam understood the Creator, and the Creator understood Adam—to a point. In fact, the biblical story explains that God brought the animals to Adam "to see what he would name them." God's curiosity appears like a father's when handing a gift to a child. *What will he say? What will his face show?*

Carriage Park. Grand Highlands. We try to breathe life into the land with our post-Babel discrete languages. Long John Mountain must have had a Cherokee name before John McCarson, a first-generation Irish immigrant, somehow came upon 140 acres of it generations ago. The land spreading into and up the mountain used to be a fox den through and through. Hunters set dogs out across the mountain's face to track foxes, and everyone got to calling the whole area "Long John McCarson's place" when they set out for a hunt. The "Long" came about because McCarson rose well above six feet; some claim he reached seven. It didn't take long for the name to be shortened to Long John's Mountain.

Then possession faded. A vanishing apostrophe, a dissolving *s*— Long John's to Long John. The man died, but in this evolution of naming he somehow became the land. No longer was the mountain his; he was the mountain.

❦

Off Bowen Terra, I turn on to a street called Fernbrook Way, then steer on to Mistletoe Trail. Now, I'm on Bay Laurel Lane, which leads farther toward Long John. As the land starts to rise, the houses thin.

From the piles of topsoil and orange flags and dirt trails becoming roads, I gather that Creekside is growing up Long John's sides.

Machines have begun preparing lots on the edges of Long John, but I don't understand entirely how houses can stand on the vertically rising land. How does the ground hold? How is it that the water doesn't wash the houses clean away? The sign at the edge of one of the unfinished lots reads, "MBDI—Mountain Builders and Development Incorporated," a company that must specialize in building up so as to build upon.

Long John is being fattened up, packed with heaps and heaps of dirt to make enough flat space to construct houses on its side. But for the new homes, there will be no view or yard, just the shaky placement in a pre-formed community. A place to be. To have.

⁓

Of course, I'm steering my way around Creekside because I'm curious about how we came up out of the land, how we've been rolled and fashioned and formed and named. Adam's Garden hadn't been lived upon. The animals could be named anything because nothing had been. But our foxes and people rise up out of historied, lived-upon land. And it must matter somehow.

It must matter to build a life on a former prison that housed a displaced people who farmed our patch of earth for a short while. It must matter to know that, in their way, those men helped Grace attend college and have a daughter who would have me. Those men helped Grace become a teacher at Edneyville Elementary, where I would reappear to teach another batch of working immigrants. This must mean something.

⁓

Yesterday, I escaped my daily schedule—second grade, kindergarten, first grade, lunch, third and fourth grade, fifth grade, translations—

to sit at a wooden table near the entrance of school. Although we are still two months from the end of the year, I was planted there to await parents coming to register their children for kindergarten.

It was strange to sit all morning and think about next school year. I could imagine myself roaming these halls next year, but I had trouble envisioning myself singing songs in the trailer out back for the rest of my life. When we returned from Honduras nearly a year ago, I figured I'd be comfortable and broken-in by now, but lately I find myself thinking of the faraway as much as I do the history all around me.

I mostly manned the table by the door to aid Spanish-speaking parents with the paperwork required to send their kids our way next school year. I began the busy morning greeting everyone in English, then switching to Spanish when Latino parents had trouble finding English words. But by the afternoon, I began calling out *"Buenas tardes"* straight away when Latino men and women entered.

During a lull, I was doodling on a free-lunch form when a woman and her bowl-cut-wearing son opened the front door. I rose and grabbed a clipboard.

"Buenas tardes," I said.

The woman approached without a word, and I went on, *"¿Viene para matricularse el niño?"*—"Are you here to register your son?"

She looked at me, at the clipboard, but said nothing.

"¿Todo bien?"—"How is everything?" I asked this as a greeting, looking also at the boy and smiling.

Finally, the woman said flatly, "We don't speak Spanish."

I stammered, faltered, changed linguistic gears: "Oh, I'm sorry. You're . . . Are you here to register your son?"

She didn't show any emotion, which I read as annoyance. "Yeah, he'll be in kindergarten next year."

After leading her through some forms and hearing in her voice that oddly familiar, yet foreign, twang—a mix of the Scots-Irish tongue and the holed-up voice of hundreds of years of hiding in the mountains—I learned that she and her son had recently moved to Henderson County from the Cherokee reservation.

I'd seen in them the hue of newcomers, when really they'd been formed of the land long before my people came along. In a language inaccessible to me, their line had named these trees and birds and mountains in what must have been close to Eden.

~

From Long John Mountain, I take back roads home. I eventually work my way to Howard Gap Road, which was an Indian trail long before pioneers and traders and bushwhackers bore in.

The road's name comes from a gunman, an armed passerby, an intruder. Before William Mills or Abraham or Andrew Maxwell, Captain Thomas Howard led his militiamen up the worn trail from South Carolina in search of Tories. Instead, they found Cherokees in the forest near Fruitland, so they set to fighting anyway. This bloodshed began decades of pushing the Cherokees deeper into the mountains. It also fixed an English name to the seventy-plus-mile stretch of trail predating Europeans—Howard's Gap Trail.

I like the *Gap*. It feels perfectly apt for the dropped land snaking between the mountains, the hole. Our mountain terms both charm and confuse me. Bearwallow is a *bald*, a place absent of trees. But we've also got *runs* and *spurs*, *benches* and *domes*—words to describe the shape of it all. Out on the West Coast, they have *buttes*, but we have *butts*. I had to look twice at the map one summer as I backpacked through Pisgah Forest and found a spot labeled "Big Butt."

We have *crags* and *sags*. One of my favorite features is *knob*, a clenched fist rising from the land. Sown into our land, we have enigmas—Shaggy Bald! Upon visiting our mountains near the turn of the twentieth century, John C. Campbell wrote that western North Carolina was a "land of paradoxes and contradictions."

~

At school yesterday, the Cherokee mother told me she and her son left the reservation to be nearer to her parents, who had moved to Henderson County last year. Her mother cleans rooms in one of the inns in Chimney Rock. The woman hasn't found a job yet, but her mom hopes to get her on at the inn soon, making beds, vacuuming. As I filled in their address—Kodiak Bear Trail—I realized they'd moved into the trailer park where most of my students live, just at the base of Bearwallow.

The Cherokees set our plateau aside, retreated from it, hid off in the gray when my people came. Now, this family has returned to move in next door to Latin American immigrants lined in rows along Kodiak Bear Trail, Koala Bear Trail, Grizzly Bear Trail. Perhaps it is fitting for them to live on roads named after animals completely unnatural to this land—the world now foreign, renamed, reclaimed.

As if by reflex, I nearly said *"Que le vaya bien"*—"Go well"— to her when they left. But instead, we exchanged a wordless wave, and I sat back down to doodle again.

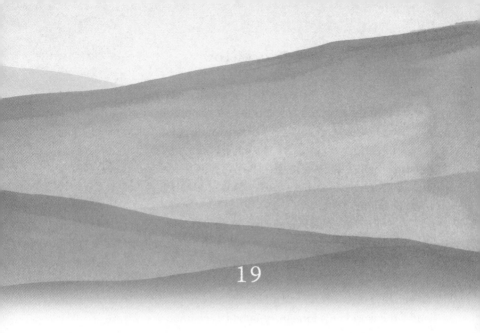

19

Appalachia is a perpetually discovered land. The Cherokees dug in; William Mills found a healing cave; the Scots-Irish took over empty space; vacationers drifted into the former Wilderness; Grand Highlands stumbled upon a foggy Bearwallow. Discovery is an amorphous concept. It blurs with the claiming; those arriving are those naming.

Hernando De Soto lost himself in these mountains in 1540. Turned around and hemmed in by the southern Blue Ridge, De Soto named the area after the natives who impeded his advancement—the Appalachees. Nearly thirty years later, the mountains first appeared on a map. Cartographer Gerardus Mercator, in his *New and Improved Descriptions of the Lands of the World*, sketched a loose mountain area he titled "Apalechen." It existed; the page proved it.

In the mid-seventeenth century, over a hundred years before Abe floated into the Wilderness, English traders worked through sections of the mountains. They abraded new trails through the forests and pieced together more accurate outlines of the topography. By the time Abraham and Bathsheba lit out, the mountain ridges appeared on most maps of the New World. Abe likely charted his journey by such maps, stabbing his seventy-five-year-old finger on the patch labeled "the Wilderness." *There*, he must have whispered.

These discoveries are myth. From them, we get our names, and

I get my genesis story—my vanishing Dutchman, my wallowed-on mountain.

Post–Civil War discovery primarily shaped the mountains I know today. The writing that emerged beginning in the 1870s named and thus explained the region. Those words essentially invented Appalachia. Travelers and writers such as Edward King (*The Great South*) and James Lane Allen ("Through Cumberland Gap on Horseback") found Appalachia for the rest of the world in the late nineteenth century. *Look*, their writing proclaimed, *a hidden land and people!* Once they turned their explorations into words, not only did the mountains exist, but their people, too, were uncovered.

Prior to this discovery, Appalachia wasn't a land entirely cut off from the world. Charlestonians vacationed; traders wore trails; deserting soldiers burrowed in. Our people had contact with outsiders and were not wholly isolated or homogenous. But once the late-nineteenth-century explorers ascended our mountains, they used the traditions and characteristics of the people to name the mountaineers as one distinct group, an ethnicity.

Here were the Appalachians—their cabins, their language, their customs. It was "A Strange Land and a Peculiar People," as Will Wallace Harney titled his 1873 essay. Suddenly, the Appalachians shifted from impeding, ignored mountains to a foreign region full of foreign people.

My third-generation return leads me to that moment—to the mountains at the turn of the twentieth century and the context of my great-grandparents. The Appalachia of the late 1800s existed on the brink of railroads and development. It was a world my grandparents saw change before their eyes. The homeland before immigration.

Writings capturing this period abound. Travel sketches and articles from 1860 to 1890 formed a popular genre of local-color writing. They often told of trips to the mountains—narratives that served to share exceptional findings and experiences. Self-conscious travelogues. This is the material I've been tilling lately, hundred-year-old accounts of the mountains. In them, I find drawings of waterfalls and mountain men; I read descriptions of farm life and banjo music. In these pages, I have Appalachia encapsulated.

Except not. The local-color writers were outsiders sending short pieces to *Harper's* and *Lippincott's* and *Scribner's* magazines for middle-class audiences. Their purposes weren't accuracy or thoroughness. The writers dropped in quickly or hiked through and sent back two archetypal impressions of the people: the backward, violent, inbred, all-consuming Appalachian or the bucolic, commonsensical, earthy, unrefined Appalachian. Either the feuding, deforesting moonshiner or the banjo-picking, funny-tongued farmer.

At first glance, I trusted these accounts of my land, since I could easily spot the same dualities around me. A quick look at Edneyville readily revealed groups of beer-drinking, NASCAR-loving, armed men and sets of quiet, abstaining, religious men—folks who lined their sentences with cuss words and folks who'd turn red at the drop of a *damn*. The plebeians and the Puritans.

But as I read more of the late-nineteenth-century reports, I found no gray in the portraits. Whether the writer found Appalachia a frightening, harsh world or an uncultured, beautiful land, the presentation was exaggerated and ultimately unbelievable. The unifying theme in all the sketches—from "A Strange Land and a Peculiar People" to "Poor White Trash"—was the *otherness* of Appalachia. Every portrait found a distinct place, a strange people. Here, hidden in our very country, were a people and a place wholly different from America. Foreign natives.

This Appalachia interested middle-class readers because of its oddity. The purpose of local-color writing was to find the quirky and exotic in everyday corners of America. And once Appalachia was discovered, it proved utterly bizarre.

The people appeared alien: "The natives of this region are characterized by marked peculiarities of the anatomical frame" ("A Strange Land," 1873); they were "tall, gaunt farmers, clad in homespun" (*The Great South*, 1875); they were "slim, slab-sided, stomachless, and serene, mild and melancholy" ("Through Cumberland Gap," 1886).

The place otherworldly: "It is useless to describe the wild and romantic scenery" ("A Week in the Great Smoky Mountains," 1860); "so accordant is it with the solemn majesty of form and color that the observer fails to separate and distinguish it as an isolated part in the grand order of Nature" ("A Strange Land"); the mountains presented "a scene of fearful elemental violence" ("Through Cumberland Gap").

The dwellings ancient: "a lonely log house" (*The Great South*); "the cabin and its indwellers were typically primitive" ("The Moonshiner of Fact," 1896); "the cracks in the walls give ingress and egress to a child or a dog" ("Through Cumberland Gap").

This Appalachia did more than captivate readers. It also concerned them. The local-color portrayals of the region drew interest by two principal means: sympathy and fear. They presented Northern readers with the untapped wonder of the land (a people "behind the times" and a world that was "one of God's great divisions") or showed the "utter barbarism" of the place (feuding, lazy men and misused land).

The success of early local-color writing from Appalachia led to more of the same—sketches such as "The Moonshine Man" and "Romance and Tragedy of Kentucky Feuds." But the writing that appeared after the 1890s shifted in focus. While the early local color discovered the mystery of the region, the later writing sought to explain it. The early writing referred to pockets of the mountains as distinct places—while the women in Kentucky, for example, rode "a jack, jennet, or a bridled ox," those of the North Carolina mountains rode "bulls" ("Through Cumberland Gap"). The later writing, though, effectively united all of Appalachia into one group, one place, one culture. And it focused less on travel tales that observed the rarity of the mountains; it instead sought to explore the causes of such queerness.

The later writing, which also started as short sketches, eventually led to longer accounts. The "community studies" of the early twentieth century stretched into books, many of them approaching the region as a distilled bit of history. A living, breathing fossil.

William Goodell Frost, president of Berea College until 1920, became a central voice in the apology for, and defense of, Appalachia. His essay "Our Contemporary Ancestors in the Southern Mountains" (*Atlantic Monthly*, 1899) began a continuing conversation that explained mountaineers as people of the past, their language Elizabethan, their stock "pure." Appalachian folk were different only because the rest of the world had moved on, not because their race was lesser. Their shortcomings were circumstantial, not genetic. They simply lived in a "retarded frontier," as George Vincent wrote of Appalachia in 1908.

Frost continually compared mountaineers to the patriarchs of the Old Testament and Homeric characters. He also began a rhetorical campaign to name the area "Appalachia America"—a region and a country. His essay and later speeches and writings were soon surrounded by similar notions of a fossilized, left-behind people in such works as *The Anglo-Saxons of the Kentucky Mountains, Elizabethan America, Our Southern Highlanders,* and *Our Appalachian Americans.*

The pronoun *our* showed up over and over in these titles. Whether the mountaineer was defined as barbaric or unrefined, he was paternally and historically connected to America. He was *ours.*

It's also no coincidence that the term *highlander* came into vogue during this period. The mountaineer was a result of his circumstances, shaped by his mountains and his lineage. He was essentially a Scotsman living in an alternate version of Scotland's highlands, writers argued. *Highlander* not only showed the mountaineer's foreignness, but also validated his so-called backwardness.

It was this post–Civil War discovery that prompted people to act. Benevolent work in the mountains began in various forms—home missions, school building, railroad planning. Many, especially those in the middle and upper classes of the North, were concerned with unity and development—with a congealed, whole America in a postwar context. Thus, the impulse appeared to Americanize this foreign land, this Appalachia, which seemed opposite to America in many ways—curious language, frontier lifestyle, untapped natural resources.

Writings in the early twentieth century offered different solutions to the "social problem" of Appalachia, but a predominant theme emerged: give these "contemporary ancestors" the same circumstances, the same context, as the rest of the country, and they would catch up in no time. The central variable that caused Appalachian oddness was simply isolation. The people had been separated physiographically. *Open the mountains!* was the cry. *Send them railroads, schools, and God.*

20

Willie Griffin works on the railroad. Every day, he crawls underneath those steel bulls in Norfolk Southern's rail yard along the French Broad River in Asheville and tightens and loosens and greases to make sure they run their freight smoothly into and out of these mountains. I haven't seen him since my return home, but my cousin Isaac sees him at the general store some mornings, and I sometimes see his mom at Fruitland Baptist on Sundays. I hear of him. I hear like everyone hears in Fruitland, in the hum of stories.

Those rails Willie hops across every morning changed everything when they reached Asheville in 1880. This came a year after they bore into Hendersonville's plateau following a treacherous three-year ordeal up the sharp 4 to 5 percent Saluda Grade from South Carolina, the steepest main rail line in the United States. Once the rails hit Hendersonville, the steel driving altogether stopped. John Henry's hammer fell silent as all the railroad money dried up. The line never intended to make Hendersonville a final destination, but the journey dead-ended there just fifteen years after the Civil War.

In my head, I hear all the old songs of steam drills and heavy steel, the work songs ("I'm swinging thirty pounds from my hips on down/ Just listen to that cold steel ring"), the don't-want-to-work songs ("Take my hammer and give to the captain/Tell him I'm gone/Lord, tell him I'm gone"). I hear Flatt and Scruggs singing of a stalled train in their version of "Nine Pound Hammer" and think of those tracks frozen in Hendersonville in 1879. The modern world lying in wait.

Finally, after months of negotiations and buying and trading, the original railway company was sold and reorganized. Money was paid, the spikes were readied, and the tracks were fixed to the earth again. The steam whistles blew, and the wheels rolled on toward Asheville, the hub, the mountain mecca.

An invisible dam was broken. The steel climbed from the south and the east and the north to all arrive in Asheville. Tuberculosis specialists and patients drifted in. Tourists dropped by and stayed for good. George Vanderbilt began building his sprawling estate. Asheville's population exploded overnight. The world was no longer knocking on the door but churning right into the living room. Rattling the dishes, loosing the rocks from the hills, sending men out the door.

It wasn't long before the railroad pushed deeper into the mountains, reaching Bryson City and Murphy, connecting up with lines across the Smokies in East Tennessee. These routes not only carried bits of modernity to the dark corners but, as the Great Smoky Mountains Railroad's website claims, "delivered thousands of mountaineers from the wilderness of their landlocked hills." Men gathered up what they needed and took off to the Piedmont's mills, not waiting for but chasing after this new industrial world.

I've recently learned to play the old song "Ruben's Train":

> Ol' Ruben made a train
> and he put it on the track
> run it 'til the Lord knows where.

It requires me to twist the pegs to land the banjo in a strange, lonely F tuning. I slide along the strings and set my hammering hand to the steady, chugging rhythm of a train. One verse charges along in the voice of this escaping mountain man:

I'm a-going where them chilly winds don't blow
Oh me, oh my, I'm a-going where them chilly winds
don't blow.

The tracks didn't only carry men rushing away after industry, they
lured many others in. To the north in West Virginia and Kentucky, coal
beckoned them. Men tunneled in and under to coax black chunks from
veins in the mountains, covering themselves in its dust and breathing in
the flecks of millions of years. But hardly anyone burrowed into western North Carolina. These mountains were worked on their edges and
on their skin; logging companies felled and dragged trees across the
land and lined the tracks with cars full of stripped timber.

Back when Abraham and Bathsheba settled into the Wilderness,
they pulled some of those trees to the ground and set to building their
inn. They framed a life out of trees that had been spreading untouched
for longer than memories.

I've come upon this land more than two hundred years later. My
twentieth-century trees managed their way into the world after the
days of the timber trains. My trees are new trees for a new world.

"There goes the Twig Man," Grandma says, spinning her recliner
toward the window.

I'm sucking on a peppermint and had been listening to her tell me
about someone she saw at the Hardee's this morning. But at the rumble
of a diesel engine, we turn to watch Isaac's big truck take off down the
road from the hayfield toward Highway 64. He waves in exaggerated
fashion at Grandma's window—she gives him grief if he doesn't wave
heading to and from his trailer. Some days, Isaac pulls right through
Grandma's front yard and flails his arms just feet from her window
chair to be certain she sees.

She calls Isaac "the Twig Man" because he spends his days creeping
into the woods to pull out old things for Russ Lyda to sell at the curb

market. He mostly collects sticks. He picks up rocks and berries, too, placing them carefully in jars and baskets. But sticks fetch the most money.

Last year, he pulled a giant stump from the ground in the woods by the end of the Yellow Brick Road trail. The stump looks like a wooden sun; the roots have all shattered to sharp points, so that the stump stands twisted and textured, wooden rays shooting out from its base. We can't believe that he manages to sell these things to tourists passing through. He ties up sticks that he whittles, and people pay for them like bouquets of roses. He rents the stump at a hundred dollars an hour. A woman took it for a wedding just last week.

Isaac doesn't like to sell the stuff; he leaves that to Russ, who stands behind the table in the market and wheels and deals. But Isaac likes to collect it, to dig it out, to unearth it. And people apparently like to buy it. They want pieces of the land—hillbilly souvenirs, accents of the mountains—and Isaac supplies them.

Sometimes, I wonder if I should buy a hunk from him. I've come back on to this land not knowing how to get into it—how to take hold of it. Isaac's pulling pieces from it, living in a trailer in the hayfield and collecting money from the army, and I have returned from another world, settling in above the family land, wondering how I know that this place is mine.

"He's off somewhere real important," Grandma says, winking, losing her earlier story about Hardee's as she spins the chair back toward me.

"Maybe out to the curb market," I guess.

~

I haven't spent much time in the curb market. I walked through earlier this year to see if Isaac was working, but I found only Russ and a few other Edneyville families selling jams and quilts and twigs. The tables lined the middle and edges of the warehouse-like building. Tourists and some locals strolled through, picking up and setting down knickknacks and hand-carved key chains before moving on to the next table. It's a slow business.

I've been reading about the curb market's beginnings, and I can see them clearly. I lived them. They're Saturday-morning Gracias. I can clearly translate those mornings of watching produce peddled on the cobblestones of Honduras to the then-dirt streets of Hendersonville.

On Saturdays in Honduras, I'd wake to staticky voices calling through rusty speakers attached to the tops of pickup trucks: "Watermelon!" "Potatoes!" "Cheese!" The old trucks would slowly bump along, watching for any sign of movement. Occasionally, a woman would open a door and sweep through the gate, and the boy hanging off the truck would jog over with a watermelon or a basket of berries for the exchange. Using a machete, a man would cut hunks of cheese from the giant, three-foot-tall block wrapped in plastic in the back of a truck.

Old men drove oxen toting warped branches of firewood. Carts of papayas and cabbages rattled by. Coolers of trout and catfish and pig feet and pig brains and pig rumps were flung open for anyone slightly interested. The tiny farm plots reaching into the mountains surrounding Gracias' plateau suddenly appeared in the streets on Saturdays. The rural edges slid right into the middle to feed us.

Hendersonville used to be Gracias, fed by Fruitland and Edneyville and the other rural edges. Farmers lugged potatoes and cabbages down off the mountains, bagged apples, and touted corn and anything else that would grow, selling their wares from the backs of carts and Model Ts. Hawking voices rang out from the street: "Cheap greasy backs!" "Fresh preserves!"

It wasn't until the mid-1920s that a market was finally established downtown. In a washed-out photograph, I catch the action stilled, everyone turned to pose for the camera. A barefoot boy, hat in hand, grins too wide. The farmers stand out clearly from the buyers, their overalls obvious against the background of suits and ties and round hats. The tables are plain planks of wood thrown over barrels, and some lucky sellers vend beneath wide umbrellas.

After a few years of bursting-at-the-seams parking lots, the farmers looked for a new space. From donated lumber and supplies, they built the first curb market off King Street. Sellers paid for tables. I know from my mom's side of the family that a curb market table was a valuable piece of property in Henderson County. They were rarely given up, often passed down generation to generation. The Maxwells held a few tables and bequeathed them for generations until nearly everyone had quit farming.

Most historians agree on two trends that marked Appalachia in the nineteenth and early twentieth centuries. As roads (like the trail Abraham built along and the soon-to-follow Buncombe Turnpike) wound through the mountains, some settlements emerged as market towns. Hendersonville, with its new railroad and status as the main route from Charleston, became one such town at the turn of the century. Fruitland, like the mountainous edges of Gracias, was the other half of the equation: a rural community. And so, after the two pieces of land were purposed by William Mills and Abraham, Fruitland and Hendersonville stood as microcosms of growth in Appalachia. The market towns grew courthouses and hotels and paved roads; the rural grew food and timber and honey.

And now, generations later, the two camps are at odds. The town appears poised to seep into the rural through a water line to the tiptop of Bearwallow. The rural wants its space, wants rid of so-called development.

And the question hangs: Is there still a purpose for the rural without the need for a market?

My mom's uncle owns a table that he rents to a neighbor, whose kids help keep up his garden. They sell quilts and woven rugs and apple butter. The curb market is wholly sustained by tourism now. Hardly anyone sells produce; nearly everyone sells handicrafts and souvenirs—bits of culture.

I know my Maxwells sold at and relied on the market, but I don't remember hearing of any of the Joneses or Prestwoods selling there, save the Twig Man, of course. I ask, "Did Great-granddaddy Albert ever sell much at the curb market?"

Grandma shakes her head. "No, not directly. He'd sell to someone who'd sell to someone, you know." She turns her wrist like she's slowly rolling dice.

I grab another mint and lean back while she looks out the window at a hummingbird darting into and out of the feeder. Then she asks, "Have you ever seen the movie of Mother on the news?"

I sit up. *Nanny on the news?*

She lived with Grandma when I was a boy, after Great-granddaddy Albert died, so I have more than mere secondhand stories with which to piece together Azalee Prestwood; I have my own boyhood memories of her bossing me around with her cane and watching professional wrestling on her tiny TV in the back room. I know Nanny as a woman who would give advice on how to best wipe oneself in the bathroom with only one square of toilet paper. Her talking on TV? No, I would remember such.

"On the news?" I echo.

Grandma gives me a long nod and waves her hand toward the TV. "I reckon the tape's under there somewhere. Tom Brokaw had her talking about her quilts."

"The national news?"

"Go dig through them tapes under the TV."

I drag out loosely bound photo albums and Ziploc bags of small, square, brown pictures—my dad and his brothers as boys at the top of Mount Mitchell, Granddaddy posing with his adoptive father/father-in-law. On the carpet, I stack old videotapes of *The Andy Griffith Show* and Humphrey Bogart movies Granddaddy liked to rewatch. I sift through shoeboxes and dig up letters and old Christmas cards of smiling families I don't recognize. I push past yellowed newspaper articles about my dad's and his twin brother's football exploits—Dad the quarterback, Uncle Danny the receiver. Jones to Jones.

As I hunt, I imagine Isaac down by the barn, surveying stones on the bank of the creek. He's bent over, scooping up the smoothest, roundest specimens—somehow careful, though it's not his nature. He grabs his rifle from the truck and walks upstream, looking out for good sticks and ducks all at once, collecting and capturing. Meanwhile, I squat here in this old house and excavate stilled memories and stories. We channel into the past simultaneously but separately.

Isaac and I were born two months apart. And seemingly overnight, we've become our fathers.

Like his daddy, Isaac tried to start farming after high school. And like his daddy, he earned a two-year agricultural degree from North Carolina State to do it. Isaac's was in turf management, since he understood our bottom land no longer grew produce or fed cattle. He'd seen the future.

After college, his dad returned and started cattle farming but eventually gave it up to join the army. After college, Isaac returned home and got in the sod business but eventually got sick of monotonous days of mowing giant plots of sod field. After a year, he, too, joined the army, leaving the fields to someone else.

After tours in Afghanistan and Iraq, Isaac has now been pulled back to our land. He lives in a mobile home below his dad's house, up the hill from Nanny's old house and just beside our great-great-grandparents' house. He harvests what he finds in the forest, and Russ, the former apple farmer, sells it at the market.

Like my dad, I never intended to become a teacher. He went to study art at a small college in a nearby county. I left the mountains to study writing. Dad came to teaching by way of coaching. I somehow found myself teaching in those eerily reminiscent Honduran mountains after I set out to explore.

Now, here I am back home, farther up the creek, teaching in the elementary school that used to feed the high school where Dad taught and coached for decades. Dad, the associate superintendent of schools, is effectively my boss. Sometimes, the older teachers at Edneyville call me David by mistake, and I don't correct them anymore.

"Is this it?" I hold up a VHS tape with what seems to be the word *Quilt* smeared in cursive on the label.

"Give it here." She can't see it well from where I sit cross-legged on the floor.

I crawl toward her chair, aware of the many times I made this trek as a child to the chair where Nanny used to sit. Now, it's Grandma's La-Z-Boy, and I'm my dad.

She snatches her glasses from the end table and looks closely at the tape. "Reckon so, stick it in."

After a blue screen and some fuzz, there's no Nanny. There's only Tom Brokaw, much younger than I've ever seen him, at a news desk in New York, leading in. Everything's the eighties: his too-bright tie, the shadowed fonts, the faded colors of the old tape. He says something about "folk art being appreciated," after which the tape cuts to a cabin at the foot of a wooded mountain. An underlined, blocky font stretching across the screen reads, "Bearwallow, N.C." The voice-over: "It gets cold in the mountains of western North Carolina."

Then we're inside, where the reporter, Kenley Jones, interviews a woman named Hattie Oaks. She's eighty-eight, sweet and soft. Her hand threads a quilt in her home as she tells about quilting as a young girl.

Then a cut. Nanny takes the stage. She's sitting in a green chair in someone else's house, leaned back, too comfortable for national TV. She's holding court, it seems. It makes me wonder if she intimidated the reporter; she's intimidating me through thirty analog years of VHS. Her voice, while full of the same accent as the previous woman, is more demanding, sure, and confident: "You grew as a child a-making string quilts—called 'em 'nine patch.' But by the time you's a young lady, if you didn't have at least three quilts for your hope chest, well, you's plain lazy."

The camera lifts to show her aged fingers as she points out the seemingly erratic pieces of her quilt: "This un's from a school dress, this a boy's shirt, here a daughter's pajamas, this un's a patch from Mother's dress."

Her quilt's pieces, small and tear-dropped, weave a bending arc across the fabric. This one, like all of Nanny's quilts, is different from those I have from the Maxwell clan. The Maxwell quilts have clear lines, borders between pieces. Nanny's are less squared and precise. They're perfectly haphazard.

Was I alive for this? The reporter says Nanny is eighty-three. I try to do the math but instead watch the camera move to a large room somewhere else, wherein women display old family quilts. Nanny's not there; these are organizers, viewers, buyers. Nanny was an everyday-use quilt woman. One of the women comments on how quilts allowed women "beauty in their daily lives." Then we're back to the not-yet-grayed Tom Brokaw. He smiles that end-of-the-broadcast, post-human-interest-story smile, and the TV buzzes with fuzz.

I must have been four or five, I decide. But I don't remember seeing this before. I have a quilt or two of Nanny's. I wonder if I even have the one from the TV segment back at our house down the creek. We don't use them; they're just for beauty now.

Somehow, strangely, it's those trains Willie works on every day that put Nanny on the news, that keep the Twig Man running. The railroad climbing into our mountains brought the craft movement of the early twentieth century.

"How 'bout that?" Grandma asks as I turn back to her.

⌁

Before the entrance of rails, before the timber boom, the Blue Ridge ran on a farm-and-forest economy. It was a land of open grazing, a world without fences. Livestock ambled through empty forest and across meadowed peaks. Land, in this way, was communal. Of course, mountain people owned and traded property, but its use was largely shared. Animals roamed and men hunted across property lines, without borders.

I can imagine this world because it feels like home. As a boy, I never knew where my uncle's property lines lay. I tramped through the woods until I hit a field or a creek or a road. Woods were woods, connected and seamless. Alive.

But those first steel rails of the nineteenth century not only swept timber from the forests but brought fences to constrain them. The emergence of "fence laws" meant forests were no longer seen or used as pasture; men couldn't wander freely when hunting bear and deer. Suddenly, Appalachian courts filled with trespassing cases as the timber industry limited access to much of the woodland. The famous Hatfield-McCoy feud began after a court battle in 1878 over a razorback hog that ran loose in the once-shared woods.

It was in this context—the building of fences, the exodus of farmers chasing mill jobs, the clearing of old growth—that the craft movement took shape. Some who rode the rails into the mountains from the North to build schools and churches found beauty in the music and handiwork here. They believed that beauty confirmed the rhetoric of the local-color writers—these were our contemporary ancestors indeed, still singing the songs of the homeland, filling their cabins with bearskins and patchwork quilts, living in the simple past.

People such as Frances Louisa Goodrich recognized not only the beauty, but also the marketability of such artisanship. Shortly before the turn of the century, many Americans, notably Northern urbanites, began filling their homes with handmade goods from Europe. So in 1895, Goodrich, a Presbyterian missionary raised in Ohio and trained in fine arts at Yale, formed a cooperative of sorts, in which older women from the communities surrounding Asheville produced coverlet weaving. Goodrich paid the women directly and sold the products in markets and through missionary magazines and Northern newspapers.

Over time, she developed a larger hand-weaving industry in the area. In 1913, Goodrich's line of products gained national notoriety when First Lady Ellen Wilson redecorated Woodrow's bedroom with the handmade goods and christened it "the Blue Mountain Room."

The folk revivalists didn't form cooperatives and schools only for profit. Goodrich, like many others who sought to encourage and capture the artisanship of Appalachia, wanted to keep the local crafts from fading away. She wanted to save the beauty, save the past, if not change the future.

Young people no longer wore homemade clothing, since trains now hauled in more fashionable attire to sell in general stores. And who needed clay hand-thrown bowls when ready-made versions were available down the road? The traditions of the mountains no longer fulfilled a need, so they began disappearing as soon as the trains chugged in.

Craft movements such as Goodrich's weaving business sought to sustain the culture while bettering the poor mountain people. Her organization, she believed, kept women active in the new industrial world; it supplied them with "habits of industry and thrift," which, she believed, were not indigenous to the Blue Ridge. "It is in a great measure the loss of these qualities that has caused the mountaineers to fall behind in the race," she wrote.

In addition to new businesses that encouraged and eventually trained people in native artisanship, folk-art schools emerged in pockets throughout the mountains. The John C. Campbell Folk School began in Brasstown, North Carolina, shortly after the death of Campbell, a believer in programs encouraging local culture. Olive Dame Campbell, his wife, spent much of her time collecting the folk music of the Southern mountains; the 2000 film *Songcatcher* was loosely based on her efforts. She started the school based on Danish models, the intention being to continue tradition while improving rural life. Olive Campbell famously said that she sought the "preservation of all that is native and fine."

In 1930, she wrote about the school's goals in a newsletter: "It must find a new approach to old subjects; it must develop a new technique of teaching. Furthermore, if the teaching is to enrich rural life, it must be rooted in a deep belief in the country; not perhaps as it is, but as it may be: its power to satisfy; to offer a full life." The goal of such folk and settlement schools was to preserve and change simultaneously, to pick out what was deemed good and leave behind what seemed bad.

Like Goodrich's weaving cooperative, which ultimately changed the coverlet weaving style while also continuing it, folk schools managed to both sustain and shape native customs. And in so doing, the movement sold the so-called backward traditions of the so-called back country to the nation. John Alexander Williams wrote in *Appalachia: A History* that "the crafts movement succeeded in making 'Appalachian' one of the leading brands in twentieth-century neotraditional home fashions and decorative arts."

This tradition not only laid the groundwork for Isaac to become the Twig Man and my Ric Flair–loving great-grandmother to appear on the national news, it also sent Willie's great-granddaddy to New York City.

His great-grandfather was a fiddler. In the early twentieth century, he and a banjo-playing Bearwallow man named Paul McKillop performed for square dances around Edneyville. As more tourists fed into the area, the duo began playing at inns like the Bee Hive and the Flack Hotel.

During the Depression, a wealthy family sponsored the two men to carry their music outside the Blue Ridge. Sometime in the 1930s, the fiddler and banjoist hopped on that rail line out of Asheville and exported their Bearwallow-bred music to New York City, where they played Carnegie Hall. After their three-month trip, they returned to Edneyville. Not long after, Paul McKillop died in an accident at a local mill, and Willie's great-granddaddy set down his fiddle for good.

The exportation of folk music allowed me the old songs and style I reproduce on my banjo. Olive Dame Campbell lured the most prominent English folk-song collector of the time, Cecil Sharp, to Asheville. From his wanderings through the Blue Ridge, Sharp "caught" 1,612 songs that he traced back to the British Isles. (He didn't have interest in catching more indigenous ballad and jigs; he wanted that pure stock he'd read of.) Together, Olive Campbell and Cecil Sharp bottled up those mountain tunes, and like weaving and pottery and carvings, the music of Appalachia gained attention in the turn-of-the-century world.

~

Grandma lets me make off with the tape of Nanny, a few pictures, and a local history book. I pile them all in an overflowing shoebox and promise to return them, then step out the front door and whistle for the dogs. Like always, Blue's just by the door, but I don't spot Banjer; I can only hear the tramping of his paws.

As Banjer comes tearing around the corner of the house, Isaac's truck barrels back in from Highway 64. I wave him down. "You find anything?" I holler, walking across the yard. Branches stick out from the bed of his truck.

"Oh yeah, man." He rubs his hands together like he's starting a fire.

I lean against his truck and peer into the back. A bucket of flowers stands in the corner, just beside a limp, dead duck.

"Flowers?"

"Yeah, man. Flowers is where's it at. Found them down by the creek. I'm gonna start planting sunflowers out by the Prestwood house next week. Russ sells those easy."

I pick through the wildflowers, balancing my box on my hip like a baby, thinking about Isaac growing curb market–bound flowers beside our great-great-grandparents' empty house. It seems right.

"What you got?" he asks.

"Some old stuff I stole from Grandma."

"Anything good?"

"Maybe," I say. I look past his truck into the Stepps' apple orchard. The air holds the tangy smell of the pesticides that must have been sprayed earlier today. The sun's starting to sink behind Bearwallow, and from the glints of light, I can make out the thin lines of towers on the peak, but nothing more. Just the bald *U* and the faint outline of my childhood bear rising up behind our overgrown hayfield.

"She got any cookies in there?" Isaac asks.

"I think so."

He nods. I nod.

"A'ight, man. I need to see if she'll cook my duck anyway."

He rumbles the truck into Grandma's driveway, I throw my arm through the air to send Blue and Banjer down the hill toward the creek, and Isaac and I change places.

21

Even though Mario is in fourth grade, I pick him up with my third-graders, Antonio and Carlos and Alicia. After struggling with this new language for the school year, Antonio and Carlos suddenly feel expert sitting at a table with a girl and boy who crossed the border recently. This has been a pleasant surprise; they speak English more often, showing off their skills. Alicia still stays pretty quiet but understands more and more. Mario follows very little but feels comfortable saying yes to everything. I haven't yet seen any of Alicia's stories, but I've been pestering her regularly.

Today, we're reading a book about a girl who takes her dog to school for show and tell, and we've stopped to name the classroom pieces inside the condo.

"Book," Carlos says, jumping up to point at the bookcase by the beanbags.

"Good. And aren't we reading a book, too?" I ask, holding up my opened text.

"Yes!" Mario blurts before anyone else.

"Light." Carlos sticks his arm straight into the air.

"No." Antonio shakes his head. *"Así no se dice, se dice* lie-it"— "That's not how you say it, you say *lie-it*." He stretches out the long-*i* sound as people often do in these mountains, nearly making it two full syllables.

"Lie-it." Mario tries it out.

"*No, es* light," Carlos says to Mario before turning to me. "*Dile*, Mr. Jones"—"Tell him, Mr. Jones."

"Light," I say, keeping my mountain voice out entirely. I go on to explain that people pronounce words different depending on their accents. I try to use a Spanish word as an example. Many Mexicans living here say something like *boss* to mean *bus*. However, the traditional Spanish pronunciation is something more like *boose*.

Antonio is incredulous. We continue reading.

In a classroom inside the building, my grandma taught for decades. That room used to be lined with cubicle-like desks and tape recorders, the tools with which she taught reading to students behind the curve. The kids worked through simple phonetic books, headphones strapped to their ears, as Grandma drifted around the room, sitting down and leaning in to correct pronunciations.

Now that it's my job to walk around a room and correct pronunciations, to decide if my students should say *light* or *lie-it*, I'm suddenly more curious about Grandma's voice. In many regards, it's wholly Appalachian, lined with *reckon*s ("I reckon that girl got a new haircut") and *like to*s ("I like to die when I saw it") and *kindly*s ("It was kindly short and choppy"). But in other ways, the grammar is standard and the pronunciations phonetic. When she hears a new word, she says it aloud once or twice to snap the sounds together correctly. She doesn't end sentences with prepositions; she steers clear of double negatives.

Papaw, on the other hand, doesn't hold to these rules. Words take on a life of their own, *shower* sounding more like *shire*, *tired* more like *tored*. His voice is muffled and throaty like those of many mountain men; he doesn't make much eye contact when talking; he never uses three words when one will do. Sarah, despite growing up just ten miles away, has trouble catching everything he says.

But Grandma never corrects Papaw's nonstandard constructions, never rights his double negatives. I sometimes wonder how this played out in her classroom. Did she manage to help her students hang on to a mountain voice while still guiding them through diphthongs and digraphs? What did she hear in their voices? Something to be changed or sustained? Or both?

When I ask about her schooling, she always talks about Mr. Rector, who taught her in sixth and seventh grades. He came to the area to help the mountain children, Grandma always says. So concerned was he with their plight that he spent his free time selling encyclopedias at cost from house to house.

Grandma remembers the set her daddy bought from him, remembers poring over the volumes in the evenings. She also remembers the rigors of Mr. Rector's class. He required oral presentations before every Friday class on randomly assigned entries in the encyclopedias. He demanded sweat-lodge-like sessions in which the class diagrammed sentences of all shapes and sizes. Her stories of Mr. Rector are always fond. It seems clear that he challenged her, assured her she could succeed, and it's no stretch to imagine his classes guided her to her teaching career. In some way, guided me to mine.

Many Mr. Rectors came into the Blue Ridge after the railroad. Teachers from the North hopped aboard to set up schools in the South. Outside the mountains, this mission mostly centered on establishing schools for emancipated blacks. But in Appalachia, it became clear from local-color accounts that the whole area needed schooling. *Save the mountain whites, the mountain children*, the thinking went.

The writing at the turn of the century made no mention of the schools that already existed in the mountains. In those accounts, the region was wholly uneducated, free of any book or teacher. President Franklin Roosevelt, discussing the purpose and placement of the TVA, described "a shack on the side of the mountain where there is a white man of about as fine stock as we have in this country who, with his family of children, is completely uneducated—never had a chance."

In reality, most communities had self-sustaining schools. Henderson County boasted over fifty autonomous schools at the turn of the century. Many of them had been established a hundred years before the outside educators arrived. In fact, Grandma's mom taught at many of those community schools. For a short time, she filled in at Bearwallow School, a small structure that had nestled on top of the mountain since well before the Civil War. Most of the time, a live-in teacher stayed on the peak for the school year. This teacher went home with local families after school and dug into the afternoon chores, hoeing cabbages and washing laundry, in exchange for a bed. The next morning, she'd lead the mountain children across the meadow to school.

When public schools were established in 1936, the county schools were incorporated and centralized, and Bearwallow School's doors were closed. Willie's great-grandfather, recently having hung up his fiddle after the death of his banjo-playing partner, decided he'd drive the bus to deliver the children to Edneyville. He took it up and down the same route Mr. Cody now drives on the second-bus run from Edneyville every afternoon.

But Willie's great-granddaddy's bus wasn't quite a bus. It had no walls, only a roof and wound wires to keep the kids from falling out around the hairpin turns. When the contraption pulled up to the school in Edneyville, the other children would taunt those monkeys in a cage, toted down from their mountain for proper learning.

I wonder if my great-granddaddy Albert often passed the bus-like creature as he delivered the mail up and over the mountain. Maybe he and Willie's great-grandfather exchanged waves, or maybe the kids made faces at him in his Model A. Maybe he made faces back.

~

I was the Mr. Rector of Honduras. I flew off to teach the poor Honduras children. I led them to the botanical gardens and the old Spanish fort to learn about history, about change, about growth. Because my teachers worked to shave the mountaineer out of my voice, I could deliver to those Honduran children a neat, boxed-up English they could use with future tourists.

Benevolent work is the phrase used to describe this phase of teachers and missionaries arriving in Appalachia. Fittingly enough, I found the job listing for my Honduras teaching position on Idealist.org.

From the history books I've been picking through, I know that many of the "outside educators" in Appalachia sought to entirely change the mountain children. They hoped to Americanize them, to catch them up, to remake in their own image those mountaineers. They built curricula to make the backward right, to make the back country their country.

Grandma's stories of Mr. Rector, however, usually involve him motivating her in some way—through high expectations or fanciful stories. Mr. Rector was a college English professor before coming to the mountains, but Grandma remembers how he always remarked on how smart the Fruitland kids were. As she tells it, he brought with him the ideas behind those words I tried to carry to Honduras: *empower, locally led.*

When I was studying in Costa Rica, a professor told me of a hardworking, idealistic Peace Corp volunteer in a small village in Belize who simply wanted to reduce litter in the streets. Her project was small but practical. She raised money and collected tools and installed trash cans along the dirt streets.

In the weeks that followed, she watched the local people pass the shiny trash cans without a glance, continuing to throw wrappers and bottles and food into the streets. The moral, the professor told me, was that the volunteer had failed to engage, failed to involve the local population. She hadn't thought about culture and tradition and—that loaded word—education. She'd thoughtlessly applied her understanding of the world to another place.

I hope my teaching in Honduras worked like Mr. Rector's in these mountains. I wanted to urge students to chase after history and language for their own ends, not because of some white man's assurance that his way was the right way. But I do sometimes worry that maybe I just dropped in, installed trash cans, and moved away.

As we walk back to the classrooms, Carlos talks about the end of school, how his dad says they may drive to see his uncle in Virginia.

"*¿Cuánto nos falta?*" Alicia asks, wondering how much school is left.

Carlos shrugs, and they all look at me.

"One month," I say, holding up one finger.

"*Un mes,*" Antonio translates for Mario.

Mario asks, in Spanish, if he will come to me with Antonio, Carlos, and Alicia next school year.

"*Sí,*" Antonio announces before I can answer.

I am glad he does because I am not sure how to respond. I can't confidently say I'll be leading them through these halls next year. When thinking about the future as a long line of this year on repeat, Sarah and I have both admitted feeling antsy. We're considering setting out for more schooling somewhere, or leaving the country altogether.

But I am conflicted. All year, I've imagined myself a square of evenly cut sod rerooting along Clear Creek after being cut free some years back. The deeper in I dig, the firmer the grip feels, but I admit to fearing the transplant can't hold for good.

And what of my mountain children? If I go, someone will follow, speaking the language of their home and taking them to the condo to practice their new voices. But of the many changing pieces in their lives, the unintelligible sounds encircling them all day, I am one constant. Their ambassador to this hazy world. And not long after I appear, I may vanish, leaving behind a few poorly placed trash cans.

After I drop Antonio, Carlos, and Alicia at their respective classes, I lead Mario back to his room.

"Good job today," I say when we get to the door.

"Yes," he says, as if I've asked a question.

Mrs. Queen walks over as Mario sits at his desk beside Adam and pulls out his math book.

"How is he doing?" she asks.

"Pretty well—understanding more, I think. It's pretty slow going, of course."

"He's lost in here," she says, lowering her voice. "I am worried about sending him on next year."

"Yeah. It seems like it's so much harder for kids after third grade to get the language quickly. One of my third-graders who got here a few weeks before him understands a lot already. Mario's sister in kindergarten is sopping up words like crazy."

"I just worry he isn't going to learn anything because he can't follow along. And the end-of-course tests are coming soon."

"How is he doing in math?"

"He's way behind."

"Should we talk to his parents about holding him back? Give him more time to settle in here before moving on?"

"I really do think so. But why don't you see what Debbie thinks?"

"Okay," I say before I head back to the trailer.

As I pass my grandma's former classroom, I wonder if another year here might give me the time I need—if it might sink me fully into this land.

22

Spring in the Blue Ridge is sometimes aloof, arriving for a string of days in March before entirely disappearing until mid-April. It has fully set in now, though. The rains settle in, the days stay warm, the mountains fill in with green. Sarah has gone off with her sisters somewhere this morning, so instead of chasing after baleadas, I head outside for the dogs.

We have a new calf in the pasture. Blue is sure she has a new sibling in the calf. The two run alongside one another up and down the fence, the calf's back legs sometimes overtaking the front, sending it tumbling. The calf's mama tolerates this only so long. She'll fashion an angry moo aimed at Blue, charge toward the fence. Banjer stands aside and barks at them all.

When I release the dogs from their pen today, Blue traces the fence toward the calf, but the mama stands between the two, and the calf doesn't dare budge. Banjer is already on his way toward the bottoms when I whistle him back. I open the back of my vehicle and beckon them in; we're headed to town.

Banjer won't be happy for long. Town means manners: wearing a leash, not peeing on everything in sight. But for now, they stick their big heads out the windows, tails slapping the paneling, and we set out. I drive toward Fruitland Road, passing what used to be Fruitland School. After the school closed its doors in 1936, the buildings lay dormant until 1946, when J. C. Canipe, a pastor from a church in Boone, came to serve as president of what the Baptist State Convention would call Fruitland Baptist Bible Institute. In Boone, Canipe had met many ministers who lacked education, so this institution was to be a preachers' school. A place of training. The school has since expanded but still stands on the site of the original community school, in view of our house, barely out of reach of William Mills's homeplace.

Across the street are Fruitland Baptist and Fruitland Methodist. My great-great-grandfather Prestwood helped build Fruitland Methodist in 1910 with the help of his son, Albert. But it didn't matter to Great-great-grandfather Prestwood's daughter-in-law, Azalee, that her husband helped drive in the nails to erect the thing. Nanny was a Baptist, and a Baptist she would stay. Marriage would not sway her an inch.

On Sundays, Albert, Azalee, and Betty (and eventually the adopted son/son-in-law, Ray) would make the short drive from Townsend Road to Gilliam, pass the spot where my house sits, and park in one lot or the other. When they got out, Azalee took Betty by the hand to Fruitland Baptist, and Albert set off to Fruitland Methodist, not fifty yards across the street.

I never doubt I'm from a line of strong-willed women when I hear these stories: my grandma Harrell wearing pants despite rules against them, Nanny marching into the Baptist church and meeting back up with her husband after the service to head home for Sunday dinner.

In the end, Azalee won out because even though Betty and Ray were married in the Methodist church, they stayed on at Fruitland Baptist. My grandma Harrell and all her Maxwells were Fruitland Baptists. Both my parents grew up Fruitland Baptist. Granddaddy was the Sunday-school director, my aunt Rhonda directs the choir, Grandma ran the kitchen, Uncle Tim delivers the announcements, Dad's a deacon, and Mom keeps the nursery.

But in the generations since Azalee, we Joneses have drifted—we haven't backslid, just slid back. Azalee always sat on the second row. I can see the back of her head clearly if I close my eyes, her hand shooting up as she sometimes chimed in with news in the middle of the service, her voice as sure as it was in that NBC video. Grandma sits somewhere in the middle of the church these days. But my parents sit near the back. We became backseat Baptists.

I'm less than a back-row-Baptist; I'm only half a Baptist. Sarah and I don't go our separate ways on Sundays. Instead, we split time between Fruitland and her family's church in town, First Presbyterian. Hers is the tradition of the Scots-Irish forefathers, mine that of the settlers, the mixing up of peoples in Appalachia. We keep a foot in each camp.

Last year, as I spent a steamy Honduran Saturday afternoon sitting in the Internet café, piecing together a lesson on the water cycle, Marshall (and his thick American accent, "*Buenas tardes*" fully and slowly enunciated) entered. An American missionary in his twenties, Marshall lived in a small community deeper in the mountains above town. Every couple of weeks, he descended into the valley to check his physical and electronic mail. Turning briefly as he plopped down at a computer behind me, I saw that he had grown a wild, scraggly beard. I wondered if he imagined himself an ancient prophet, bearded in the heathen wilderness.

On any given day, Marshall and I were the only two American men in Gracias. I resented him for this. My resentment was ridiculous, but I enjoyed my foreign-resident role. I liked that everyone knew me as *Meester* simply by my skin color. Marshall wrecked this when he set foot in town. Once, even the old woman in the post office—a woman with whom I had regular conversations—mistook me for him and tried to give me a package addressed to Marshall. "No, I'm *Meester*," I wanted to say.

In the Internet café, I kept my eyes on *National Geographic*'s website. Other than a teenage girl chatting online, Marshall and I were the only patrons that afternoon, facing opposite directions.

Eventually, two teenage guys who worked in the place ambled over and sat down beside Marshall. They were hip for our patch of rural Honduras, dressed in designer jeans and T-shirts and Pumas. They liked to talk about music, but their tastes were like a time capsule. It was 2005, but they loved eighties metal—"We mostly listen to Guns," they told me once in Spanish, meaning the band Guns N' Roses.

The guys were bored. It was a lazy afternoon in the café, so they chatted with Marshall, asking him if he thought their friend sitting behind the counter (with headphones over his ears) would go to hell because he was gay. The friend, clacking away at a keyboard, didn't look up. Marshall didn't understand the word they used for *gay*. He surely didn't understand that the guys were having fun with him. And at their friend's unbeknownst expense. Their friend who, to the best of my knowledge, was straight.

"*¿Cómo?*" Marshall asked.

One of the guys asked again, this time using *homosexual*, an easy cognate.

"*¿Cómo?*"

After a few more tries, one of the guys finally cried out in English, "Gay, Marshall! Nestor is gay!" Nestor still sat behind the counter, bobbing his head to his music.

Marshall launched into a short speech about salvation with the few Spanish words he owned. The guys egged him on, mostly out of boredom. But there also seemed a genuine curiosity to their questions. They asked about God. Marshall didn't respond specifically to their questions—he pitched his standard evangelical steps to salvation. Eventually, one of the guys asked Marshall if he thought the world would end soon. He did.

After I settled my bill, I walked toward home and imagined the bearded Marshall digging deeper into the mountains as the end of the world came from just behind the clouds resting upon Celaque.

⌒

Passing Fruitland's churches and institute this morning, I understand those Honduran highlands as a contemporary version of the Appalachia of eighty years ago. The same trends emerging in Honduras today appeared in 1920s Appalachia: new roads weaving in, missionaries descending, electricity sparking from newly dammed rivers. Back on this land, digging into the past, I know my discomfort with Marshall had historical prompting. It may be in my blood. My Scots-Irish forefolk who were jammed into Ulster to spread Presbyterianism joined with the Baptists or Methodists once they holed up here. Circuit-riding preachers swept through, some settling in for good. Edneyville takes its name from Asa and Samuel Edney, eighteenth-century Methodist circuit-riding preacher brothers. My great-great-granddaddy built Fruitland Methodist a century later. In these new mountains, my people clung to their religion.

But upon the "discovery" of Appalachia, missionaries climbed aboard the shiny, new rails to carry the gospel into this unchurched, heathen-filled land. A place without God. That same rhetoric sends many into the Honduran mountains to do good. It sent me there in many ways, to become Mr. Rector. Missionaries and *Meesters* alike drop in to better the irreligious, uncultured, uneducated *others*.

I know now my annoyance with Marshall had to do with more than his encroaching on my resident-white-guy role. I resented his mission. Not because he came to do good but because he ignored the preexisting place. He came to Christianize an already Christian world.

Honduras, like most of Latin America, is Catholic, with bits of indigenous tradition and belief meshed in. Most families in Gracias clicked down the cobblestone streets to the bell-ringing Catholic church for Mass; women crawled up the aisle on their knees in fervent belief.

But Marshall, like many evangelical missionaries in Latin America, came to convert the Catholics. He didn't carry the gospel to a world that had never heard it; the gospel had come here on the edge of a sword centuries ago. Yet Marshall, like those first conquerors, seemed sure he carried the right version of this gospel and ignored everything else.

Like the missionaries to Appalachia eighty years prior, Marshall brought the right beliefs, and he intended to take them blindly and narrowly into the unbelieving mountains.

~

In his 1921 essay "God's Plan for the Southern Mountains," William Goodell Frost urged readers to carry the gospel into the mountains because, he believed, mountaineers would become the church's backbone under the right "conditions." They would carry American Protestantism forward to become "a source of religious power through long coming generations."

Soon after missionaries landed here early in the twentieth century, we mountain folk were raising up preachers and missionaries to send into the world. Just as we Scots-Irish were thrown into Ulster to spread Protestantism to Ireland before coming to the New World, we carried forward the Word again. We were "a source of religious power."

At Fruitland Baptist, I came up hearing the calls—as William Goodell Frost predicted—to carry the Word outward, beyond the mountains. As a child in the 1980s, I learned "the Roman Road"—verses plucked from the New Testament to lead someone to salvation, the same verses Marshall shared in the Internet café in Honduras. The Reverend McKinnish, the preacher when I was a boy, seemed to preach salvation every Sunday, his King James Bible glued to his hand, expression even, voice rising into that high, lonesome sound of old-time singers. But evangelism always made me uncomfortable. Although I knew the stakes, I never felt right approaching strangers with the steps to salvation, wielding tracts and end-times questions.

I always worried about the altar calls at the Billy Graham service the youth group traveled to in the Charlotte Coliseum. Would they stick? Were lives forever altered or emotions only fleetingly charged? I imagined conversion happened as it happened to me, a slow lapping instead of a sudden rush, family ever-present. Not just grandparents and parents but the gray-haired Sunday-school teachers, the ever-young youth leaders, the old farmers praying for rain, the perfumed women hugging everyone with a pulse. Relationships, not revelations.

Of course, I'd never argue that road-to-Damascus experiences don't result in changed lives, but I felt uncomfortable being the light and voice on someone else's road. Maybe this was just my lineage of hiding in these hazy mountains. Maybe it was my ancestors pushing me inward, instructing me in keeping my beliefs to myself.

But I suspect what made me uncomfortable as a teenager was what made me uncomfortable sitting in a cinder-block Internet café in the Honduran mountains: power.

Marshall, like those missionaries in Appalachia, came from the modern world into the backwoods. They came not only with their personal faith but with a prepackaged, passing-through, take-it-or-leave-it religion. They came with a new culture and ethic. They came to pat the heads of the poor natives and single-handedly pull them from the muck. To remake the mountaineers in their image. And then leave.

In their wake, a power shift came. Many religious scholars have predicted the world will soon turn upside down. Over the past century, the Northern Hemisphere shipped missionaries south. North America to South America. Europe to Africa. Marshall to Honduras. However, in recent decades, the evangelical movement in the Southern Hemisphere has grown so swiftly that South America and Africa have begun sending missionaries north, into the United States and Europe. Soon, a Honduran missionary may come knocking on Marshall's or my door, asking if we have the right beliefs. The student now the teacher, the heathen the missionary.

William Goodell Frost warned against these power dynamics. While he, too, ignored the preexisting churches and widespread faith of Appalachia in that 1921 essay, he predicted the coming wave of condescending help that flooded our mountains. And he argued for "brothers," not missionaries—people who would work with, not over. He sought to foster relationships, to balance the power.

I witnessed this even-footed approach when Mike Smith took the helm of Fruitland Baptist in my adolescence. The Reverend McKinnish was an old-timer, a local who'd been preaching since he was eighteen. We listened down in the pews, nodding our heads week after week to the same washed-in-the-blood sermon. But when Mike came, my understanding of the Bible and my faith deepened. His sermons moved beyond the basic gospel story; he contextualized his messages with history and translations and outside sources; he didn't require the King James Version. He yelled less than other Baptist preachers. Suddenly, the story became more complicated, but in ways I loved. I started reading the Bible myself, bought different translations, learned the word *theology.* He provided me with tools, lit my interest, made my belief personal, not passed-down—real, not ready-made.

Mike was pursuing a Ph.D. at a seminary in Kentucky. Even though he was from the mountains of North Carolina, he represented a new line of preachers. We didn't call him "Reverend"; he insisted on "Brother Mike."

From him, I learned that evangelism isn't a quiz offered scornfully to strangers or a checklist used to measure foreigners; it's not a power trip on secret knowledge. It's the sharing of a lived life, as much listening as speaking.

~

I unload the dogs near Main Street, hook them up, and try to keep Banjer from pulling us along like a sled dog. As we're walking down Third Avenue, a vehicle slows in my periphery. I turn to see a beige minivan with a man leaning across the seat toward the rolled-down passenger window. I step toward him, assuming he wants directions; the coming of spring means tourists. I smile a local smile and wait.

"Jesus loves you," he says, his face flat and serious.

I nod, step closer, not sure what sort of response the statement demands. I can't exactly say "Thanks." I'm certainly glad to know Jesus loves me. I'm glad he does, but I can't rightly thank a stranger driving a minivan for this love.

I try to revive the smile that has fallen limp on my face. "I appreciate it," I say. This seems valid enough. A vague pronoun—I appreciate the man reminding me, and I appreciate Jesus's loving me.

I half expect the van to move on, a drive-by Jesus-loves-you. Instead, the man reaches in his pocket, leaning awkwardly in the seat, and pulls out a stack of tracts. He shuffles the top one to his left hand and reaches back across the van to stick it out the window.

"Take one of these," he insists. "Read it."

"I appreciate it, but hang on to it for someone else," I say, tugging Banjer back toward me.

"Do you have salvation?"

"I hope so."

"Are you born again?"

"Every day."

"Do you go to church?"

"Yes, sir."

This feels like the lightning round on a game show called *Inquisition.*

"What church do you go to?" he asks.

"Fruitland Baptist."

His arm stretches farther across the passenger seat, offering the tract. "Take one anyway." He's suspicious. "Look through it. Give it to someone else."

A few cars are backed up behind him. The dogs are pulling me onward. I think of giving in to get this over with, to keep everything moving. But I'm stubborn for some reason, still standing on the edge of the sidewalk, holding the leashes tightly and refusing to take his message. *Proselytize* comes from a late-Latin noun meaning *stranger* or *alien resident. I live here,* I want to say. *My family's been building and attending churches in these mountains since the eighteenth century. Who are you? You're not my Damascus, not my Marshall.*

"No thanks," I say instead. "You're too late."

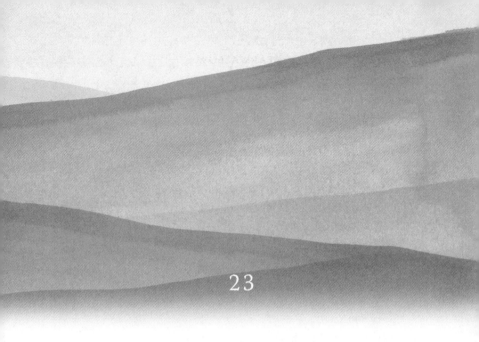

23

It takes some nagging, but I finally talk Alicia into bringing me one of her stories. As I lead her group back to class one day, she asks me to wait at her room's door. She returns with a notebook—"*Mi cuento*," she says, sticking it in my hand and dashing to her seat.

At the end of the day, I read through a story about a princess who is forced to leave her castle but soon gains magical powers. She learns to fly and eventually soars back home. It is clear from the careful print and the lack of strikethroughs that she has rewritten the story into the otherwise empty notebook.

The next day, I eat my sandwich quickly in the trailer instead of with Terry and Jayne and use my remaining time to fetch Alicia from her classroom. Angie says it's fine for me to borrow Alicia for a few minutes, so we head to the trailer to talk about princesses and shark-men.

I let her read through "Sharkman vs. Bear." I try to explain the oh-so-complicated plot in Spanish, but I'm not sure how well "man of shark" translates. I have her read her story aloud in Spanish. She moves through it quickly and quietly, not looking up. When she's finished, I list what I like about it: the description of the castle, the nice ending.

She blushes and agrees to bring me another one soon.

As we walk back to her classroom, I ask if she is looking forward to Field Day next week.

She shrugs. "I won't be here," she says in Spanish. "We are leaving."

"Leaving? To where?"

"Back to Mexico," she says.

"Back to Mexico?" I'm a broken record. "When?"

"I don't know. Soon."

We stop walking shy of her classroom. I'm confused. Her family just arrived. Her mother is looking for work; they're happy to be all together, she said.

"Is your father returning, too?"

She looks farther up the hall, tucking her story under her arm. "Yes, we will all return."

⁓

After school, Beth and I wait inside her classroom. I am nervous, not sure how Mario's father and mother will react to our suggestion of returning Mario to fourth grade next year. Debbie, too, believes this will be the best course of action, after meeting with Mario a few times and talking with the principal. She has supplied me with talking points, prominent among them the idea that Mario will be better prepared for middle school, for everything that follows. Still, I wonder how his parents will feel about a plan that seems to suggest moving backward, returning to already-traveled terrain.

When the father appears in the door, Mario and Susi are attached to his hands. Susi smiles and leans into her dad. Mario raises one stiff arm to wave. Beth and I shake hands with José; he explains that his wife couldn't get out of work. I suggest that Mario and Susi might read some books across the hall, and Beth leads them over to make sure the teacher there will keep an eye on them. Mario holds Susi's hand.

As I invite José over to the table, he asks how Mario and Susi are doing. "Well," I say, "Susi is learning quickly, and Mario is working hard."

"I wanted to ask you," he says in Spanish as we sit down, "my wife and I were talking, and we wondered if it might be best for Mario to stay in his grade again. Can this be done?"

Beth walks back in the room.

"Yes, yes," I say to him as Beth takes her seat beside me. "We wanted to suggest the same today."

I tell Beth what he asked, and she looks as relieved as I feel. I work through the reasons anyway; I translate for Beth as she explains what Mario is doing well and where he needs more help. The father listens, his hands resting on the table. When we stand, he shakes our hands and thanks us as if we've just granted him a favor.

"Well, that was easy," Beth says after he retrieves Mario and Susi.

"Too easy." I hum sinister-sounding music.

～

When I get home, the mail holds its usual junk. I sort through it, looking for bills and acceptance or rejection letters. Sarah and I both sent away applications for graduate school, testing the waters. So far, we've been welcomed to a few places (and I've been rejected by a few), but none of them match, so we're undecided about our plans, not sure if we're willing to set up two households for a few years. Unless the stars align, we may, like Mario, be repeating this year, wedging ourselves more tightly between Clear Creek and Bearwallow Mountain.

I find nothing except coupons for Pizza Hut and a promise to lower our phone bill. I drop my bag and the mail inside before giving the calf some relief from the dogs. After they're freed, we sink farther down, both dogs springing ahead of me, toward the perpetual pull of the water.

～

The next morning, I am on gym duty. From my post at the door, where I usher the kids in with a reminder to quietly find their places,

I see Mario and Susi amid a batch of students tramping down the hill from their bus. As they come inside, Mario waves and leads Susi by the hand past me to her line of kindergartners. She hardly seems awake, her face wearing faint pillow lines, frizzy hair escaping the ponytail. Mario drops his backpack behind a fourth-grader and assumes the position: crisscross applesauce.

After the next rush of bus riders, I start the rounds. I stop to make a third-grader put his bouncy ball away, then head over to Mario.

"Good morning," I say.

"G'morn," he says, bouncing his knees on his shoes.

I ask if he knows about Field Day. He seems to have a pretty good understanding that we will play outside all day.

Then it comes: "¿Mr. Jones, es verdad que me voy a quedar en cuarto?"—"Mr. Jones, is it true I'm going to stay in fourth grade?"

As I squat beside him, I unearth the same talking points I'd prepared for his father: "Yes, it's true. This will be good. It will give you more time to practice your English. And you will already have friends—Antonio, Carlos, and Alicia will be in that grade, too."

He turns his head on its side to consider this.

"Do you like class?" I ask.

He shrugs. "Sometimes." He starts tying his shoe, then shoots his head up, as if struck by electricity. "Me gusta PE." He says the letters in English as if one word: pee.

"Think how much better class will be when you understand more, can speak more English."

"Will Antonio or Carlos be in my class?"

"Maybe," I say.

"But we will still go with you to practice?"

Too easy indeed. "Maybe," I say, realizing Antonio won't answer for me this time. "You will come to practice English. But if I am not the teacher, someone else will be there."

"Where are you going?"

"I don't know yet. Maybe nowhere. Maybe to go to school somewhere."

"You haven't finished school? How old are you? Fifteen?"

"Old," I say. "I might go to school so I can teach at a university."

"Oh." He's fidgeting with his shoes again. "When is Field Day?"

"Next week." He smiles, and that's it. I stand and walk over to a group of second-grade girls talking too loudly and leave Mario, undevastated, to think about the promise of Field Day.

Perhaps, like a stone tossed into the creek, my plopping into this school will ripple for merely a moment. Another Mister Rogers will drop in; students will arrive, set down roots; others will disappear, pulled home.

The noise in the gym is beginning to bounce off the walls. The other assistant is already moving toward the light switch; I try to catch her eye, to show on my face *not yet*. But she doesn't see me and everything goes dark and quiet too soon.

24

I realized recently that I now look forward to the *K* more than any other block on my schedule. After some early chaotic months, I finally learned to set clear boundaries: I made rules about chairs, about places in line, about touching each other at the table. I defined our spaces—beanbags for reading, standing beside the table for singing. I tried to make the trailer predictable and exciting all at once.

And now this time is rewarding. The short period passes quickly, the children picking up English in leaps and bounds. And it's easy; they don't mind singing the same songs over and over, and it doesn't take much to rouse them.

Since those early days, my short line of three has grown to five. One boy and four girls. It is hard, though, to remember whose turn it is to lead our convoy. Some days, I forget, but they never do. *"Me toca"*— "My turn," they say.

Today, I know it's Angel, so I stop by his class first. Susi sees me from Mrs. Salatino's class next door while I wait for Angel; she skips my way as Angel slogs from his class.

"You're the leader today, Angel," I say. The edges of the smile show, but he hides them and steps in front of Susi. Some days, my only mission during the *K* period is to try to see Angel's smushy down-turned face erupt into that radiant smile.

"Aw, Mr. Jones. *¿Por qué?*" Susi whines.

"It's Angel's turn."

I can speak to Susi mostly in English now, but she usually responds in Spanish and with a comical whine. She smiles and twists her body sideways, leaning against the wall.

When Susi arrived last month, she tried to speak to Angel in her native language. She couldn't understand why his brown complexion and presence in my line didn't equal Spanish. He looked back at her blankly. Finally, after a few moments of one-way questions, he whispered without looking at her, "I don't speak Spanish." I explained to Susi's scrunched-up face, in Spanish, that Angel didn't speak her language, but she kept her brow wrinkled, unsatisfied. I didn't tell her I'd made the same mistake registering incoming kindergartners a month before.

We step across the hall to get Maricruz's attention. She drifts from her class, thinks about cutting in front of Susi. But Susi presses clumsily into Angel's back. He looks back with a scowl, and Maricruz takes the caboose.

"Good morning," I say to Maricruz.

"Hello," she says. "How are you?" Maricruz attended an English-speaking preschool and has more English stored up than the rest of the group. She likes to use it, but sometimes her brain moves faster than her English tongue will allow. She blurs languages and words and has to stop completely to collect herself.

Lupe strolls from the class next door and fills out our line. Lupe is grabbing up English remarkably fast. She sings as loudly as any of the other kindergartners. She tries out new words without hesitation. She smiles goofily at the other kids in her class, making friends despite the language barrier. She loves the phrase *my name is* and often says it without filling in the blank: "Hello, my name is." "How are you? My name is." "What is your my name is?"

After her sister Alicia's proclamation yesterday about moving, I halfway expect Lupe to be gone today. But here she is, petting Maricruz's hair at the back of the line.

"Lupe, Alicia told me you're leaving. Is that true?" I ask in Spanish. She shakes a low-eyebrowed no.

"You're not moving to another house or anything?" I ask.

She shrugs. "¿*Vamos a cantar 'La Canción del León' hoy?*"—"Are we going to sing 'The Lion Song' today?"

"Maybe." I say. "Okay, Angel, lead us."

He turns and plods our line toward my condo.

                         ⤳

After we read and act out *Brown Bear, Brown Bear, What Do You See?* and sing "The Lion Song," we play I Spy to practice the colors. Before I know it, we're back in line, and Angel is leading everyone down the ramp from the trailer back to the kindergarten hall.

Once at his classroom's door, Angel walks quietly into a sea of napping kindergartners balled up on pastel towels. He unrolls his towel and plops down.

Susi finds her room empty but for Mrs. Salatino.

"Susi, honey, they're on the playground." Mrs. Salatino points outside, and Susi needs no translation. She shoots out the door.

Lupe returns to her desk, but Maricruz is tugging on my pants and saying she needs to tell me something. This has been happening more and more. She lingers outside the classroom after everyone's gone and pulls on my shirt and hand. Some days, she doesn't really seem to have anything to say. She thinks hard and tells me what she had to eat. Or she smiles and says nothing.

Other days, though, she begins in English and after a few *um*s and stalled sentences switches into Spanish. She's been telling me about her dad coming home. About how he's moving back into the house, about how she's happy. But then sometimes she's frightened. A man came to her house, she told me once. It was scary. He banged on the doors. The police came. Sometimes, her dad's back home; sometimes, he's coming soon. The stories shift but uniformly contain anxiety.

I caught her mom one morning as she walked Maricruz into school. I asked about the police and the dad, and the mom looked confused and worried. "Her dad has been gone for years," she said. "He's not coming home."

"Did someone try to break in or something?" I asked.

"No. And the police have never been to our house."

"Oh, just stories, I guess," I said.

Last week, I asked the teacher about Maricruz's stories; she told me she has gotten disconnected and confusing tales from Maricruz as well. Maricruz has lied about being hit in class; she hit one of the boys on the playground and then lied about it. She's lied about which lunchbox is hers, which work is hers. The teacher wondered aloud if we should schedule a conference with Maricruz's mother. The end-of-term conferences are coming in a week, so we decided to wait until then.

"I have a hurt," Maricruz tells me today, pulling up her shirt and pooching out her tiny belly.

I don't see anything, but I ask how she got hurt.

"Hit," she says.

I switch to Spanish. I ask if someone in class hit her, and her story begins with a man but then changes to her dad.

"Your dad came back?" I ask.

She looks up for a long moment, then says in English, "Yes."

"Where were you hit?" I make use of Spanish's easy passive voice.

She points to a spot on her stomach. She sticks out her arm, but I don't see any sign of injury there either. Then she turns, says her back, too. A faint discolored circle of a bruise sits at the base of her back, just at the edge of the elastic waist of her jeans.

"He hit you here?" I point to her back.

She nods. "Yes," again in English.

Maricruz lifts her shirt while she stands beside the counselor's desk. Kelley, the school's counselor, looks for the bruise I spotted. It's light and seems old, but we both see it. Maricruz says she was hit yesterday, which seems unlikely. Kelley takes pictures of the spot, asks a few questions that I translate: "Does it hurt?" "Did you tell your mom?" "Is your dad still at home?"

Yes, no, no.

Kelley wants to talk more with Maricruz, but she's required to take the next steps without asking too much. I walk Maricruz back to class, descending the hill on a breezy, warm day.

"Bye," she says as she glides through her classroom door, arms stilled by her sides.

Back in Kelley's office, I sit as she calls the Department of Social Services. I feel ill at ease. I want to call Maricruz's mom to ask about the story and the father and the bruise. But I also want Maricruz to feel and be safe. I understand how and why we're legally bound to call DSS to have it followed up, but I still feel unnecessarily clandestine behind the counselor's closed door.

Kelley is on a first-name basis with all the social workers and knows which ones will take a request seriously. She dreads hearing a few of the voices on the other end of the line. Often, no one answers and she leaves messages and waits for any response. Many of the workers are buried in cases, and many are lazy. It's hit or miss, Kelley says. I pardon the pun.

At first, it seems Kelley is speaking to an automated system. She gives specific answers—name, age, address. A long pause follows each of her answers. I wonder why no one is asking what happened, what the problem is, what should be done. It feels too flat and formal. She eventually puts the call on speakerphone, and I hear a live human voice asking the questions. After each of Kelley's answers comes the clacking of keys. No follow-up questions or discussion, just her responses and his typing. Eventually, the man asks about the injury. Kelley is finally able to explain Maricruz's bruise and story. I fill in bits of information, since Maricruz told me the story in Spanish. More typing.

Earlier in the year, I brought a student to Kelley's office because of suspected abuse. I didn't stay for the phone call or conversation, since the student spoke comfortable English. After the report was filed, Kelley had to call and call to catch the social worker to find out what happened, what the plans were, if the student was safe at home. The abuse was "unfounded," the social worker finally said—not enough evidence. It often takes multiple reports and calls before any significant action.

After the standard questions, Kelley asks the voice on the other end of the line when he plans to talk with the student. He says he'll try to come to the school but will likely visit the house today or tomorrow. She shows on her face a knowing annoyance.

At the end of the call, I begin to leave, but Kelley calls behind me, "Oh, also . . ."

I turn.

"Could you take a ride with me to a student's house after school today?"

"I think so," I say. "What for?"

My after-school duties are varied. Aside from bus duty and the many parent-teacher conferences, I often accompany the school nurse when she makes home visits to Spanish-speakers. I try to bone up on Spanish medical terminology during those rides, punching words into my electronic dictionary. Since that secret ride with Debbie on the first day of school to retrieve Manuel, my job description has been ever-expanding.

"I'll show you," Kelley says as she stands.

We walk next door to the principal's office. The principal isn't in, but in the corner of her office stands a pink bike with lavender streamers hanging from the handlebars and training wheels holding it upright.

"Alicia Rodriguez won this bike," Kelley says. I'm suddenly touching the streamers and fingering the tread of the tires. "A bike shop donated it, and we pulled her name out of a hat. Pretty cool, huh?"

Instead of climbing on and taking it for a tour around the school like I want to, I say, "Yeah, it is."

"So I want to deliver it today after school, but they don't speak English, do they?"

"No, not much."

"It'll be a surprise," Kelley says. "Alicia doesn't know. Maybe we can head by after the bus drops them off today. I think they live in that trailer park below Bearwallow."

"Sounds good," I say. Something good to cover something bad.

Once we manage to squeeze the bike into the backseat of Kelley's car, we head up Bearwallow Road. I think about my great-granddaddy Jim climbing the mountains in his car with treasures stuffed in the back: calves, pigs. We've got only a pastel bike.

We climb slowly past apple orchards and houses, stopping just shy of the road leading up the mountain itself. The orchards across the street from the trailer park belong to the Nixes. Mrs. Nix used to cut my hair in her basement when I was a boy. While she gave me my monthly bowl cut, I listened to complaints about the trailer park's plan to spread over the former farmland. Years later, here I am delivering a bike to a child of the age I must have been then.

The plot of land is five or so acres, but fifty to sixty trailers lie across it. The population is largely Latino, with at least one Cherokee family in the mix. Kelley creeps the car past the rows of trailers as we try to spot trailer number 38 on Kodiak Bear Trail.

I suddenly feel like Ed McMahon. I wish we had balloons and a giant check to accompany the bike. I'm thinking about logistics. Should we leave the bike in the car and break the news empty-handed first? Or should we knock on the door and run, leaving the bike waiting there like magic? Maybe I should ride up to the front door on the bike and honk the horn, streamers blowing in the wind. I check the backseat: no horn.

After we climb out, we pull the bike from the car in front of trailer 38. From the outside, all the trailers look the same—off-white paneling, two windows per side. There's hardly any grass in the park, so the trailers stand side by side like they're in the desert or on the moon. The roads are dirt paths, and there are no clear boundaries, except for the creek to the left and the forest in back, marking where the trailer park ends.

I carry the bike up the wooden stairs leading to the front door—I couldn't have ridden it up the steps anyway.

Alicia and Lupe's mom answers the door. She's surprised and cordial and invites us in before I can explain why I'm toting a pink bike.

The walls inside are colorful, the living space ordered and warm—a flowery couch and thick rug in front of the TV. Alicia and Lupe come from another room with the same shocked looks they wore in the Mexican grocery store.

Rosa offers to make us coffee. We decline, and I tell why we've come, why a kid's rosy bike trails me. Alicia turns the same color as the bike as I explain in Spanish. Rosa says "*Gracias*" and "Thank you." She tears up, and I'm embarrassed for feeling responsible, when all I did was hop in Kelley's car and imagine myself riding Alicia's new bike. I've merely dropped onto this land, into this school—a resident interloper. Still, I'm happy to push the bike toward Alicia.

While the girls pull at the streamers and touch the purple seat, I decide to ask if they are indeed returning to Mexico soon. By Alicia's telling, they should be packing up and hitting the road in mere hours, but I see no boxes or signs of shipping out.

"Return?" the mom asks. "We just arrived. Why would we return?"

"Alicia said you were going back. Soon."

"No. We're here to stay. Soon?" She shakes her head. "We just moved in. Why would she say that?"

"I don't know. How is she adjusting to everything?"

"Good, I think. I don't know. She needs to meet more girls."

Lupe starts to climb on the bike. It's too big for her, and Alicia pulls her quickly off.

"Can we take it outside?" Alicia calls to her mom.

"Not yet. In a minute."

"Juana, another girl in third grade, lives here," I say. "Alicia knows her, I think. But I don't know which trailer she's in."

"We'll see," the mother says. "She's being shy. Is she behaving herself at school?"

"*Sí, sí.*"

"Every day when she comes home, I ask her to talk to me in English, but she never does. She stays quiet. Is she learning anything?"

"Yes, it will be slow at first, but she's doing well."

"Going back to Mexico. ¡*Que niña!*"

As we leave, the mother carries the bike outside for Alicia. They huddle around it. I worry about my Alicias and Maricruzes—the students who can't quite set down roots here. Students like Alicia hold on to Mexico, a place and past that escape them daily. They fight hard against a new language. They can't move on or go back. They're stuck. Students like Maricruz long for something else—a full family or a place and time that feel right. Mexico is a hazy place from a dream. They can't get comfortable here.

I wonder how this land will tease them out. How will the mountains that sprouted my chest hair and fashioned my kin's futures get a hold on these reluctant immigrants now living at the foot of Bearwallow?

"Bring me another story tomorrow?" I ask Alicia as we climb in the car.

"Okay," she says, and we're off.

～

Once I'm home, I change and climb on my bike—still no horn, but at least it fits me. After passing between Fruitland Baptist and Fruitland Methodist, I turn right on to Mills Gap Road, William Mills's route from South Carolina to Fruitland, and the opposite direction of my usual ride up the mountain. I push past miles of sod fields, irrigation shooting across the green expanses. Eventually, I turn left on Bearwallow Road. I try to keep my cadence steady up the slow climb, retracing the bending road Kelley and I drove after school.

The apple orchards are empty and the packing houses closed. A few trucks pass. The sun nears the mountains, not yet hiding but transmuting its color into a sepia wash of light. I imagine myself in an old photo, wonder about my ghost grandchildren recomposing my youth through stories and pictures.

I slow as I near the end of the rolling road. Before I cross the one-lane bridge above the creek and churn up the familiar serpentine route to Bearwallow's peak, I drift alongside the trailer park. It's quiet, but I hear whispered laughs in the distance and the hint of bolero music. A few high-school-age girls walk in a cluster down one of the dirt paths.

Just before I roll entirely by, I spot the pink bike and Alicia and her bob cut circling the park. She's alone at the edge of the lot, gliding in front of empty forest and the rising baldness of Bearwallow. As she comes around the corner, I see the streamers shimmering and a smile covering her face. She's somewhere else. Maybe at home, in her castle.

I stand on the pedals and try out a smile of my own before groaning up the unmoved mountain.

25

Until now, Grand Highlands' progress has been smooth-running, like water evenly and effortlessly streaming from faucets. It's been a distant, unstoppable force—a waterfall unseen but heard. The lots mapped out, the land cleared, the roads carved, the money paid. But like that pipe reaching from Gracias into the haze of Celaque, it's now clogged, backing up. No one's building, no one's coming.

But soon, the debris will be cleared. Someone's hands will dig in and scoop it all out. Then it's all going to erupt. One way or another.

When Grand Highlands put together its initial plan, it mapped out 99 lots across the peak. It started digging for water but soon realized there wasn't enough room for all the houses, septic tanks, and wells across Bearwallow's meadow. After the company struck its deal with the city, the lots have shrunk in size and more than tripled in number. The development's plan now charts 320 water-needing plots on barely 407 acres.

But the trenching hasn't started, and Grand Highlands can't get anyone to build a million-dollar house on a mountain without water. Yet the development continues in *Field of Dreams* fashion—if the roads and lots and fences and clubhouse are built, they will come, water or not.

I learned a few days ago that the county is asking questions about these city plans. The county commissioners argue that if the water reaches outside the city limits, then it's not the city's decision to send water to Bearwallow; it's a county matter. The commissioners are planning to take a vote of their own, to have the final say. A yea or nay on Grand Highlands' water line, and in that way, on Grand Highlands itself.

And so the fight swells. Centuries of tandem growth—Fruitland feeding Hendersonville, Hendersonville supporting Fruitland, apples from the country, the festival selling them in town—are pouring into this debate. City versus county. Market town versus rural area. Twenty-first-century Appalachia.

Out here, they talk about it as outside change, like the North encroaching 150 years ago. In town, they talk about progress, about growth. It's a battle, like nearly all battles, over borders.

And I'm leaving.

⌁

Finally: Field Day.

I loved this day as a kid. I love this day as an adult. Trailing me outside is a group of eight students, some white, some Latino—a random mix of fifth-graders. This is their last hurrah of elementary school, and we're first off to a game of crab soccer down the hill, the sun steady and full across the field. On our way, we pass Mr. Cody and some other old men unpacking instruments near the playground. I make my troupe stop. They're not happy about it.

Before long, the men set into a bluegrass number, "Clinch Mountain Backstep." A couple of kids roll their eyes. Mr. Cody flat-picks his guitar, keeping the rhythm, and it's not long before one kid is tapping a toe. It must be unintentional, intuitive.

We smatter applause when they end. Then Mrs. Cody steps in. She sings "I'll Fly Away" for their next number. Her voice is high and right. When she moves into the last verse, I allow my students to move on. They're itchy for action.

Sarah and I are heading to Ecuador for a belated honeymoon in a couple of weeks. We saved some money, bought open-ended tickets, and plan to disappear into the Andes for the summer. We've started packing up our little brown house, standing the red light beside boxes of clothes and dishes.

Come August, we'll move away to the Midwest for more schooling. I received my matching acceptance letter a few days ago. We know now that I want to write—fulfilling one of Debbie's predictions—and teach college; Sarah wants to be a lawyer, to follow in the line of her grandfather and father. So we're off to get trained. It feels right.

But I am worried about the flatness. We flew to Iowa over the weekend to look for a house, and it was the most foreign place I'd ever been. Land stretched farther than it ought to. No trees blocked the horizon; only baby cornstalks rose from the even land. I felt exposed with nowhere to hide.

As the kids run across the field, I look back at the Codys, wrapped up in song. I try to picture them on their porch, just off the peak of Bearwallow, singing those same songs. I wonder if their yard will be dug up for the coming water line. I think about how, again, it's water disrupting the earth around Mr. Cody. His family moved from Fontana to make way for electricity. He settled on the highest spot he could after being flooded out of that low-lying land. He retreated, hid out. Now, nearly seventy years later, he's in the midst of a water debate again, this time not to fill a valley with a lake but to flood a peak with houses.

～

Water was the city's first business. The first public facility Hendersonville established was its waterworks. Twenty years after the Civil War, nearly a decade after the railroad, the city made plans to provide water to its citizens. The world was changing. Paved streets, electricity, telegraphs, sidewalks. Water would make it all run.

The city started building a dam and reservoir, but money problems and political debates and injuries made the process a decade-long affair. It wasn't until 1897 that the system streamed water beneath the city streets. And as soon as it was installed, the system struggled to keep up with the town's growth. People were moving in, and the water was coming too slowly. The train outran it at every turn.

In 1963, a new, modern facility took shape. Today, the city's water comes largely from the Mills River, named after William Mills. But the city is again looking to expand. It has plans to tap the French Broad for another raw source. Should water rush across the county and up Bearwallow's side to hundreds of new residents, that source may quickly be needed to sustain the development of our land.

~

On the sideline, I watch my small crew take on Jayne's students.

"Heard you're leaving us," Jayne says as the game starts.

"Yeah." I shield my eyes. "For now, anyway."

The kids wheel around on four limbs across the softball field on which I practiced Little League years ago. Bouncing off the brick building behind us and the small herd of trailers up the hill are screams and shrieks and laughs—the soundtrack of Field Day, of the end of the school year.

"Reckon me and Terry will have to find somebody else to eat with."

"Yeah, somebody else to pick on." The ball rolls over to us; I kick it back in play. "What do you think will happen up on Bearwallow?"

"Who knows? There's no predicting, really." My team scores, and the crabs return to their sides. "I don't know. I figure they'll get their houses up there eventually."

We talk down a couple of roughhousing boys near the goal and cheer on the kids until the PE teacher blows the whistle to convert the crabs into kids again.

"Water slide, here we come," I say to Jayne as the students rush over.

"I'm off to the egg toss," she says. "Hey, y'all gonna take that red light with you when you go?"

I shrug, waiting for a big fifth-grader, Chris, to tie his shoe before we go on. "May leave it for whoever comes after us. Give you something to look for on the way to church."

᠆᠆

The water slide is actually a humongous blue tarp the PE teacher coated in water and dish soap this morning. It looks fast and steep, laid out across the hill above the softball field. At the top of the hill, I can hear the Codys' music, but it's too faint to make out. As the first boy blurs down the tarp, I stand back. I can't get wet and dirty. I'm Mister.

But this is my last hurrah at Edneyville, too. Classes end tomorrow; we're leaving the country in a couple of weeks. So once the students are sopped and bored and ready to move on to some game involving balls as weapons and mats as barricades, I take off down the hill.

I announce my 180-pound presence with a warning yell and go head first. Water has pooled at the bottom of the hill, where the kids have formed a divot of worn grass. I close my eyes as I rush into it, thinking I should have screamed "Cannonball!" before sending the waiting water flying. I let everything stay black and wet for a moment, once my body finally stops. I wonder if, when I open my eyes, I might just for an instant shrink into my former self.

"Mr. Jones!" I turn to see Chris skidding down the hill, right at me and my daydream. I slosh to my feet and move on.

᠆᠆

Even as I tromp around Field Day, the county commissioners institute a drought on Bearwallow. In a three-to-two vote, they deny the water line extension that the city agreed to over a year ago. The nays cite the high-density nature of Grand Highlands, the problematic shift from 99 houses to 320. They speak of keeping the rural rural. They fear pumping the water would set a precedent for coming—and oh, they're coming—developments.

And that's it? No water, no growth? Grand Highlands will dry up? I'd already resigned myself to a new Bearwallow, a Bearwallow swarming with roads and houses. I'd started thinking of it with hundreds of residents on top, a vacation destination. A new place.

I haven't been all the way to the peak in months. I've found new rides, new spots. I still swoop down Terry's Gap between Bearwallow and Hightop Mountain and climb the ridge lines. But past the Codys' place and up above Willie's house to the wide meadow, I haven't been. Until I began hearing the rumblings of the water fight a few weeks back, I'd assumed dozens of houses were springing up, garages tacked on, porches spread out.

Now, I'm not sure what to think. The peak must bear a skeleton of the development, the lines clear and sharp, looking like the opposite of Abraham's Wilderness nearly 250 years ago. The soil holds not the traces of history but the markings of the future, a future that will never come. And now the development will rest like my cripple finger, its foundation grown but its tip stunted. I imagine it will soon be sold off in sections, dissected, stillborn. That leaves me to wonder if the mountain will simply become its former self, if anything can ever truly return.

26

Abraham grew rich. Men bought his whiskey and rooms, covering him in gold and silver on the frontier of Appalachia. He claimed over a thousand acres across the plateau; everything he saw was his.

Before long, the surge in traffic to his inn brought in its wake thieves who hid in the thick woods along the pioneer road—bands of ruthless bushwhackers and renegade Indians banished from their tribes. They swept through the forests in the dark, surrounding caravans and taking all they could carry. Abraham worried for his wealth. He stockpiled the coins in locked wooden boxes strapped with iron. Now in his nineties, he feared his fortune simply lay bound and waiting for someone to cart off, the gangs pushing him easily aside.

Perhaps more than the bushwhackers, though, Abraham worried about his wife, Bathsheba. As traders came through the tavern with packsaddles full of jewels and dresses, earrings and powder, Bathsheba traded Abe's gold and silver for what caught her fancy. Living in a wild land of men and pirates, she enjoyed buying anything soft and bright and new, slipping in the back on a whim to unlock the boxes and pilfer his treasure. This made Abraham nervous, suspicious, and protective. Paranoid, perhaps.

Late one night, he woke two slaves and had them dump a great portion of his fortune into a giant iron wash pot before blindfolding them and ordering them into the pitch-black forest with him. Circling and zigzagging to keep them muddled about his path, he led them by torch deeper and deeper into the Wilderness. The three men crossed Pheasant Branch back and forth and back and forth until finally Abraham was satisfied.

He removed the slaves' blindfolds and handed them shovels as their eyes tried to adjust to the forest's dark. There, at the base of a white oak tree, they dug a hole deeper and deeper until Abraham finally raised his hand to stop them. They lowered the pot of gold and buried it, leaving no trace of the opening in the earth. Abraham threatened the men with death to keep them quiet before covering their eyes again and returning home, weaving them back and forth across the branch.

His gold lay for years until one day when Abraham needed to unearth a bit to complete some business. He disappeared again into the wild at nightfall, a man of ninety-four. He wound his way through the woods in case he was followed, crossing Pheasant Branch again and again and again.

The next morning, when he wasn't in bed or at the still or tending the animal pens, his employees and Bathsheba searched the Wilderness, calling his name through the trees—"Abraham!"—and sending the birds into frightened flight—"Abraham!"

They found his body crumpled and face down in Pheasant Branch. No one knew why he had absconded in the darkness, but when pressed, the two slaves admitted to helping bury treasure deep in the woods years before. They couldn't say exactly where the pot lay because they had been blindfolded and bullied, but they both remembered a gnarled white oak standing near the fortune's tomb.

Some reckoned Abraham had tripped on a root near the branch, falling and hitting his head and drowning in the shallow water. Others believed he'd been followed and mugged, the pirates making off with his treasure and burrowing deeper into the mountains.

Men sought his treasure for generations. They dug at the base of many oak trees, leaving holes throughout the woods but always coming away empty. In the century following Abraham's passing, all the trees in the Wilderness were cut for lumber, thinning the forest and leaving only new, slight trees to work their way toward the sky. Nothing remains of the old growth; no sign stands to mark the buried fortune.

Yet for centuries, men and women and children have claimed to see the ghost of an old man on the roads and paths near Pheasant Branch, wandering, desperately searching for what was lost.

27

They take it back.

Nine days after the Grand Highlands' water line was denied, the county commissioners reconvened. Yesterday morning at nine o'clock, they reversed the decision; the commissioner from Edneyville switched from a nay to a yea. Three votes to two, for.

Already, there's talk of corruption, of money exchanged, of a gifted lot on the mountain—rumors fly around the general store and the Walmart alike. For his part, the commissioner claims he changed his mind after Grand Highlands agreed to reduce the number of lots from 320 to 249. They'd shrunk it, made it more reasonable, he believed. He didn't mention or rationalize how the number was still higher than the one first agreed upon. Regardless, the water is coming, and the bald peak of Bearwallow will sprout once it's flowing. Once I'm off somewhere else.

We're flying out in a few days. I turned in my keys, said my goodbyes to the teachers last week. When I told my students in the final days of class, they asked when I'd return. No one asked *if*, only *when*. I wondered if they knew something I didn't. If they already knew of the Pull.

I've neglected the dogs for the banjo this afternoon. They're waiting outside for me, chasing one another around in slobbery circles, but
I'm sitting at my desk with the Saga on my lap, playing one of the love/
murder ballads I've learned. This one's called "Little Sadie." As with
most of them, the singer has to kill and then flee because he loves so
deeply. I don't feel murderous, but I can fathom the bitter mix of con-
flicting emotions. I give the banjo one final empty strum and pat a stack
of labeled boxes on the way outside.

As I round the back of the house, the dogs are bounding up and
down the hill. Turf Mountain has started cutting sections of the sod
field below our house. Squares of the landscape are now checkered
brown in the corners, green skin cut and rolled away to be planted elsewhere to reroot. "What A Friend We Have in Jesus" bounces off the
hills and sweeps through the bottoms from Fruitland Baptist Bible Institute. A tractor hums unseen in a nearby field.

I imagine the bottom land lined with corn and potatoes and beans,
not this sod for golf courses and developments. I try to conjure a Maxwell-
looking man, clad in neutral browns and a wide hat, wiping a day's work
from his head. I stick a young boy down there, my great-grandfather,
maybe, about the age of my students. He's throwing dirt clods toward
the creek, then charging through the field to skip rocks on the bank I'll
soon claim.

But before I free the dogs and set out after the boyhood ghost of
my great-grandfather, the bells and the tractor hum disappear. A dark
crash resounds. It falls on top of all the afternoon noises, smothering
them entirely. The blast rings and hushes in a blink. Then the chimes
continue as if never muffled—*All our sins and griefs to bear.* I question
my ears.

I scan the field, looking for a cause of the boom, invented or real. I
see only the trees lining Clear Creek and the quilted browns and greens
of the partially harvested sod field. I head toward the barn to stand

higher above everything, but I still can't spot anything *kaboom*-worthy in the miles of land below us.

Baffled, I walk back toward the fenced-in dogs. It is then that I hear the cracking, the snaps of flame running under the chorus: *All because we do not carry everything to God in prayer.* I survey the field again, holding my hand up to shield my eyes from the full spring sun. Behind the thinly forested creek, I catch smoke curling above the tree line.

I try to find any reason for an intentional burn along the creek on a dry afternoon. But the smoke is so dark, so opaque, that it seems unnatural. I leave the dogs penned and head down past the horses to the field. I'm not running, but my pace is rushed by the steep downhill route to the field and an unwelcome, nagging worry.

Once I'm in the bottoms, I catch sight of flames in the openings between trees. The smoke is rising high now. I march through the brown patches of the field. From here, it's clear the fire is across the creek. Before I reach the bank where my imagined great-grandfather was meant to skip rocks, a thunderous pop sends me jumping backward. I cover my head for no reason.

"Hello?" I holler, gathering myself.

"*Hello?*" I try louder, but no one calls back from the other side.

I hear an engine running beneath the crackling fire. The blaze seems high enough to reach tree limbs, but I can't discern what is actually burning. The blasts are enough to keep me from hopping into and across the creek to explore. Instead, I jog back up the hill to jump in the car and drive across the bridge to see what's fueling the fire.

I fly down Gilliam Road and pass over the water, taking up all of the narrow bridge five feet above the lazy stream. Once across, I see a rusty green tractor fully ablaze along the water. I jerk the car off the road and on to the dirt trail outlining the field and speed toward the flames, trying to spot any sign of a body, of life, near the burning machine.

Once I'm close, I jump out. I've left the vehicle fifty yards from the fire, but I feel it when I'm out in the open. It's somehow fuller, heavier than the late-afternoon heat. The wind sends waves of it past me. I get closer and trot around the tractor, trying to see if someone was tossed off the back. A giant hose snakes from the water and into the field. It's an irrigation line that connects to a giant metal sprinkler, a machine larger than the tractor, hard at work sending spears of creek water across the field, in the opposite direction from me and the dissolving tractor. I'm standing exactly between shoots of water and shoots of flame.

The engine's still running, but as I circle the thing, I don't see any trace of a person. I soon realize the tractor had been standing still and empty all afternoon, its engine pumping the water from the creek to the irrigation system. No one mans it. Nothing's in danger but for these trees and this tractor. And maybe me.

Despite the fire burning through the hood, the motor still sends water into the thirsty field. The tractor fuels the water and the fire all at once.

I call Fred Pittillo and find myself lurching backward again. A hollow explosion bellows out, and the machine and the ground both seem to resettle. *A tire*, I think. I see the back of the tractor sink on the now-airless rubber.

"Fred?"

"Yeah."

"It's Jeremy Jones. You got a tractor on fire down here."

"What?"

"This tractor running the irrigation down here near the church is on fire."

"Man alive. I'll be . . . I'm coming."

He hangs up before I can say okay or ask about the fire department.

Soon, Fred's and another truck send dust across the field. They park much closer than I did, and Fred and the other man, Harvey, jump out, leaving the doors open. They circle the thing. Harvey sees about pulling the keys to cut the engine. He weaves back and forth, looking for a way to reach the ignition. The burn's too hot to get close, so he tries to get in behind it with a pair of gloves to kill the engine altogether.

"It blew one or two of the tires," I say, worried the impact of the escaping air and burst of oxygen to the flame might catch Harvey. Fred brought a fire extinguisher, likely assuming the blaze was small. But this is a bonfire, licking the branches of the trees. He shoots the pasty liquid for a minute while Harvey dances with the flames, but Fred eventually realizes the small extinguisher won't do much and steps back.

Harvey inches in but eventually jumps back, too. He can't make his arm long enough to maneuver past the heat and fire. He grabs the extinguisher and tries to quench enough of a path to cut the engine. But the fire's hungry.

It's not long before a volunteer fireman charges into the field, red light flashing on the dash of his jacked-up pickup. Behind him comes a fire truck, blaring down Gilliam from the station up the road. Fred and Harvey drive their trucks from the path, and the red rig sidles up to the tractor. The volunteer jumps out, a wad of tobacco jutting out his bottom lip. The firemen climb out, too, holding up their hands to block the sun.

I step back and lean against my vehicle as the spectator, the messenger. I can't hear the men from here, but after some circling and chatting and pointing, they unwind hoses and douse the thing. The smell of this fire is odd. It's chemical and thin. It permeates the air as the firemen soak it. I don't care for it. I like the smell of a campfire, the wood cooking and releasing itself into the air; it sends my brain to the woods, surrounds me with nostalgia. But this smell is empty of memory.

I can still conjure the tangy, smoky smell of scorched earth that filled my nose and brain when I landed in Honduras. As a man named Luis drove me and the backpack full of my life from the city to Gracias, the air whipping through the windows was steeped in burnt land, burnt manure—fired restoration. Farmers set fire to their land after a crop, incinerating the soil to release the nutrients into the earth. The tactic turned the land over, allowing farmers to stick corn in the ground and watch it grow posthaste. It was Honduras, to me. The smell of a new country.

Searing the land was a quick fix, a way to revive used dirt. The method, though, I knew to be unsustainable. Soon, the land would be used up, tired, infertile. Farmers in our mountains used to do the same thing. I knew the smell in Honduras to be a faint taste of my childhood.

As a boy, I caught the same whiffs drifting over our land. And so my first sensory connection to my new country was a harking back to the country of my childhood.

Hardly anyone fires fields in Henderson County these days. People burn ditches to keep grass low, but it's rare to set an entire field ablaze. They now know the effects.

While I lived below the foggy Celaque in Honduras, fires would occasionally flare up on the mountainside and stretch across the forest. I remember always finding it odd—fire on a mountain covered in water. Farmers igniting their land to make ends meet would sometimes lose control, and the flames would dive into the forest, leaking into trees and undergrowth.

From Gracias, we could see these blazes like sparks on the giant mountain. Shimmers of destruction. Aside from the smell—a mix of campfire and acidic, smoldering land—we felt the effects in the escaping animals, the refugees. A puma migrated to Gracias to evade the burning trees a few times. The radio always warned of the roaming beast once it was spotted. We closed the doors of the school; people cleared the streets; rumored sightings passed along the sidewalks. The cat always worked its way back up the charred mountain to start over in a changed world, its eerie, shrieking howl echoing down.

In the earliest travelogue I've found of southern Appalachia (1860), an anonymous writer, R, wrote of sitting with a family in the Great Smoky Mountains. Suddenly, the son rushed into the cabin: "Daddy, there's fire in the mountains!"

R wrote that, to a mountaineer, such a cry was "more fearful than was, 'the Philistines be upon thee,' in the days of yore." But despite this fear, despite the possibility of fire taking everything in a windy instant, R mused on the magic of living, breathing fire:

> But what a sublime sight a fire in the mountains is! The whirlwind of flame leaps to the highest tree tops, stripping them of every leaf in a moment. Here and there, all through the forest, stand dead trees, rendered thoroughly combustible

by the summer's sun. Around these the fire seems to flap its wings with wild and savage joy, leaving them for days and nights after as burning pillars to mark the line of its victorious march.

A few years after R wrote of fire in the mountains, General Sherman made his fiery march from Atlanta to the coast, lighting trees and buildings like kindling. He scorched a trail, a *V* from Georgia to the Carolinas.

Meanwhile, another march pushed into western North Carolina. General George Stoneman fanned his ten thousand Union men across the Blue Ridge in search of Jefferson Davis, effectively connecting with the *V* of Sherman's route to form a pillaging triangle. Not as wholly igneous as Sherman's violent parade, Stoneman's Raid destroyed roads and warehouses, the beginnings of railroads and industries. It broke supply lines and pillaged farms and camps. It tried to drive out bushwhackers and deserters and guerrillas.

I read in one of his men's journals about Stoneman's march through North Carolina. I found entries describing how the men "marched all day through pine forests" in the middle of the state. They eventually entered the mountains, crossing back and forth below the Virginia border. Captain Weand, the journal writer, eventually complained, "We crossed the Blue Ridge again. . . . While we are now experts at mountain climbing, it gives us no pleasure."

Two divisions of Stoneman's men broke off and trudged through Henderson County in search of "Jeff," as Weand called Jefferson Davis. One division ransacked its way toward Asheville, up Howard Gap Road, following that same trail on which Thomas Howard and his men had met the Cherokees nearly a hundred years before. The other camped in Hickory Nut Gap near Bat Cave, on the backside of Bearwallow. This second division, resting before setting out toward Salisbury to burn bridges, took its horses up Bearwallow to graze on the meadow.

In Weand's account, I expected to find more grumbling about the marching and climbing and descending. Instead, this trek to Bearwallow in the midst of Stoneman's fiery, violent charge lingered as a moment of respite and calm:

> Our march today was through the grandest scenery we have looked on during our term of service. We went up through Hickory Nut Gap in the mountains, along the Broad River, up to its source. Towering above us almost to the clouds, were the precipitous crags of the Hickory Mountains, and at High Falls the water drops 380 feet from the summit. It was so imposing that the usual chat of the riders was hushed, as they gazed with awe on the sight. As we rode along we plucked the fragrant magnolia from the forest trees, and the wish of all was to stay longer with it, but that could not be done, and we went on up to the top, where plenty of forage was found.

After the horses grazed, the soldiers had to descend and leave Bearwallow behind. "It was of some disappointment to the men," Weand wrote. After dropping back into the world, they received orders to do "all the damage possible."

Both Sherman's and Stoneman's marches set out to smash to make new. Burning the South was for its own good. To save the South, it had to be destroyed, turned over, dissipated. Like our mountain forebears and Honduran farmers, those Civil War soldiers charred the earth to replenish it, to make it what they wanted.

Before the timber trains, before development and benevolent missions, Stoneman's men filed down Howard Gap Road and broke it all down. They tried to leave no place to hide, to level any of those lingering pockets where one could pass from sight. They sought to expose the very skin of our mountains.

Eighty years later, Nazis set Bearwallow's fire tower upright. They helped make sure a watchman could keep us free of fearless, furious fire.

Both elements fueled by the tractor—fire and water—can lay waste to the land. Each can enliven, each has its place and its purpose—old farmers and lightning bolts enflame the earth to clean it, to clear it, to replenish it; rain and irrigation chutes sprout it, feed the seeds, bring up the fruit of Fruitland like Adam from the dust. But in excess, they wipe out everything.

I worry that Grand Highlands' water might be excess, that it will mark a coming wave of water that, like fire, will cover the land so that the skin of our mountains is exposed, with nowhere left to hide. And these days, the tower on Bearwallow stands empty, with no watchman to warn.

~

The firemen's hose shrinks enough of the flame to shut off the tractor. Once the engine's off, the irrigation system slowly stops, water streaming through the air in shorter, thinner gushes. The fire truck's flow continues, though, and I decide the fire won't reach the trees or hop the creek or tear a path toward my house. I've done my duty; I drive back across Clear Creek to pick up where I left off, releasing the dogs to pour through the field.

We stomp through the grass and the empty squares where sod used to grow, passing the smoke and the fire truck across the water. We follow the creek downstream, push past the barn and up the hill past the Prestwood house. We press into the woods to cut through the trail to Grandma's backyard. Granddaddy's truck waits at the opening of the forest.

The maze of rhododendron that thickens the forest in front of me stood as my second home as a boy. It was a hideout, an escape. "The mountain man, in the Southern Appalachians," wrote Donald Culross Peattie in 1943, "is not a real mountaineer, as are some of the Swiss living at giddy altitudes; he is a forest man." We lined our boyhood forest with traps and filled it with things—baseball bats, a homemade map of our land, Tonka trucks. We stashed and stored. We gave the woods what we wanted saved.

Josh, the eldest cousin, took as his shelter a circular cave of rho-

dodendron. Inside it, he became Cobra Commander, the enemy of the
G.I. Joes—the rest of my cousins and me. He plotted within, and we
planned lines of defense and attacks from our larger, deeper base just
across the dirt path. No one could see us inside. We peered out between leaves and mangled branches. We receded from view and created what we wanted inside.

Cobra Commander's post, Josh's patch of rhododendron, went up
in flames. Playing Legos with my sister inside Grandma's house that
day, I heard popping outside the window. From the front porch, I saw
the forested hideout smeared in jumping orange flames.

Granddaddy had been burning leaves and trash in a rock pit at the
edge of the woods—cleaning by flame. He'd driven down to the barn,
and in his absence the fire bolted. It wore a path across the leaves and
underbrush and made a home in the rhododendron, seeping inside the
safe house. I wanted to fill buckets. I wanted to hop on my bike and
chase after Granddaddy. I wanted to do something. But Grandma sent
me inside and walked to the back of the house. She reached in her open
car window and bleeped three steady blares from the horn. And we
waited.

I snuck back to the porch to watch what had once been impen-
etrable melt away. I feared the burn might reach the house; I wondered
if the G.I. Joes had won once and for all. Suddenly, I didn't want them
to. I wanted the dance of good and evil to always carry on.

Eventually, I heard the rumble of Granddaddy's truck over the
crackling of the fire. He saw the flames, jumped out, and spent the afternoon fighting the shifty fire with a garden hose and a shovel. He'd sit
and observe for a bit, then attack again.

Once he quenched it and the sun began to fall, Josh's lair stood
black, exposed, and empty of imagination. I was afraid the whole thing
would collapse if I got too close. The thickness that had kept us out had
vanished, leaving scarred branches and holes betraying the inside. A
scorched skeleton.

Only now, with Granddaddy ten years passed and Josh nearly thirty years old and living near Kings Mountain, has the giant patch filled

in again. Granddaddy's truck wastes away immediately between Cobra Commander's regenerated fort and the G.I. Joes' labyrinthine shelter. Bits of our childhoods still hide inside. Like Granddaddy's decaying truck, our Tonka Toys rust away in the woods. Except for the oxidation and the spreading forest, everything seems stilled in amber.

Instead of setting out up the path to Grandma's house to grab a peppermint and holler hello, I duck inside the regrown fort. I thumb the new branches and thick leaves. Stunted limbs rise above me. I sit on a horizontally growing branch. It creaks and dips, and I put weight on my legs to keep everything together. I'm half in the air, half on the ground. I hear the dogs tramping through the woods and wonder if they can find me burrowed away in this living cave. I squint through the leaves and imagine I've disappeared, that I've become part of the woods, that this land is unchanged after flames.

28

As if to fully squelch the fire, all day we were drenched in rain. Even as I drive home from delivering boxes to my parents' basement, where they'll wait for us to return from South America, the clouds keep it all dark, pouring heavy shadows on the valleys of Edneyville and Fruitland. Yet in the garage, I stubbornly tune up my bike and throw on this awkward spandex. When I open the door—tires inflated, helmet at the ready—the clouds have thinned and worn away and retreated into the hollows. I know the sun has won out for the moment; darkness, though, still threatens the edges.

I decide to turn it around. This may be my last ride for a while. I push out Gilliam, cut down the short road separating Fruitland Baptist from Fruitland Methodist—I imagine Nanny and Albert going their separate ways on Sundays—and turn right instead of left. I'll find my way back to this spot eventually, but I flip the loop. Instead of dipping down Terry Gap Road, I head down Mills Gap, William Mills's ancient path into these mountains after his home in South Carolina was destroyed over two centuries ago. I wind past the sod fields, where migrant workers and tractors cut and roll the dry squares of manicured grass. As I work toward Bearwallow and pass the trailer park full of my former students, I look for Alicia and her pink bike, but I see no one in the water-soaked field. I push on toward the mountain, following the path the water line will take in the coming months.

This backward route slows the speed of the formerly swift sections of my ride, as if the weight of everything has shifted and my top-heavy orbit is suddenly upside down. The pieces of Bearwallow I normally blur down become sedate and still. As I strain up the switchbacks I usually fly around, I notice sections of forest I've never seen.

On this side of the mountain, I parallel a thin stream around the tight turns. Patches of forest-canopied road seem forever wet, like pockets of rain forest. The trickle I hear from the stream becomes the unified cry of the woods; the babbling comes from all sides and from nowhere all at once.

Beside the road up the mountain, an old mill wheel waits, suspended above the thin stream. Despite the day's rain, the water leaking down the mountain isn't fast or full enough to put the wheel to work. In fact, the wooden planks are strangled with vines, as if the earth has reached up and stopped the spinning. It stands here as a wheel without purpose, left behind by time. Soon, city pipes will bore into the soil below this stilled wheel, defying gravity and running upward alongside the stream tricking down the mountain.

I work my way higher and higher, the tree line growing closer. After months of ignoring the peak, I have decided to head to the top on this final ride, to stop and see what's been done. To suck it up.

Eventually, I pass the Codys' trailer in a gap off the road. No one seems to be home. I cycle past Willie's house, just on the edge of Grand Highlands. And then the fences marking the development start. I brace for the changed topography, the climbing mansions, the marks of passing time, the preparations for the promised water.

But once I curve into the meadow, all is mostly the same as on my last visit months ago. A few horses amble around the barn. The giant rock sign stands beneath its ever-running fountain. The stained wooden fence lines the entire peak. And signs sprinkle the land. No houses or foundations, only markers. Boundaries. Claimed land.

I stop beside the giant rock sign. The sun has burnt off nearly all the clouds. Splotches of moisture still cling to crannies of the mountains, but the sky's eyes are clearing as I walk the bike along the Grand Highlands' drive. The immense wooden gates are open, and I feel tiny entering them without a vehicle. The newly paved road leads to the spot where the clubhouse will stand. For now, though, it's a road to nothing.

At the dead end, beyond the gates to nowhere, I survey this land I'm from. I make out a truck traversing a thin road down below, a fleck of worn red slipping around turns. I wonder if it's Isaac, chasing sticks, or Willie, heading home. Wide stretches of fields are broken by patches of trailers and wild tracts of forest. Houses pop up sporadically. Nothing below me is square or predictable; the lines of the land, the creeks and roads and ridges, are all impulsive and free of easy geometry. Like Nanny's quilts, they're haphazard and beautiful.

I can't quite spot the house we'll vacate tomorrow, but I can follow the trees that line Clear Creek to the sod fields below it. I think I find the site where the tractor blazed, a few hundred yards before the low bridge on Gilliam Road. I wonder if the pitch-black plume and the flames themselves were visible from this spot yesterday.

The highest spot on Bearwallow rises to my left. Upon that bald waits the fire tower, along with a few utility towers. They stick from the mountain like missiles awaiting orders. I'm sure the smoldering tractor was on display from the top of the tower. I decide to roll toward it.

~

In Sunday school at Fruitland Baptist down in the valley, I never learned that the Bible starts with a contradiction. I learned the Bible was an errorless document, seamless and sure. I memorized its verses and sang its psalms. But in college, I signed up for an Old Testament class, only to learn on the first day that the Bible immediately opens with options. Like a choose-your-own-adventure book, its first two chapters offer two paths, two beginnings—perhaps two understandings of the world and our relationship to it.

Genesis 1 outlines the creation of the earth. The world is "formless" before God starts lighting everything up. He speaks, and stuff happens. He invents days, then uses those days for different purposes, eventually making mankind in his image. He says to Adam and Eve, "Be fruitful and increase in number; fill the earth and subdue it. Rule over the fish in the sea and the birds in the sky and over every living creature that moves on the ground." *It's yours*, he seems to say.

But Genesis 2 gives another account. God pulls Adam up from the dust, breathes life into his nostrils. He shows him around, instructs him on how to water and take care of everything. This second story presents humanity's "house-sitter" role. The earth, Eden, is God's, and we should care for it in his stead. Enjoy it but just don't eat that apple, we're told. I half expect God to tell Adam where to leave the mail and which animals have special diets.

In the two accounts, I see the diverging impulses that send people into these mountains: they come to either conquer or camouflage. In my people, I see the two courses. My Scots-Irish came in swinging, drawing bold borders, forcing the land to their will; my Dutchman passed from sight, becoming a ghost to always roam.

It's impossible to climb up here and not feel something. The hazy blue ridge lines blur into the sky as though the mountains are breathing, exhaling on a cold day. Everything that is waits below.

The word *awe* was invented for such moments. This land will change one's perspective, the Grand Highlands' literature claims. People get that shiver, that nearly transcendent awareness of time. And they want to keep it.

Conquerors try to claim it, to stake the land right then and there. They build upon it, set fences around it, scream *Mine!* They want the awe perfectly contained. The camouflagers try to drift deeper into it, to become part of it. They hope to seep into this land so it sustains them, becomes them, covers them up. They don't want to be noticed for fear they'll throw it all off, upset the awe.

Over the past century, Appalachia has mostly endured conquerors, waves of everyone else's ideas—missionaries and teachers, politicians and companies. *Do it this way, give us that.* Of course, those outside actors bettered and developed this place in many ways. I'm proof: world-traveled and college-educated. But the region has been taken from as much as it has been given to. One only need drive through West Virginia or eastern Kentucky to see that coal mining hasn't eradicated poverty but has likely increased it.

All year, in the shadow of this mountain, digging into my families' histories, I have uncovered the past. I've been able to find this world anew, to understand it in a way I never could have without leaving. My return allowed me to find and feel the mixed loyalties: the immigrant and native, the fleer and pursuer, the shooter and victim, the conqueror and camouflager. It gave me an answer—or answers—to my question: How am I mountain folk? My mountain-ness is this tension, this ease with contradiction, Genesis 1 and 2. Like Bearwallow with its two peaks, its two minds, rising on either side of me, the people in my skin and in the bones of these mountains made a home with the discord.

～

I let gravity carry me slightly downhill toward the beginning of the final peak. Not far from Grand Highlands' gates, the paved road turns to gravel as it starts to drop down another side of the mountain. I stop. I know this rocky road trapezes the ridge line down the mountain into Gerton, west of Bat Cave, but I never cycle down it for the loose rocks. This must have been the route Captain Weand and the other men climbed on the way to the peak from Hickory Nut Gorge 150 years ago. I try to imagine their steadily slow march of silence, entranced by Bearwallow.

I straddle the bike, looking for a route to the towers. To my right, a gate marks a rough dirt road leading higher up the ridge line. Neither my bike nor I could make it up this steep gravel path after the last thirty minutes of climbing. Plus, the gate's closed and locked. So I duck into the forest, portaging my bike over my shoulder. Once I'm fairly deep in, fifty yards or so from the road, I stash the bike behind a tree. Its blue handlebars peek out beyond the trunk, but it's mostly camouflaged. I glance back at it as I emerge from the woods, halfway afraid it will follow me like a too-loyal pet. I doubt anyone will drive this section of road in the next hour, much less notice my bike and take off with it, but I don't want to be stuck on top of Bearwallow on a late afternoon without wheels to help me descend.

I squeeze past the gate and start hoofing it toward the top. The path is a narrow cut up the mountain's edge, and when the trees beside and below me open up enough, I'm offered a fully forested stretch of mountains and valleys leading toward Asheville. This must have been the view Stoneman's men had marching to the top. But the openings appear rarely, as the gravel road is caved in by trees on both sides.

It's warm today, but the shade and the breeze sweeping across the mountain give my sweat a chill as I trudge up the road, cycling shoes clicking on the gravel. Vast outcrops of rock come forth from the mountain above me. They're dark, coated in water. Moss carpets fallen trees and the undersides of these rocks, spreading green to the ends of this patch of earth. The sopped, perpetually green forest reminds me of the peak of Celaque, not only in its dampness but in its constricting nature. The limbs and vines and rocks all seem to be spreading, moving too slowly for anything but their effects to be noticed.

Soon, I find myself not looking out over the ridge line or up into the slow-moving forest but instead watching my feet. Just steps back, I narrowly missed a few-days-old cow patty waiting in the road. Now, bovine droppings pock the road like a minefield, and I'm being sure not to put my foot in one.

I've not seen any other evidence of cattle, and it's odd to imagine them off in the forest or milling about down in the forested gaps. I zigzag past the patties and climb and climb. Eventually, the trees surrounding me grow shorter. Soon, I'm above them all. The deep green that had hemmed me in transforms into a soft khaki-colored meadow. Tall grass stretches out as the route curves up to the peak. What was closed is now open.

Up here, the mountain has lost its edges entirely. No trees or fences or lines circle or mark the crest of the mountain. It's an exposed space rounding slowly back down into forests and valleys. Cows moo all across the field. The dirt path cuts straight through the pasture, and as I pass, a few spring calves stumble behind their mamas, while older cows chew indifferently at me.

This feels like a foreign world. Nothing but clear blue sky backdrops the strolling cows. They're not held in by anything but land—no barbed wire or electricity, only the choice between a meadow full of grass and a forest full of water. The place feels timeworn and enduring. This scene could be three hundred years ago or tomorrow. It's not placed in time. There's nothing but dirt and cows and grass and trees. The forest hides the meadow covered in lot signs and lined with fences, and I'm not yet high enough to get a view into the valleys. The modern world is hidden from me, and I know this must be the Bearwallow of always.

Then the ancientness breaks, the towers rise from the earth, and I trudge through the pasture toward them, farther up the meadow.

The fire tower stands above a small structure that must have been the watcher's house. The tower and house are both fenced in, protected by a sign reading, "No Trespassing, Property of USGS." The fire tower is steel and not nearly as tall as the cellular or radio towers that have moved in to climb into the sky beside it. But it has a ready, wide perch atop. I try to imagine those Germans lifting the thing upright sixty years ago. I wonder if they ever stopped to take in the view.

I circle the tower; I stand and spin—360 degrees of open land above everything. But I'm not thinking about this view, about the panorama of Bearwallow. I'm thinking about the view from up there, from the tip-top of the tower. I've already visualized myself up there, and it's everything I can do not to hurdle the six-foot fence and set out up the ladder.

No one lives in the small house; no one's here to man the tower. I give the pasture another survey and decide the herd of mountain cattle won't rat me out if I scale the fire tower to have a look. I want to be the watchman, the eyes of the mountain.

I jump into the chain-link and start scaling. I'm nearly over, with one leg swung atop the rail, when I spot the camera. It's perched in a tree beside the small house and has a sign of its own. I read the word *surveillance* and stop, caught red-handed, dangling on the fence. I hang there, letting the camera get too good a look.

And so I'm stuck in a bad pun on my mountain. I'm literally on the fence, pushed over the top by my Scots-Irish blood and my Rebel kin but pulled back down by the hiding Dutchman and the loyal deserters. Here's the balance I set out for on Bearwallow.

I finally decide to dismount before I break any laws or bones. I've known for some time that I'm a camouflager, a hider, not an invader.

Once down, I break free of the camera's eye and, minding the cow patties, sit in the field. I lean back, try to forget the allure of the tower, try to forget that high view and the chance to spot my house and the ghost of yesterday's fire. No, I'm happy here. This is good enough. Yes.

I squirm.

⌒

Abraham—my Rip Van Winkle, a Dutchman disappearing into the allure of these mountains—begat a long line, a clan of sleepy Van Winkles who sank in here and closed their eyes. For over a century, the Wilderness hemmed them in. They built hard, somnambulant lives while the rest of the world charged along.

Then the twentieth century. Then ways in and out. Then trains and cars and mill jobs and vacation homes. My people, who'd been drowsily outlying, suddenly saw the world around them. It appeared before them as if always there. Their eyes opened. Electricity! Factories! Dynamite!

We twentieth-century Van Winkles see only hints and hear stories of Rip and the dream. I'm merely a catnapping Van Winkle. I drift off in the woods and up here on Bearwallow, but I always wake to descend back into modernity.

I try to get comfortable on the higher of Bearwallow's peaks, the right side of its *U*. This is Barnwell land, the acreage Nancy Lyda assured me would never be sold. It's separated from Grand Highlands by forest and this higher crest, above it all.

Here, I feel like I've landed on a Western range filled with cattle.

I wait for a stampede or cowboys. I wait for a fire down in the valley, some smoke to set me in motion. I wait for something.

Nothing. Only occasional shimmering cars and the trucks in the fields lifting the earth in tight sod rolls. Everything moves, but nothing changes.

So I imagine Abe, my Rip, down in the waterlogged valley, a weighty fog settling in, darkening the periphery, shrinking the world. As the haze covers the forests and the clouds tighten around the land, Abraham stumbles from the woods pawing at his eyes. He wears a long beard and a misshapen hat. He stops briefly, rifle tossed easily over his shoulder, to survey what he can amid the burying gray.

Suddenly, sun shoots straight through the edges of the dark. The fog cowers, retracts, sulks away. And there stands Abraham, shabbily clothed, 294 years old, groggy-eyed. He does not recognize the mega church before him, the golf course beneath his feet, the paved road circling him. Lost and dizzy, he nearly starts to run in search of Bathsheba, his inn, his dog. But first, he stoops and sticks his hand as far as he can in the ground. He digs his fingers in deep to learn, to somehow know that this place is home and foreign all at once.

I stick my hands into the grass, reach into the dirt, try to feel something. I think about Captain Weand sitting up here 150 years ago during a brief respite from fire and war: "The wish of all was to stay longer." I wonder if he thought of leaning back into this grass and sleeping, of turning Rip Van Winkle on the soft top of Bearwallow Mountain.

I'm wiggling, trying to stay comfortable as the sharp grass spikes through my spandex. I shift my weight but can't settle in. Not yet. "But that could not be done," wrote Weand.

I hop up, take another look at the tower, the edgeless edges of the mountain, the soon-to-be Grand Highlands splayed out below me. Then I set my shoes to clicking back down the cow-patty-lined road.

～

Once down, I retrieve my bike, survey the sky for any lingering rain clouds, and push off. I dive down, giving in to gravity. I slow for the tight turns much more than I need, but I'm doing this backward, descending what's usually ascended, and I want to be sure and safe.

As I lean over and slowly curl around a switchback, I try to find the dog that usually bursts from nowhere when I'm climbing. I don't see or hear any sign of him, but I spot a young, chubby boy standing in front of a small house a short way off the road. I don't know him, but I catch his eye as I release the brakes and let the straightening road pull me faster forward.

Is he dancing? Not quite. Twirling batons? I can't make it out exactly; he waves his arms and spins. As I near, I realize he's swinging nun-chucks in the empty yard. They blur through the air. There's no one but him and me; at this moment, we are Bearwallow Mountain. I'm chasing ghosts, leaving behind my patrolling bear, and he's digging in, fighting unnamed, unseen enemies.

His T-shirt is too tight. He can't keep his belly hidden as he flings his arms up and down. But he doesn't seem to mind. He must be a student at Edneyville, but I've never seen him before. Maybe he just arrived, or maybe his family has lived on this spot like mine, generations piled upon generations. It's impossible to know from looking at him, but he's wearing that timeless crew cut Willie always owned in elementary school, nearly see-through, sharp, and fierce. Maybe he's a cousin to Willie, a nephew. A ghost.

As I pass, I hear a "Hi-yah!" and see his stout leg kick as high as he can—barely to his waist. He swirls the nun-chucks through the rainless air and punches with his empty hand. I want to catch his eye again, to let him know I see him, I know him, but he's somewhere else entirely. So I set my sights back on the falling road, trying to remember which curve comes next, and pray that the boy is winning.

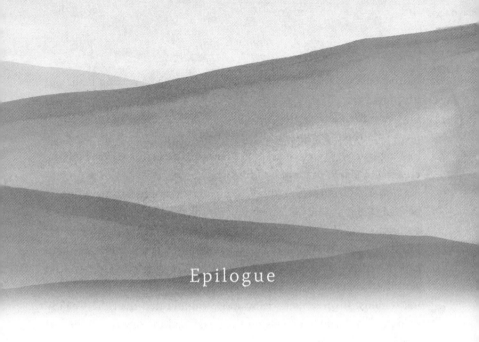

Epilogue

Nearly a decade later, Bearwallow stands mostly empty. The town tore up the land and ran water to the base of the mountain, dropping millions along the way. The pipes now lie in wait beneath Bearwallow's soil, gurgling, ready to release their water, but no one's building. No one's coming. The market crashed, the bubble burst.

The Grand Highlands' office on Main Street closed up, and the owner moved into a small rock house on the peak, into what used to be the only structure in the meadow. Like Abraham sitting on that flat rock among faint, empty trails centuries ago, the man waits there for the world to come.

Who knows if it will, if the development will fold or flourish? But for now, any action is stopped. On the Barnwell land holding the fire tower above Grand Highlands, an environmental group, the Carolina Mountain Land Conservancy, built a trail. With the help of this group, the Barnwells established an easement on the peak, ensuring it can never be developed. They allowed a trail to stretch from the pasture down the backside of Bearwallow into Hickory Nut Gorge. Locals and tourists alike can now make that trip, following a similar route to Stoneman's men 150 years ago, to explore and understand the mountain. People get their awe, the Barnwells keep their grazing land, and life moves on.

After the water fight, people in Edneyville put together a "community plan." The 104-page document begins with a "Historical Overview," looking backward before coming forward. The plan lays out how the area might allow for more building while protecting the resources and community. It suggests methods to protect Clear Creek, the water that has long fed my family's history. It demands that the county limit forest cutting, especially on ridges, and that it begin to reforest some areas. It outlines ways to increase tourism while supporting sustainable land use. The plan intends to control high-density development and also slow the proliferation of trailer parks, requesting other affordable housing options. It presents a vision more complicated than the wealthy living in comfortable houses on the peaks and the laborers toiling in trailers down in the valley.

While it's unclear what, if any, action the plan will spur, and while only twenty-six members of the community attended the public forums at the elementary school to prepare it, it's something. It's a soft voice for these changing mountains.

～

Sarah and I eventually left the flatlands of the Midwest to arrive in the lowlands of Charleston, South Carolina, a place from which many people have found their way to the Blue Ridge over the last two centuries. And like those before us, we now follow the Pull home.

In a few months, I will begin teaching at Western Carolina University. We will pack up, slide again into these hazy mountains, and set down roots alongside centuries of my people's. Yesterday, I followed the wide interstate that subsumed the wagon trail from the coast, and this morning, I write on the tiptop of Sugarloaf, in an old rock house standing on the edge of an immense rockface extending to the westward edge of the mountain—the top of William Mills's closed-up cave, the Devil's Smoke House.

Alone, I sit overlooking everything. Through the window in front of me reach verdant mountains into which I'll soon return; they seem softly draped in a bushy blanket—nothing too sharp, too defined, just easy rising and falling. On a clear spring day like today, I can make out what I'm leaving behind, the flatness of South Carolina just beyond the blue haze. Last night, Greenville's lights reached up beyond the ridge line like stage lights backing the valley holding Edneyville and Fruitland. It's all below me. Somewhere beneath my feet reached a hole in the earth where that first settler found himself healed. And down in that valley stretches a place where a young boy like me found his way.

Bearwallow is behind me, but I haven't forgotten it. My bike's atop my car. After lunch, I'll rush down this mountain—still marked with my father's old scribbles—to climb it. On the way, I'll think of the mountains' parabolic beginnings, of the piling up of history, of the pieces of mountain now falling back into the valley. After I grind my way upward, I'll rest as long as I can on Bearwallow's silent peak before I finally leave it alone again, blurring down the moving mountain.

Geologists doubt these mountains will ever entirely flatten out again. At least not for long. Even as they wear away now, they will in time take new shapes. These rocks will become roots for later generations of mountains, melting or breaking into the earth to build a new base for rising land and people. They will find purpose even as their world shifts. And this is how Sarah and I will soon drift back here, into this remade wilderness, carrying in our arms our son, Abraham.

Acknowledgments

For their early support and guidance, I thank the editors of the following publications in which pieces of this book first appeared, often in altered forms:

"Mountain Mobility" in *Cheat River Review*
"The Disillusionment of Bearwallow Mountain" in *Jelly Bucket*
"The Disappearing" in *Black & Grey Magazine*
"Marshaling the Mountains" in *Rock & Sling*
"The Twig Man" in *Visions Magazine*
"Fiddlin' Tongue" in *Code Meshing as World English: Pedagogy, Policy, and Performance*

I am grateful to the people at Wildacres Retreat for the artist residencies that gave me the time and space (not to mention food) to work on this book during the summers. Much of *Bearwallow* came to life in that solitary cabin.

For their never-ending care and backing, I'm indebted to my parents, David and Joy; my sister, Kristie; and the closest extended family that exists. Too, I have received floods of needed support from the

Massagees—my second family. My wife, Sarah, believed in this book when I didn't, always graciously giving of time and love when I so desperately needed it.

I want to thank the people of the Villa Verde School and Edneyville Elementary School. Foremost among those teachers who will always be my teachers is Debbie Lunsford, who knew I'd be a writer well before I did. Thanks to the Henderson County Historical Society and Dr. George Jones, the sharpest and farthest-reaching mind I know, even at ninety-four years old. *Bearwallow* found its earliest and wisest reader in Kenneth Youngblood, whose care and concern for these mountains puts us all to shame.

I have been urged along and shaped by tremendous writing teachers who helped grow this book from the tiniest of seeds: Jane Stephens, Cassie Kircher, Kevin Boyle, Susan Lohafer, David Hamilton, Jo Ann Beard, Lia Purpura, and Mary Ruefle. I'm especially grateful for my MFA thesis committee members, who stuck it out in the trenches of my early manuscript: Robin Hemley, James McKean, and the late Huston Diehl.

Countless shrewd readers had hands in improving this book along the way, but I am profoundly thankful for Torrey Peters, who read with such depth of insight and care that I gobbled up every bit of her advice. I am grateful to the good people of John F. Blair, who shared my vision for this book, especially my editor, Steve Kirk, whose eye and edits crafted this book into its best form. Thanks to the hardworking people at Anderson Literary Management: Claire Anderson-Wheeler and my agent, Kathleen Anderson, who believed in this project in its messy infancy. And now here it is, full-grown.